MARK BITTMAN'S QUICK AND EASY RECIPES FROM THE NEW YORK TIMES

MARK BITTMAN'S

QUICK AND EASY RECIPES

FROM

The New York Times

MARK BITTMAN

Broadway Books   New York

BROADWAY

PUBLISHED BY BROADWAY BOOKS

Published in the United States by
Broadway Books, an imprint of The
Doubleday Broadway Publishing
Group, a division of Random House,
Inc., New York.
www.broadwaybooks.com

BROADWAY BOOKS and its logo, a letter
B bisected on the diagonal, are
trademarks of Random House, Inc.

Book design by Elizabeth Rendfleisch

Library of Congress Cataloging-in-
Publication Data
Bittman, Mark.
    Mark Bittman's quick and easy
recipes from the *New York Times* / by
Mark Bittman.
        p. cm.
    Includes index.
1. Quick and easy cookery. 2. Cookery,
International. I. Title.
    TX833.5.B556   2007
    641.5'55—dc22
    ISBN-13: 978-0-7679-2623-2
                        2006030529

PRINTED IN THE UNITED STATES OF AMERICA

10   9   8   7   6   5   4   3   2   1

First Edition

For Emma, Kate, Murray, and Gertrude

CONTENTS

ACKNOWLEDGMENTS ix

INTRODUCTION 1

SOUPS 5

SALADS 41

SHELLFISH 61

FISH 93

POULTRY 119

BEEF AND VEAL 157

LAMB 185

PORK 199

VEGETABLES 215

BREAD, NOODLES, AND RICE 247

SAUCES AND CONDIMENTS 293

DESSERTS 309

INDEX 331

ACKNOWLEDGMENTS

In 1995 Trish Hall, then editor of the *New York Times* Living section, asked me to develop a weekly column. Two years later, when the section was re-launched as Dining In/Dining Out, that column became "The Minimalist." The column title, and indeed its theme, were the brainchildren of Rick Flaste, an inspired and inspiring editor and person. Though there are dozens of people I'm grateful to for their help and support in my work at the *Times* and on my cookbooks, Trish and Rick were largely responsible for beginning a weekly relationship that as of this writing is going on eleven years, and I'm eternally grateful.

During that period I have outlasted a slew of editors but have enjoyed none more than my current chief, Nick Fox. I've happily worked with deputy Pat Gurosky from the beginning. I'd also like to single out Sam Sifton, now a big honcho at the paper, who not only reinspired me during a rough patch but had the savvy to bring Nick on board.

Scores of chefs, fellow food writers, and home cooks, especially in the New York area but all over the world, have given me great ideas for "the Mini"—trying to single them out would only offend those I miss. Special thanks go to Jennifer Josephy, my editor at Broadway, to Bill Shinker, who brought the Minimalist books there about ten years ago, and to Steve Rubin, my publisher and friend. Peter "The Kid" Meehan and Chris Benton also played key roles in pulling this book together.

Many of my close friends and colleagues have made my life easier and fuller over the years, but again to mention them individually would only get me in trouble. The exceptions are my closest confidants, companions, and spiritual advisers: Angela Miller, John H. Willoughby, Charlie Pinsky, and the indefatigable Reverend Dr. L. Serene Jones. My family—in all its forms—has played a big role in inspiring and supporting me and in eating the food I cook, like it or not. Though the days of raising a young family have passed for me, they are a constant reminder of the importance of cooking in daily life. I wish I could talk about this with the first great cook I knew, Helen Art, who would probably love the Minimalist—critically, of course.

INTRODUCTION

THIS COLLECTION OF RECIPES includes just about everything I've published in the *New York Times* Dining section in the last ten years. "The Minimalist," my weekly column, was launched then, with the idea of offering people a simple and easy recipe (sometimes three or four recipes) every week, recipes that more often than not could be put together quickly, on a weeknight. The idea is no longer novel, but it was fresh then, and it's more valid now than ever.

Looking back on these recipes, I'm happy about how useful they remain. Which is as it should be: good, simple recipes are not trendy but timeless, or nearly so. Simple, as a friend of mine said to me, need not mean simple-minded. As much thought and work may go into figuring out a great three-ingredient, thirty-minute recipe as one that includes thirty ingredients and takes three hours. The fact that the preparation and execution are faster and easier does not make the recipe less sophisticated, complex, or desirable—indeed, it may make it more so.

Many of these are traditional recipes from around the world, updated. Almost all of them require a minimum of technique and/or a minimum number of ingredients; when they're not fast, they're "largely unattended," a phrase I adore for describing the kind of cooking that lets you leave the kitchen for long stretches. In general, my approach is less-is-more, an attempt to produce recipes that are so sophisticated, savvy, and fresh that they will inspire even experienced cooks while being basic and simple enough to tempt novices.

As you look through these recipes, you'll see that my style of cooking is more flexible than that of many other cookbook writers; it's not the style of chefs but of traditional home cooks, who've always made do with what they've had. Sometimes the success of a dish hinges on a single ingredient (obviously, you can't roast a chicken without a chicken), but more often it does not—herbs and spices can be omitted and substituted for one another, chicken can pinch-hit for fish and pork for chicken (and vice versa), many fish are interchangeable, many vegetables can be treated the same. To a beginning or only slightly experienced cook, these recipes and variations can be followed step by step; eventually, these cooks will gain the confidence to begin creating their own variations. To a veteran cook, these recipes—like all others—are just descriptions of a general technique applied to a preferred set of ingredients, not to be taken too literally. But veterans will find plenty of good ideas here, too.

This way of thinking, that cooking is not a set of dogmas but a craft that can be learned and enjoyed, is no longer the most common approach. By the thousands, people go to cooking schools to learn standardized skills; this approach didn't exist a hundred years ago and barely had any traction at all until the 1980s. For people who want to go into cooking as a profession, I have no problem with this (though I always encourage young people to do things the old-fashioned way, by finding a chef who will work them to death for a couple of years). But when faced with the choice between iron-clad recipes or those that encourage flexibility, I always opt for the latter.

Nor is this a theory; I learned it by cooking tens of thousands of meals at home, almost always for my family, almost always without adequate time or planning. The organized chef knows what he or she is going to cook and has all the ingredients at hand. But most of us decide what to prepare based on what's in the fridge, pantry, or shopping bag. Minimizing the required number of ingredients, then, is a top priority. Recognizing that some ingredients can almost always be switched or dispensed with is an important axiom.

Stripping recipes to their bare essentials and seeing ingredients as interchangeable are big parts of the Minimalist plan, but there is more. Home cooks in the United States are seeing the introduction of a new set of basic recipes, not the French classics revisited or the Italian staples revealed—although these are certainly parts of the trend—but the informal, quick, everyday food of households from all over the world.

In cultures where cooking is thousands of years old, most recipes are little more than combinations of the ingredients that appear seasonally. Now, for the first time in history, the standard ingredients of many of those cuisines are available at most supermarkets, opening new possibilities to both novice and experienced cooks. The result is that cooking no longer has to be complicated to be interesting and unusual. What's common to a home cook in Mexico, Greece, or Thailand may be exotic to us; what's new is that the ingredients are sold at supermarkets, and the expertise needed to put them together is available in cookbooks like this one.

Thus the recipes here not only provide great weeknight dinners. They will change the repertoire of experienced cooks while demonstrating contemporary cooking basics and teaching home cooks how to develop the sixth sense that comes with experience.

Again, it all starts with simplicity, which is not a compromise but a treasure.

SOUPS

NEARLY INSTANT MISO SOUP WITH TOFU

MAKES 4 SERVINGS   TIME: 15 MINUTES

"REAL" MISO SOUP is a little more complicated than this quick version, which begins with dashi, a basic Japanese stock made with kelp (kombu) and flakes of dried bonito (a relative of tuna). Although dashi has definite character and is easy enough to make, it is a light stock, pretty much overpowered by the miso anyway. So I just whisk or blend a tablespoon of miso into a cup of water and put my energy into turning the soup into a meal, adding cubed tofu and a couple of vegetables at the last moment. If you don't find tofu alluring, you might throw some shrimp or boneless chicken into the soup, where either will cook in a couple of minutes.

The only trick lies in getting the miso to dissolve properly, creating a smooth, almost creamy soup rather than a lumpy one. But this is in fact a snap: you just whisk or blend the miso with a few tablespoons of hot water before adding the rest of the liquid. Any cooking from that point on must be gentle to preserve the miso's flavor and aroma.

$^1/_3$ cup dark or other miso (see
   Note)
$^1/_2$ pound tofu, cut into $^1/_2$-inch
   cubes

$^1/_4$ cup minced carrot
$^1/_4$ cup minced scallion

NOTE

Buy traditional, unpasteurized, even organic miso, which is common enough, inexpensive enough (it's tough to spend more than $8 on a pound of miso), and better than quick-made miso, which is comparable to quick-made Parmesan or quick-made wine. All miso has a long shelf life, keeping for at least several months in the refrigerator with little or no loss of quality. Traditionally, thick, dark brown hatcho miso is used to make soup, but the lighter varieties, which are more often used to make dressings and sauces, are fine too.

1. Bring 6 cups of water to a boil in a medium saucepan. Turn the heat to low, then mix about $^1/_2$ cup of the water with the miso in a bowl or blender; whisk or blend until smooth. (If you have an immersion blender, the fastest and easiest tool here, carry out this operation in a tall measuring cup.)
2. Pour the miso mixture back into the hot water and add the tofu and carrot; stir once or twice and let sit for a minute, just long enough to heat the tofu through. Add the scallion and serve.

COLD TOMATO SOUP WITH ROSEMARY

MAKES 4 SERVINGS   TIME: 15 MINUTES, PLUS TIME TO CHILL

GOOD TOMATOES ARE bursting with potential. The difference between consuming a tomato out of hand and slicing it, then sprinkling it with a pinch of salt and a few drops of olive oil, is the difference between a snack and a dish. And the great thing about tomatoes is that it takes so little to convert them from one to the other.

In this instance—though not always—peeling and seeding the tomatoes is worth the effort. To do so, bring a pot of water to a boil. Meanwhile, cut a small X on the smooth (flower) end of each tomato. Drop them into the boiling water. In about thirty seconds, you'll see the skin begin to loosen. Immediately remove from the boiling water and plunge into a bowl of ice water. When they're cool, peel, then cut them in half through their equator. Squeeze and shake out the seeds. (For best flavor, do this over a strainer and recombine the reserved juices with the pulp.)

Use fresh thyme (1 teaspoon), dill (1 tablespoon), basil (^{1}/4 cup), parsley (^{1}/4 cup), chervil (1 tablespoon), chives (^{1}/4 cup), or a mixture of herbs to make this even better; garnish with fresh herbs, too, if you like.

2 slices good-quality stale white
    bread, crusts removed
3 pounds ripe tomatoes, peeled,
    seeded, and roughly chopped
1 teaspoon fresh rosemary leaves

1 small garlic clove, peeled
1 cup chicken stock or ice cubes
Salt and freshly ground black
    pepper
Juice of 1 lemon

1. Soak the bread in cold water briefly; squeeze dry and combine in a blender with the tomatoes, rosemary, and garlic (you may have to do this in 2 batches). Add the ice cubes if using them. Turn on the machine and drizzle in the stock. Turn off the machine and pour the mixture into a bowl.

2. Season with salt and pepper to taste, then add lemon juice to taste. Chill and serve.

TOMATO-MELON GAZPACHO

MAKES 4 SERVINGS   TIME: 20 MINUTES, PLUS TIME TO CHILL

I LIKE GAZPACHO, but the ultimate minimalist version—take a few tomatoes, a red pepper, some onion, oil, and vinegar, and whiz it in a blender—doesn't always cut it for me. When I confessed this to my friend and sometime co-author Jean-Georges Vongerichten, he suggested I abandon tradition entirely and combine tomatoes with another fruit of the season: cantaloupe. These, combined with basil and lemon—in place of vinegar—produce the mildest, most delicious, creamiest gazpacho I've ever tasted. Make sure to use ripe cantaloupe and tomato at the height of the summer for the best results.

4 tomatoes (about $1^1/2$ pounds), peeled and seeded

One 3-pound cantaloupe

2 tablespoons olive oil

10 fresh basil leaves

Salt and freshly ground black pepper

Juice of 1 lemon

1. Cut the tomato flesh into 1-inch chunks. Seed the melon and remove the flesh from the rind; cut it into chunks. Put a tablespoon of olive oil in each of two 10- or 12-inch skillets and turn the heat under both to high (you can do this sequentially if you have only one skillet). Add the melon to one skillet and the tomatoes to the other and cook, stirring, until they become juicy, no longer than 2 minutes.

2. In a blender, puree the melon, tomato, $1^1/2$ cups water or 1 cup water plus $1/2$ cup ice cubes, and the basil, along with some salt and pepper. Chill, then add lemon juice to taste and adjust the seasoning. Serve.

ASIAN-STYLE CUCUMBER SOUP

MAKES 4 SERVINGS   TIME: 30 MINUTES

FOR YEARS I was stuck on blended or cooked cucumber soups, until I was served a clear, chunky, ice-cold soup laced with soy and with the sour-sweet-salty-spicy combination characteristic of so much Southeast Asian cooking. After I duplicated that, it occurred to me to make a similar preparation with nam pla (fish sauce) and coconut milk, an equally spicy but wonderfully creamy concoction. I know I'll never use either the blender or the stove to make cucumber soup again.

VARIATION

Cucumber-Coconut Soup
Substitute 2 cups coconut milk and 1 cup water for the stock and, if you have it, nam pla (fish sauce) for the soy sauce. You can turn this simple soup into a hot-weather main course by topping it with some pre-cooked shrimp (simply grilled would be my first choice) just before serving.

3 cups chicken stock, preferably chilled

2 medium cucumbers

3 tablespoons soy sauce

2 tablespoons rice or white wine vinegar

1 small fresh chile, stemmed, seeded, and minced, or $1/4$ teaspoon cayenne, or to taste

2 teaspoons sugar

$1/2$ cup minced scallion

1 cup chopped watercress or arugula (optional)

1 cup roughly chopped fresh cilantro, mint, Thai basil, or a combination

1. If the stock is not cold, throw it in the freezer while you prepare the cucumbers. Peel them, then cut them in half the long way; use a spoon to scoop out the seeds. Slice them as thinly as possible (a mandoline is ideal for this). Mix them in a bowl with the soy sauce, vinegar, chile, and sugar and let sit, refrigerated, for about 20 minutes.

2. Add the stock, scallion, and watercress or arugula if you like and stir. Taste and adjust the seasoning, then chill or serve. Just before serving, garnish with the herb(s).

EUROPEAN-STYLE CUCUMBER SOUP

MAKES 4 SERVINGS   TIME: 30 MINUTES

MOST OF THE time spent making soups like this one and the preceding Asian-Style Cucumber Soup goes to chilling: refrigerate the cucumbers as their moisture is drawn out; refrigerate the stock, yogurt, or sour cream that is their base; and, if time allows, refrigerate the soup itself so you can serve it not cool but really cold. And remember, the lively flavor of these derives largely from a load of herbs—vary them to your heart's content, but don't leave them out.

$1^1/_2$ cups chicken stock, preferably chilled

2 medium cucumbers

Salt and freshly ground black pepper

$1^1/_2$ cups yogurt, preferably whole-milk

2 shallots, minced, or about $^1/_4$ cup minced red onion or scallion

1 cup chopped watercress (optional)

1 cup roughly chopped fresh dill or mint

1. If the stock is not cold, throw it in the freezer while you prepare the cucumbers. Peel them, then cut them in half the long way; use a spoon to scoop out the seeds. Slice them as thinly as possible (a mandoline is ideal for this). Mix them in a bowl with 2 teaspoons salt and let sit, refrigerated, for about 20 minutes.

2. Add the stock, black pepper, yogurt, shallots, and watercress if you like and stir. Taste and adjust the seasoning, then chill or serve. Just before serving, garnish with the herb.

COLD PEA SOUP

MAKES 4 SERVINGS   TIME: 30 MINUTES, PLUS TIME TO CHILL

THIS SOUP IS on the thin, almost drinkable, side. If that doesn't appeal to you, use sour cream, perhaps a bit more than the quantity recommended here, or throw a peeled, diced potato in with the peas, which will give the final soup quite a bit of heft.

1 pound peas in the pod, snow peas, or sugar snap peas (frozen are perfectly acceptable)
1 quart chicken or vegetable stock
Salt and freshly ground black pepper
2 tablespoons heavy or sour cream, or more to taste
Chopped fresh parsley for garnish (optional)

1. Combine the peas and stock in a saucepan and bring to a boil over medium-high heat. Reduce the heat to simmer and cook until the peas are bright green and tender, 10 minutes or so. Cool for a few minutes. If you're using peas, remove some from their pods for garnish (refrigerate until serving).

2. Pour into a blender and carefully blend until pureed. Add salt and pepper to taste, then force through a fairly fine strainer, discarding the solids. Stir or whisk in the cream and refrigerate (up to 2 days) before serving cold. Garnish with the reserved peas or some parsley.

PEA AND GINGER SOUP

MAKES 4 SERVINGS   TIME: 30 MINUTES

FRESH PEAS ARE inestimably better than frozen for munching, but by the time you cook them and mix them with ginger, they have lost much of their advantage; if you can't find them or deal with them—the shelling does take a while—by all means use frozen.

2 cups peas, fresh or frozen

2 tablespoons roughly chopped peeled fresh ginger, or more to taste (up to $1/4$ cup)

Salt and freshly ground black pepper

1 quart chicken or other stock

1. Combine all the ingredients in a saucepan and bring to a boil over medium-high heat. Reduce the heat to simmer and cook until the peas and ginger are very tender, about 15 minutes. Cool for a few minutes.

2. Pour into a blender and carefully blend until pureed. Return to the pan over medium-low heat and reheat gently, stirring occasionally. When the soup is hot, adjust the seasoning and serve.

EGGS IN SOUP

WHEN YOU USE eggs to thicken a sauce or stew, you keep the heat low to gain a smooth, creamy result. In egg drop soup, whether it is Chinese or Italian or Greek, you do just the opposite—keep the heat relatively high so the eggs cook in shreds, or curds. The result is lightning-fast soup of real substance.

EGG DROP SOUP

MAKES 4 SERVINGS   TIME: 15 MINUTES

EGG DROP SOUP is best flavored with soy sauce, plenty of chopped scallions, and a bit of sesame oil. Starting with a good chicken stock will yield the best results, but purchased stock can be substituted in a pinch.

1 quart chicken stock

4 eggs

1 tablespoon soy sauce, or to taste

Salt and freshly ground black pepper

$1/2$ cup chopped scallion

1 teaspoon sesame oil, or to taste

1. Bring 3 cups of the stock to a boil in a 6- to 8-cup saucepan over medium-high heat. Beat the remaining stock with the eggs and soy sauce until well blended.

2. When the stock is boiling, adjust the heat so that it bubbles frequently but not furiously. Add the egg mixture in a steady stream, stirring all the while. Stir occasionally until the eggs gather together in small curds, 2 or 3 minutes.

3. Taste and add salt (or more soy sauce), if necessary, then add plenty of pepper, the scallion, and the sesame oil. Taste again, adjust the seasoning, and serve.

===============

STRACCIATELLA

MAKES 4 SERVINGS   TIME: 15 MINUTES

EGG DROP SOUP, a cliché in American-Chinese restaurants for at least fifty years, has a less-well-known Italian counterpart called *stracciatella*. Both are based on the simple fact that eggs scramble or curdle in boiling water or stock, and each demonstrates the ease with which a basic dish can be transformed in spirit, moving from one cuisine to the other almost as quickly as you can change your mind about which you prefer.

1 quart chicken stock

4 eggs

1/4 cup freshly grated Parmigiano-
    Reggiano cheese, or a little
    more for garnish

A tiny grating of fresh nutmeg

2 tablespoons minced fresh parsley

Salt and freshly ground black
    pepper

1. Bring 3 cups of the stock to a boil in a 6- to 8-cup saucepan over medium-high heat. Beat the remaining stock with the eggs, cheese, nutmeg, and parsley until well blended.

2. When the stock is boiling, adjust the heat so that it bubbles frequently but not furiously. Add the egg mixture in a steady stream,

stirring all the while. Stir occasionally until the eggs gather together in small curds, 2 or 3 minutes.

3. Taste and add salt and pepper to taste, then serve. Garnish with a little more cheese if you like.

AVGOLEMONO

MAKES 4 SERVINGS   TIME: ABOUT 30 MINUTES

IF STRACCIATELLA IS egg drop soup's less-well-known cousin, avgolemono is its neglected stepchild and it can be prepared easily, quickly, and almost effortlessly from ingredients that most of us always have on hand.

5 cups chicken or vegetable stock, preferably homemade

1/2 cup long-grain rice or orzo

Salt and freshly ground black pepper

1 cup chopped tomatoes (optional)

2 eggs

1 teaspoon grated lemon zest

3 tablespoons fresh lemon juice, plus more to taste

Minced fresh dill or parsley for garnish

1. Put the stock in a large, deep saucepan or casserole and turn the heat to medium-high. When it is just about boiling, turn the heat down to medium so that it bubbles but not too vigorously. Stir in the rice and cook, stirring occasionally, until the rice is cooked, about 20 minutes. Season with salt and pepper and add the tomatoes if you're using them; turn the heat under the soup to low.

2. Use a whisk to beat the eggs in a bowl with the lemon zest and juice; still beating, add about 1/2 cup of the hot stock. Gradually add about another cup of the stock, beating all the while. Pour this mixture back into the soup and reheat, but under no circumstances allow the mixture to boil.

3. Taste and adjust the seasoning, adding salt, pepper, or lemon juice as necessary. Garnish and serve.

Thai Garlic Soup

Like egg drop soup, a simple soup like this has relatives from around the globe. This is one of my favorites. To make it, add a minced fresh chile, or a few small dried chiles, to the oil along with the garlic (discard dried chiles after cooking). Omit the bread; add 2 cups cooked rice to the soup along with the shrimp. Substitute fresh cilantro for the parsley, and serve with wedges of lime.

NOTE

To make a stock from the shrimp shells, put the shells in a pot, cover with water, bring to a boil, and simmer for about 5 minutes; strain. (The liquid can be used in many shrimp dishes or in place of fish stock in most recipes. You can accumulate shells and freeze them over a period of months if you like, and there's no need to defrost them before making the stock.) The amount of stock made by the pound or so of shrimp in this recipe isn't enough to complete the soup, but its volume can be increased with water or enhanced with chicken stock; the combination is wonderful.

GARLIC SOUP WITH SHRIMP

MAKES 4 SERVINGS   TIME: 30 MINUTES

MOST SOUPS HAVE simple origins, but none more so than this Mediterranean one of France, whose antecedent is usually called something like *boiled water.* At its most impoverished, this is no more than garlic simmered in water to give it flavor, with a few crusts of bread added for bulk. Simple as it is, boiled water is the perfect example of how an almost absurdly elementary preparation can be converted quickly and easily into one that is nearly grand.

Use stock in place of water if you have it. This is a fine place for canned stock, because the garlic-scented oil will boost it to a higher level.

Remember to cook the garlic very gently to add complexity and color; by then browning the bread in the same oil, you increase its flavor immeasurably. Also consider doubling the amount of bread given in the recipe here; like me, you may find the allure of bread crisped in garlic-scented oil irresistible.

$1/4$ cup extra virgin olive oil

8 to 16 medium to large garlic cloves, peeled

Salt and freshly ground black pepper

4 thick slices French or Italian bread

6 cups shrimp stock (see Note), chicken stock, water, or a combination

1 to $1/2$ pounds shrimp, peeled

Minced fresh parsley for garnish (optional)

1. Combine the olive oil and garlic in a deep skillet or broad saucepan, turn the heat to medium, and sprinkle lightly with salt and pepper. Cook, turning the garlic cloves occasionally, until they are tender and lightly browned all over, about 10 minutes; lower the heat if they seem to be browning too quickly. Remove the garlic with a slotted spoon.
2. Turn the heat to low and add the bread (in batches if necessary); cook on each side until nicely browned, a total of about 4 minutes. Remove the bread, add the stock, and raise the heat to medium-high.

3. When the stock is nearly boiling, add the shrimp and salt and pepper to taste. Cook until the shrimp are pink, about 4 minutes. Put a piece of bread and a portion of garlic in each of 4 bowls, then ladle in a portion of soup and shrimp. Sprinkle with the parsley if desired and serve.

PROSCIUTTO SOUP

MAKES 4 SERVINGS   TIME: 30 MINUTES

WATER-BASED SOUPS are great, but many soups are indisputably better when made with meat stock. Of course you don't always have stock, and there are short cuts that produce in-between soups. One of the easiest and most effective ways of making a potent soup quickly and without stock is to start with a small piece of prosciutto or other dry-cured ham. The long aging process this meat undergoes—almost always a year or more—ensures an intense flavor that is quickly transferred to anything in which it is cooked, including water.

To save time, chop the vegetables and add them one at a time while you're rendering the ham; by the time you're done chopping, you'll have added all the ingredients except water. And if you bring the water to a boil before you begin chopping, you really minimize cooking time, producing a thick, rich soup in less than thirty minutes. Do not omit the final drizzle of olive oil; its freshness really brings this soup to life.

3 tablespoons extra virgin olive oil

$1/4$ pound prosciutto, in 1 chunk or slice

4 garlic cloves

1 medium onion

$1/2$ pound greens, like spinach or kale

$3/4$ cup small pasta, like orzo or small shells

Salt and freshly ground black pepper

VARIATIONS

The basic recipe, though delicious, is on the meager side, the kind of soup people make when times are hard or no one's been shopping lately: a small piece of meat, some common vegetables, a little pasta. But you can make it as elaborate as you like and even convert it to a stew by doubling the amount of meat, vegetables, and pasta. The chopping time will be extended slightly, but the cooking time will remain more or less the same.

(continued)

(Variations, continued)
• Add more root vegetables, like thinly sliced carrots or chopped celery, or diced potatoes or turnips.
• Vary the greens: Shredded cabbage is perfect for this soup and will cook as quickly as kale. Collard, mustard, and turnip greens are also appropriate. Some peas and/or corn will work nicely, too, even if they come from the freezer.
• Use any starch you like in place of the pasta: Rice and barley, each of which take a few minutes longer than pasta, are good choices.
• Add tomatoes, either fresh, canned, or paste, for color and flavor. To use tomato paste, just stir a couple of tablespoons into the sautéing vegetables before adding the water. Tomatoes should be added with the onions so they have time to break up.
• Leftovers are great, like a bit of chopped chicken or some vegetables from a previous meal (rinse them with boiling water if they were sauced).
• Consider the chopped-up rind of hard cheese, like Parmesan, which will not only soften enough to become edible during cooking but will add great flavor to the soup.

1. Bring 6 cups of water to a boil in a pot or kettle. Put 2 tablespoons of the olive oil in the bottom of a saucepan and turn the heat to medium. Chop the prosciutto (remove the fat if you must, but remember that it has flavor) into $1/4$-inch or smaller cubes and add to the oil. Brown, stirring occasionally, for about 5 minutes, while you prepare the garlic, onion, and greens.

2. Peel the garlic and chop it roughly or leave it whole. Peel and chop the onion. Wash and chop the greens into bite-sized pieces.

3. When the prosciutto has browned, add the garlic and cook, stirring occasionally, until it begins to color, about 2 minutes. Add the onion and cook, stirring occasionally, until it becomes translucent, 2 or 3 minutes. Add the greens and stir, then add the boiling water. (You can prepare the dish in advance up to this point. Cover and refrigerate for up to 2 days, then reheat before proceeding.) Stir in the pasta and a good sprinkling of salt and pepper; adjust the heat so the mixture simmers.

4. When the pasta is done, taste and adjust the seasoning. Drizzle with the remaining olive oil and serve.

VICHYSSOISE WITH GARLIC

MAKES 4 SERVINGS   TIME: 40 MINUTES, PLUS TIME TO CHILL

IN ITS TRADITIONAL form, this cold potato-and-leek soup borders on boring: potatoes, leeks (or onions or a combination), water or stock, salt and pepper, butter, and cream. What little complexity the soup has comes from butter, lots of salt and pepper, good stock, and, of course, cream. But if you add other vegetables, like garlic and carrots, things become more interesting. And you can nudge the soup over into gazpacho territory by adding a tomato to the mix, along with basil. Some protein, like shrimp, can turn it into more of a whole-meal soup.

1 quart water, stock, or a combination

1 pound potatoes, peeled and cut into slices or chunks

1 pound leeks or onions (or a combination), the leeks well washed, the onions peeled, either cut into slices or chunks

1 whole head of green garlic, plus its stem, chopped into pieces, or 3 garlic cloves, peeled

Salt and freshly ground black pepper

$1/2$ to 1 cup heavy cream or half-and-half

Chopped fresh parsley, chervil, or chives for garnish

1. Combine the water or stock, potatoes, leeks, garlic, and salt and pepper to taste in a saucepan, cover, and turn the heat to high. Bring to a boil, then lower the heat so the mixture simmers steadily but not violently. Cook until the potatoes are tender, 20 to 30 minutes. Cool or chill, then season to taste.

2. Puree in a blender, then chill fully. Stir in the cream, then adjust the seasoning and serve, garnished with parsley.

THE MINIMALIST'S CORN CHOWDER

MAKES 4 SERVINGS   TIME: 30 TO 40 MINUTES

ANYONE WHO'S EVER had a garden or raided a corn field knows that when corn is young you can eat it cob and all and that the cob has as much flavor as the kernels. That flavor remains even when the cob has become inedibly tough, and you can take advantage of it by using it as the base of a corn chowder—a corn stock, if you will. Into that stock can go some starch for bulk, a variety of seasonings from colonial to contemporary, and, finally, the corn kernels. The entire process takes a half hour or a little bit longer, and the result is a thick, satisfying, late-summer chowder.

4 to 6 ears corn

1 tablespoon butter or neutral oil, like corn or grapeseed

1 medium onion, chopped

2 medium potatoes, peeled and cut into $1/4$-inch pieces

Salt and freshly ground black pepper

2 tomatoes, seeded and chopped (optional)

1 cup milk

$1/2$ cup chopped fresh parsley (optional)

1. Shuck the corn and use a paring knife to strip the kernels into a bowl. (Catch any liquid that seeps out and add it to the soup.) Put the cobs in a pot with 1 quart water; bring to a boil, cover, and lower the heat to simmer while you continue.

2. Put the butter or oil in a saucepan and turn the heat to medium-high. When the butter melts or the oil is hot, add the onion and potatoes, along with a sprinkling of salt and pepper. Cook, stirring occasionally, until the onion softens, about 5 minutes; add the tomatoes if you're using them and cook, stirring, for another minute or two.

3. After the corn cobs have cooked for at least 10 minutes, strain the liquid into the onion-potato mixture; bring to a boil, then turn the

VARIATIONS

Corn Chowder with Bacon and Cream

In step 2, substitute 1/2 cup chopped bacon for the butter or oil; cook over medium heat until it renders some of its fat, then add the onion. Proceed as directed. In step 3, use heavy cream or half-and-half in place of milk.

Curried Corn Chowder

In step 2, use oil and add 1 tablespoon curry powder, or to taste, and 1 tablespoon minced peeled fresh ginger to the onion as it cooks. Proceed as directed. In step 3, use sour cream in place of milk; garnish with minced cilantro in place of parsley.

heat down so the mixture simmers. When the potatoes are tender, after about 10 minutes, add the corn kernels and milk and heat through. Adjust the seasoning, garnish with the parsley if you like, and serve.

═══════════

CLAM CHOWDER

MAKES 4 SERVINGS TIME: 30 MINUTES

ALTHOUGH CLAM CHOWDER takes many guises, the best is a simple affair that has as its flavorful essence the juices of the clams themselves. And as long as you begin with fresh clams, these juices are easily extracted and reserved; the minced clam meat becomes a garnish.

Hardshell clams, often called *littlenecks, cherrystones,* or *quahogs,* are a must for this chowder; cockles, which are smaller, will also work well. Steamers (which have softer shells) will make the chowder sandy.

If you like, try finishing the chowder with a little cream for both color and silkiness.

NOTE
Remember that live clams have tightly closed shells; reject any whose shells are open or cracked. Those that do not open fully during steaming are perfectly fine; simply pry them open with a knife.

At least 3 dozen littleneck clams (3 pounds or more), or an equivalent amount of other clams (see Note)
1 medium onion, peeled and minced

2 large potatoes (about 1 pound), peeled and cut into $1/4$-inch dice
Salt and freshly ground black pepper

1. Wash the clams well, scrubbing if necessary to remove external grit. (You can wash the clams hours or even a day in advance; keep them in a large bowl or colander set over a bowl, uncovered, in the refrigerator.) Put them in a pot with $1/2$ cup of water and turn the heat to high. Steam, shaking the pot occasionally, until most of the clams are open, 7 to 10 minutes. Use a slotted spoon to transfer the clams to a broad bowl; reserve the cooking liquid.

2. When the clams are cool enough to handle, shuck them over the bowl, catching every drop of their liquid; discard the shells. If any clams remain closed, use a thin-bladed knife to pry them open (it will be easy).

3. Chop the clams. Strain all the liquid through a sieve lined with a paper towel or a couple of layers of cheesecloth. Measure the liquid and add enough water to make $3^1/2$ cups. (You may prepare the dish in advance up to this point; refrigerate, covered, for up to a day before reheating.)

4. Combine the liquid with the onion and potatoes in a saucepan; cover and bring to a boil. Reduce the heat to simmer, still covered, and cook until the potatoes are tender, about 10 minutes. Stir in the clams, season to taste with salt and pepper, and serve.

CLAM STEW WITH POTATOES AND PARSLEY PUREE

MAKES 4 SERVINGS   TIME: 30 MINUTES

THIS IS ESSENTIALLY a clam chowder but one that is less soupy, more colorful, and more "clammy" than most. The departures from American tradition include a strong whiff of garlic and a bright green puree of parsley.

4 pounds small clams, like cockles or butter clams (see Note, page 21)

$3/4$ pound waxy potatoes, peeled and cut into $1/4$-inch dice

$3/4$ cup dry white wine

1 bunch of fresh parsley, thick stems removed and tied in a bundle

1 garlic clove

$1/4$ cup extra virgin olive oil

Salt

1. Wash the clams well, in several changes of water, until the water contains no traces of sand. (You can wash the clams hours or even a day in advance; keep them in a large bowl or colander set over a bowl, uncovered, in the refrigerator.) Put them in a wide, deep skillet or saucepan along with the potatoes, wine, and thick parsley stems. Cover and turn the heat to high.

2. While the clams and potatoes are cooking, combine the parsley leaves and thin stems in a blender with the garlic and oil. Puree, adding water as necessary (it will be $1/2$ cup or more) to make a smooth puree. Add salt to taste and transfer to a bowl.

3. Cook the clam-potato mixture until the potatoes are tender, about 15 minutes. Remove the bundle of thick stems, then stir about half the puree into the mixture and serve, passing the rest at the table.

====

LEMONGRASS-GINGER SOUP
WITH MUSHROOMS

MAKES 4 SERVINGS   TIME: 30 MINUTES

THIS THAI SOUP, like most European soups, begins with chicken stock. You can use canned stock if you like, because the added ingredients here are so strong that all you really need from the base is a bit of body. (Good homemade stock has better body than canned stock, of course; use it if you have it.)

You can find all of these ingredients at almost any supermarket, and if you don't have luck at yours, try an Asian market, where they are as common as carrots, celery, and onions. (And if you do go to an Asian market, pick up some rice or bean thread noodles, which require almost no cooking time and turn this dish into a meal.)

You don't need oyster mushrooms, by the way—fresh shiitakes or even white button mushrooms are just as good. All you really need to know is that lemongrass must be trimmed of its outer layers before being minced and nam pla (fish sauce) keeps forever in your pantry (and tastes much better than it smells).

6 cups good-quality chicken stock

3 lemongrass stalks

4 nickel-sized slices peeled fresh
    ginger

3 to 4 small fresh hot chiles, minced
    (optional)

2 tablespoons nam pla (fish sauce),
    or to taste

6 to 8 ounces roughly chopped
    oyster mushrooms

Salt (optional)

2 teaspoons minced lime leaves or
    lime zest

Juice of 1 lime

$1/4$ cup minced fresh cilantro

1. Heat the stock over medium heat. Trim two of the lemongrass stalks of their toughest outer layers, then bruise them with the back of a knife; cut them into sections and add them to the stock with the ginger and about one-fourth of the minced chiles if you're using them. Simmer for about 15 minutes, longer if you have the time. (You can prepare the recipe in advance up to this point; cover and refrigerate for up to 2 days before proceeding.) Peel all the hard layers off the remaining stalk of lemongrass and mince its tender inner core.

2. When you're just about ready to eat the soup, remove the lemongrass and ginger. Add 1 tablespoon of the nam pla and the chopped mushrooms. Taste the broth and add more chiles if you like, as well as some salt if necessary. In the bottom of each of 4 warmed bowls, sprinkle a little chile if using, lime leaves or zest, lime juice, cilantro, and minced lemongrass. Ladle the soup into the bowls and add a teaspoon of nam pla to each bowl. Serve piping hot.

CREAMY MUSHROOM SOUP

MAKES 4 SERVINGS   TIME: 30 MINUTES

EVEN AS THEY become increasingly common, there remains something special, even exotic, about mushrooms. And combining their various forms allows you to make a splendid and impressive soup in less than half an hour.

The best-tasting dried mushrooms are dried porcini (also called *cèpes*), which have come down about 50 percent in price over the last few years (do not buy less than an ounce or so at a time—you can buy them by the pound, too—or you'll be paying way too much). Or you can start with inexpensive dried shiitakes, readily available in Asian markets (where they're also called *black mushrooms*), or any other dried fungus, or an assortment. An assortment of fresh mushrooms is best, but you can simply rely on ordinary button (white) mushrooms or shiitakes (whose stems, by the way, are too tough to eat).

2 ounces dried mushrooms (about 1 cup)

2 tablespoons butter

6 to 8 ounces fresh mushrooms, trimmed and sliced

Salt and freshly ground black pepper

2 tablespoons chopped shallot

1 cup heavy cream

2 teaspoons fresh lemon juice, or to taste

Chopped fresh chervil or parsley for garnish (optional)

1. Put the dried mushrooms in a saucepan with 5 cups of water; bring to a boil, cover, turn the heat to low, and simmer for about 10 minutes, or until tender.

2. Meanwhile, put the butter in a skillet and turn the heat to medium-high. When the butter melts, add the sliced fresh mushrooms and turn the heat to high. Cook, stirring occasionally and seasoning with salt and pepper, until they give up their liquid and begin to brown, about 5 minutes. When the dried mushrooms are tender, scoop them from the liquid with a slotted spoon and add them to the skillet along with the shallot. When all the fresh mushrooms are browned and the shallot is tender, about 3 minutes later, turn off the heat.

3. Strain the mushroom-cooking liquid through a cheesecloth-, napkin-, or towel-lined strainer; measure it and add water or stock to make sure you have at least 1 quart. Rinse the saucepan and return the liquid to it. Add the mushrooms and cream and heat through; taste and adjust the seasoning. Add the lemon juice, taste once more, garnish if you like, and serve.

PAN-ROASTED ASPARAGUS SOUP WITH TARRAGON

MAKES 4 SERVINGS   TIME: 40 MINUTES

ASPARAGUS IS ONE of the few vegetables that remains true to its season; though you can buy it earlier than ever, and it stays around later than ever, it's still pretty much a spring vegetable.

You can save yourself some time by using thin asparagus; if you use thicker stalks, peel them first or the soup will be fibrous. Be especially careful whenever you puree hot liquid; do it in smaller batches to avoid spattering.

1^1/2 pounds thin or peeled thick
    asparagus
2 tablespoons butter or extra virgin
    olive oil
10 fresh tarragon leaves or
    ^{1}/2 teaspoon dried

1 quart chicken or other stock
Salt and freshly ground black
    pepper

1. Break off the bottom of each asparagus stalk and discard. Coarsely chop the rest of the stalks, leaving 16 of the flower ends whole. Put the butter or oil in a large deep skillet or broad saucepan and turn the heat to medium-high. A minute later, add the asparagus and tarragon, raise the heat to high, and cook, stirring only occasionally, until nicely browned, about 10 minutes. Remove the whole flower ends; set aside.

2. Add the stock and some salt and pepper; bring to a boil, then reduce the heat and simmer until the asparagus is very tender, about 10 minutes. Cool for a few minutes.

3. Use a blender to puree carefully in batches. Return to the pan and reheat gently over medium-low heat, stirring occasionally. When the soup is hot, taste and adjust the seasoning. Put 4 of the cooked flower ends in each of 4 bowls; ladle in the soup and serve.

CABBAGE SOUP WITH APPLES

MAKES 4 SERVINGS   TIME: 40 MINUTES

THIS IS A CABBAGE soup with a difference; the apples add sweetness, crunch, and complexity.

1 tablespoon olive oil

2 tablespoons butter

1 large onion, sliced

1 pound trimmed and cored cabbage, shredded

10 fresh thyme sprigs

Salt and freshly ground black pepper

5 cups chicken or beef stock

3 Golden Delicious or other good-quality apples, peeled and cubed

1. In a medium saucepan, combine the oil and 1 tablespoon of the butter and turn the heat to medium-high. When the butter melts, add the onion and cabbage and cook, stirring occasionally, until the vegetables wilt and begin to brown, 5 to 7 minutes. Add 5 of the thyme sprigs and cook for a few minutes more. Sprinkle with salt and pepper.

2. Add the stock and turn the heat to medium; stir occasionally as it heats. Put the remaining butter in a skillet and turn the heat to medium-high. When the butter foam subsides, add the apple pieces. Cook, stirring occasionally, until browned and tender, about 10 minutes. Strip the leaves from the remaining thyme sprigs and sprinkle them over the apples along with a bit of salt.

3. Taste the soup and adjust the seasoning; remove the thyme sprigs. Serve the soup hot, garnished with the apple chunks.

A NOTE ON CREAMY VEGETABLE SOUPS

IT ISN'T OFTEN that you can apply a simple formula to a broad range of dishes, but when it comes to creamy vegetable soups—whether hot or cold—there is one that actually works. The soups have three basic ingredients, and their proportions form a pyramid: three parts liquid, two parts vegetable, one part dairy.

The pyramid's foundation is chicken stock (you can substitute vegetable stock or water, but the result will be somewhat less substantial). The middle section is any vegetable, or combination of vegetables, that will puree nicely and produce good body and flavor. The peak is cream, or nearly any other liquid dairy product—milk, yogurt, or sour cream (though some vegetables, like winter squash, are so dense that they create their own creaminess, reducing the amount of dairy needed in the final step).

To make four servings, the three-two-one measurement is in cups, conveniently enough, because a total of six cups is the perfect amount of soup for four people. Aromatic vegetables, like onions, carrots, or celery, which are almost always welcome additions, count as part of the vegetable portion, but seasonings like salt, pepper, herbs, spices, or garlic or shallots are extras and can be added pretty much to taste. Add seasonings that require cooking, like garlic and onions, with the vegetables. Those that do not, like herbs and spices, are best added before pureeing the cold mixture so they retain their freshness.

The recipes on pages 29–31 are basics—use them as templates. Here are a few more creamy vegetable soup ideas to try that follow the general guidelines:

- **BEET** Add some minced scallion or chive before pureeing. Puree with sour cream and garnish with chives and a teaspoon of sour cream per serving.
- **SPINACH** Start with $1/2$ pound of leaves (remove thick stems). Cook quickly, adding a bit of garlic if you like.
- **TURNIP AND PARSNIP** Or turnip and potato. Cook with a small onion and some thyme.
- **RED PEPPER AND TOMATO** Peel and seed both before cooking. Puree with sour cream to thicken the mixture, which will be thin. Garnish with chervil (ideally) or parsley.
- **CARROT** Nice with a pinch of cayenne and a teaspoon or more of minced peeled fresh ginger, added after cooking.
- **PEAS OR SNOW PEAS** Make sure to remove the strings from snow peas. Cook with thyme or mint.
- **CELERY OR FENNEL** Cook a few garlic cloves along with the vegetable.
- **ARTICHOKE HEARTS** If you use canned hearts, simply puree with cold chicken stock; there's no need to cook.
- **TOMATILLOS OR GREEN TOMATOES** Season with chili powder, puree with sour cream, and garnish with a teaspoon of sour cream.

CREAMY BROCCOLI SOUP

MAKES 4 SERVINGS   TIME: 30 MINUTES

LEFTOVER BROCCOLI—maybe that you boiled or steamed as a simple side dish—is a super candidate for this soup. (You may even find yourself making more broccoli than you can eat, as I do, specifically so you can turn it into this soup the next day.)

To use leftovers, rinse off any remnants of dressing with hot water, add it to the pan after you've cooked away the garlic's raw taste, and proceed without any additional cooking.

2 cups broccoli florets and peeled stems (about $1/2$ average head), cut into chunks

3 cups chicken stock

1 garlic clove, peeled and cut in half

1 cup milk, cream, or yogurt

Salt and freshly ground black pepper

1. Combine the broccoli and stock in a saucepan and simmer, covered, until the broccoli is tender, about 10 minutes. During the last minute or so of cooking, add the garlic (this cooks the garlic just enough to remove its raw taste). If you're serving the soup cold, chill now (or refrigerate for up to 2 days or freeze for up to a month before proceeding).

2. Puree in a blender, in batches if necessary, until very smooth. Stir in the milk, cream, or yogurt and reheat gently (or chill again); do not boil (yogurt will curdle). Season to taste—cold soups generally require more seasoning than hot ones—and serve.

POTATO AND ONION SOUP

MAKES 4 SERVINGS   TIME: 30 MINUTES

ALWAYS COOK THE vegetables for a creamy soup until tender, but no more than that. Spinach is tender in a couple of minutes; potatoes, cut into chunks, will require no more than ten or fifteen. Almost nothing will take longer than that. Cover the pot while the vegetables cook to prevent too much of the stock from evaporating.

1 cup peeled potato chunks (about 1 large)
1 cup roughly chopped onion or leek, the leek well washed
3 cups chicken stock

1 cup milk or cream
Salt and freshly ground black pepper
Chopped fresh parsley or chives for garnish

1. Combine the potato, onion, and stock in a saucepan and simmer, covered, until the potato is tender, about 15 minutes. If you're serving the soup cold, chill now (or refrigerate for up to 2 days or freeze for up to a month before proceeding).
2. Puree in a blender, in batches if necessary, until very smooth. Stir in the milk or cream and reheat gently (or chill again); do not boil. Season to taste—cold soups generally require more seasoning than hot ones—garnish with the parsley or chives, and serve.

PUMPKIN SOUP

MAKES 4 SERVINGS   TIME: 40 MINUTES

USUALLY, PUMPKIN MEANS pie, a limited role for a large vegetable that is nearly ubiquitous from Labor Day through Christmas. But soup based on pumpkin—or other winter squash like acorn or butternut—is a minimalist's dream, a luxuriously creamy dish that requires little more than a stove and a blender.

If there is a challenge here, it lies in peeling the squash. The big mistake many people make is to attack it with a standard vegetable peeler; the usual result is an unpeeled pumpkin and a broken peeler. A quicker and more reliable method is to cut the squash up into wedges; then rest each section on a cutting board and use a sharp, heavy knife to cut away the peel. You'll wind up taking part of the flesh with it, but given the large size and small cost of winter squash, this is hardly a concern.

2 pounds peeled pumpkin or other winter squash	4 to 5 cups chicken or other stock Salt and freshly ground black pepper

1. Place the pumpkin or squash in a saucepan with stock to cover and a pinch of salt. Turn the heat to high and bring to a boil. Cover and adjust the heat so that the mixture simmers. Cook until the pumpkin or squash is very tender, about 30 minutes. If time allows, cool.

2. Put the mixture, in batches if necessary, in the container of a blender and puree until smooth. (The recipe can be prepared a day or two in advance up to this point; cool, put in a covered container, and refrigerate.) Reheat, adjust the seasoning, and serve.

VARIATIONS

Pumpkin, stock, and black pepper are all you need to make a good pumpkin soup. But when you have more time and ingredients, try one of the following:

• Add 1 teaspoon ground ginger (or 1 tablespoon finely minced peeled fresh ginger) or 1 teaspoon curry powder (and, if you have it, $1/2$ teaspoon ground turmeric) to the simmering soup.

• Add $1/2$ teaspoon ground cinnamon, $1/4$ teaspoon ground allspice, and a small grating of nutmeg to the simmering soup.

• Garnish each bowl of soup with 3 or 4 grilled, sautéed, or roasted shrimp; or about $1/4$ cup crabmeat or lobster meat per serving.

• Garnish the soup with chopped fresh chervil, chives, parsley, or dill.

• Stir 2 tablespoons to 1 cup crème fraîche, sweet cream, sour cream, or yogurt into the pureed soup as you are reheating it.

• Stir about 1 cup cooked long-grain rice into the pureed soup as you are reheating it.

Or make a variation on the main soup:

Pumpkin and Apple Soup
This screams autumn: Add $1/2$ teaspoon ground ginger or 1 teaspoon minced peeled fresh ginger to the soup. Peel, core, and thinly slice 2 apples; cook them in 2 tablespoons butter until lightly browned, turning occasionally. Garnish the soup with the apple slices.

Creamy and Chunky Pumpkin Soup
Measure about 1 cup pumpkin or squash (you will almost always have extra), cut into $1/4$-inch dice, steam until tender, and stir into the soup about 2 minutes before removing from the heat.

Pumpkin and Mushroom Soup
Sauté about 1 cup sliced mushrooms—chanterelles are best, but shiitakes (stems discarded) or button mushrooms are good—in 2 tablespoons butter or extra virgin olive oil until they give up their liquid and begin to get crisp. Garnish the soup with them.

BLACK-EYED PEA SOUP WITH HAM AND GREENS

MAKES 4 SERVINGS   TIME: 45 MINUTES

THE SOUP DRAWS its main flavors from olive oil, cured meat, and watercress. It gains substance and supporting flavors from the peas and a little onion. The combination is delicious, warming, and celebratory in a rustic way. I like to serve with a bottle of Tabasco or any vinegar hot sauce at the table.

2 tablespoons extra virgin olive oil

2 ounces ham, prosciutto, or bacon, chopped

1 medium onion, chopped

2 cups cooked, canned, or frozen black-eyed peas (see Note)

2 cups watercress, trimmed and chopped

Salt and freshly ground black pepper

NOTE

Frozen black-eyed peas (and white beans, chickpeas, and others) can be found in the super-market freezer, and their convenience and quality are unparalleled; they're faster and easier to use than dried beans or peas and far better tasting than canned ones. In the case of black-eyed peas, they need about half an hour to become fully tender. If you use precooked peas or those from a can (please rinse them first), that time will be reduced to almost nothing.

1. Put half the olive oil in a deep skillet or casserole over medium-high heat. Add the meat and cook, stirring, for a minute; then add the onion and cook, stirring occasionally, until it softens and begins to brown, about 10 minutes. Add the peas and 1 quart of water and bring to a boil; turn the heat to medium-low and simmer, uncovered, until the peas are completely tender—10 minutes for cooked or canned, about 30 minutes for frozen.

2. Stir in the watercress and cook, stirring occasionally, for just a couple of minutes, or until it wilts. Add more water if the soup is very thick. Taste and adjust the seasoning, stir in the remaining olive oil, and serve.

CARROT, SPINACH, AND RICE STEW

MAKES 4 SERVINGS   TIME: 45 MINUTES

THIS IS A stew of carrots, spinach, and rice cooked, you might say, to death. I first ate it at a Turkish lunch counter and was taken by its depth of flavor. The whole is definitely greater than the sum of its parts.

$1/2$ pound carrots, cut into $1/4$-inch dice

$3/4$ cup long-grain rice, preferably basmati

Salt and freshly ground pepper

1 pound fresh spinach, thick stems removed, roughly chopped

3 garlic cloves, minced (optional)

2 tablespoons butter (optional)

1. Combine the carrots with 3 cups of water in a saucepan over high heat. Bring to a boil, then stir in the rice and a large pinch of salt. When the mixture returns to a boil, add the spinach, then adjust the heat so that it simmers gently.

2. Cook, stirring occasionally, until the rice and carrots are very tender, about 30 minutes, and the mixture takes on the consistency of a thick stew. When it reaches this stage, stir in the garlic or butter (if you're using either or both) and cook for another 5 minutes. Taste and adjust the seasoning and serve.

ROASTED CHESTNUT SOUP

MAKES 4 SERVINGS   TIME: ABOUT 1 HOUR

CHESTNUTS HAVE A subtle but distinctive flavor; another, less-well-known attribute is their ability to lend a rich, creamy texture to anything in which they're pureed—making cream completely superfluous. This soup is a perfect example, and if you can find frozen, peeled chestnuts, it's the work of a moment. But even if you cannot, the chestnut-peeling process takes about twenty minutes start to finish, and much of that

VARIATIONS

I like to elaborate on this soup in two ways, depending on what I've got in the fridge and whether meat eaters are coming to dinner:

Chestnut Soup with Bacon

Start by rendering $^1/_4$ cup or so of diced slab bacon; scoop out the solids and reserve them for garnish, then sauté the celery and onion in the rendered fat and proceed as directed.

Chestnut Soup with Shiitakes

Garnish the soup with a cup or so of shiitake mushrooms (caps only), sliced and sautéed in butter or oil until crisp.

time is unattended; you can use it to chop and cook the vegetables. In a way, starting from scratch with whole chestnuts is preferable, because they gain a bit of flavor as you toast them lightly to remove the skins.

10 large chestnuts, peeled or unpeeled
2 tablespoons extra virgin olive oil or butter
2 cups chopped celery
$^1/_2$ cup chopped onion

Salt and freshly ground black pepper
1 quart good-quality chicken stock
Chopped celery leaves or parsley for garnish

1. If you have skinned chestnuts, proceed to step 2. If your chestnuts still have their skins, preheat the oven to 350°F. Use a sharp (preferably curved) paring knife to make an X on their flat sides. Roast them in one layer in a baking pan for 10 to 15 minutes, or until their skins begin to open away from the meat. They will then be easy to peel; remove both outer and inner skins while they are warm. (The peeled chestnuts will cook faster if you chop them roughly, but it isn't necessary.)

2. Meanwhile (if you have skinned chestnuts, start here), put the olive oil or butter in a deep skillet or casserole over medium heat. A couple of minutes later, add the celery, onion, and a good sprinkling of salt and pepper and cook, stirring occasionally, until the onion is translucent, about 10 minutes. Add the stock and the chestnuts, bring to a boil, and partially cover. Adjust the heat so that the mixture simmers and cook until the chestnuts are mushy, about 30 minutes.

3. Carefully puree the soup in a blender (if you are not in a hurry, cool it slightly first for extra caution). Measure and add water to make 6 cups of liquid. Reheat, adjust the seasoning if necessary, garnish with celery leaves or parsley, and serve.

CURRIED SWEET POTATO SOUP
WITH APRICOT

MAKES 4 SERVINGS   TIME: ABOUT 1 HOUR

THIS CARIBBEAN-INSPIRED sweet potato soup is always appropriate in hot weather and makes an unusual starter for a meal off the grill. Serve it hot or cold; by all means chill it in warm weather, but remember it in winter. Whether you're reheating it or serving it cold, make the soup as far in advance as you like, up to a couple of days. If you're so inclined, you can make this soup even richer and sweeter by using half chicken stock and half canned coconut milk.

1 tablespoon butter

1 1/2 teaspoons curry powder, or to
    taste

1 large sweet potato (about
    1 pound), peeled and cut into
    chunks

1 cup dried apricots (about
    1 pound)

Salt

1 quart chicken or other stock

1. Put the butter in a casserole or Dutch oven over medium-high heat; when the butter melts, add the curry and cook, stirring, for about 30 seconds. Add the sweet potato and the apricots and cook, stirring occasionally, until well mixed, a minute or so.

2. Season with salt and add the stock. Turn the heat to high and bring to a boil. Cover and adjust the heat so that the mixture simmers. Cook until the potatoes are very tender, 20 to 25 minutes. If time allows, cool.

3. Put the mixture, in batches if necessary, in a blender and puree until smooth, adding a little water or stock if necessary if the mixture is too thick. The recipe can be prepared a day or two in advance up to this point, cooled, and then chilled or reheated to serve.

LIKE ANY BEAN, chickpeas can be cooked without soaking, though they will cook somewhat more quickly if they are soaked for six to twelve hours beforehand. Soaked or not, cooking time for beans is somewhat unpredictable, depending largely on how much moisture they have lost during storage (older beans, being drier, require longer cooking times). Generally speaking, soaked chickpeas will take about one and a half hours to become tender; unsoaked ones will take about thirty minutes longer.

Canned chickpeas do not have as much flavor as cooked dried chickpeas, but they are incomparably more convenient, as dried chickpeas can take three hours to soften. Your choice.

CHICKPEA SOUP WITH SAUSAGE

MAKES 4 SERVINGS   TIME: ABOUT 2 HOURS

THE COOKING LIQUID of chickpeas, unlike that of most other beans, tastes so good that it makes the basis of a decent soup. Season the beans and their stock as they cook—with garlic, herbs, and some aromatic vegetables, for example—and you have the basis of a great soup. Puree some of the cooked chickpeas, then stir them back into the soup, and it becomes deceptively, even sublimely, creamy.

VARIATION

This soup can be made with canned chickpeas: Substitute 4 cups canned chickpeas for the dried chickpeas and combine with 6 cups chicken or vegetable stock and the vegetables as in step 2. Cook until the vegetables are tender, then proceed as directed.

$1^{1}/_{2}$ cups dried chickpeas

5 garlic cloves, sliced

3 fresh rosemary or thyme sprigs

1 medium to large carrot, cut into small dice

1 celery stalk, trimmed and cut into small dice

1 medium onion, cut into small dice

Salt and freshly ground black pepper

1 teaspoon minced garlic

$^{1}/_{2}$ pound sausage, grilled or broiled and thinly sliced (optional)

1 tablespoon extra virgin olive oil, or to taste

1. If you have the time, soak the chickpeas for several hours or overnight in water to cover (if not, don't worry). Combine the chickpeas, sliced garlic, and herb in a large saucepan with fresh water to cover by at least 2 inches. Bring to a boil, turn down the heat, and simmer, partially covered, for at least 1 hour, or until fairly tender. Add water if it is boiling off and skim any foam that rises to the top of the pot.

2. Scoop out the herbs and add the carrot, celery, onion, salt, and pepper to the pot. Continue to cook until the chickpeas and vegetables are soft, at least another 20 minutes. Remove about half the chickpeas and vegetables and carefully puree in a blender with enough of the water to allow the machine to do its work. Return the puree to the soup and stir; reheat with the minced garlic, adding water if the mixture is too thick.

3. Stir in the sausage if you are using it and cook for a few minutes longer. Taste and adjust the seasoning, then serve, drizzled with the olive oil.

WHOLE-MEAL CHICKEN NOODLE SOUP, CHINESE STYLE

MAKES 4 SERVINGS   TIME: 30 MINUTES

FRESH ASIAN-STYLE noodles are everywhere these days—even supermarkets—and they're ideal for soups, because you can cook them right in the broth. It takes only a few minutes, and, unlike dried noodles, they won't make the broth too starchy. Do not overcook the noodles; if you use thin ones, they'll be ready almost immediately after you add them to the simmering stock.

Start with canned chicken stock if you must, but don't skip the step of simmering it briefly with the garlic and ginger, which will give it a decidedly Asian flavor.

6 cups chicken stock

10 slices peeled fresh ginger

2 garlic cloves, peeled and lightly
crushed

1 tablespoon peanut or vegetable
oil

1 teaspoon minced garlic

1 1/2 cups chopped cooked chicken

1 cup broccoli florets, no larger than
1 inch on any side

1 pound fresh thin egg noodles
(labeled "soup noodles" or
"wonton noodle" or simply
"noodles")

2 tablespoons soy sauce, or to taste

1 tablespoon sesame oil

1/2 cup minced scallion

1. Heat the stock with the ginger and crushed garlic while you prepare the other ingredients. Keep it warm and simmering until you are ready to use it.

2. Put the oil in a broad, deep skillet or saucepan over medium-high heat. Add the minced garlic and stir, then add the chicken. Turn the heat to high and cook, stirring occasionally, until the meat begins to brown. Add the broccoli and cook, stirring occasionally, for about 5 minutes.

3. Strain and add the stock; adjust the heat so that it boils gently. Add the noodles and cook, stirring occasionally, until they are separate and tender, about 3 minutes. Stir in the soy sauce and sesame oil, then taste and adjust the seasoning. Divide the soup among 4 bowls; add a little more stock to each if you want the mixture soupier. Garnish with the scallion and serve.

RICH CHICKEN NOODLE SOUP
WITH GINGER

MAKES 4 SERVINGS   TIME: 30 MINUTES

BUY RICE "VERMICELLI," the thinnest rice noodles sold. Substitute angel hair pasta (you'll have to boil it separately) if you like.

Scant $1/2$ pound fine rice noodles

6 cups chicken stock

1 small dried chile

1 tablespoon finely minced peeled fresh ginger

1 bunch of scallions

$1/2$ pound skinless, boneless chicken breast, cut into $1/2$-Inch cubes

$1/4$ pound fresh shiitake mushrooms, stems removed, caps sliced

2 tablespoons nam pla (fish sauce) or soy sauce, or to taste

Salt if necessary

$1/4$ cup roughly chopped fresh cilantro

1. Soak the rice noodles in very hot water to cover. Meanwhile, put the stock in a saucepan with the chile and ginger over medium heat. Trim the scallions; chop the white part and add it to the simmering stock. Chop the green part and set aside.

2. After about 8 minutes of simmering, remove the chile. Drain the noodles and add them, along with the chicken breast and mushrooms. Stir and adjust the heat so the mixture continues to simmer. When the chicken is cooked through, about 10 minutes, add the nam pla; taste and adjust the seasoning—add more nam pla or soy sauce or some salt if necessary, along with the cilantro and reserved scallions, then serve.

MUSHROOM-BARLEY SOUP

MAKES 4 SERVINGS   TIME: 45 MINUTES

A GOOD MUSHROOM BARLEY soup needs no meat, because you can make it with dried porcini, which can be reconstituted in hot water in less than ten minutes, giving you not only the best-tasting mushrooms you can find outside of the woods but an intensely flavored broth that rivals beef stock. A touch of soy sauce is untraditional but really enhances the flavor.

$3/4$ ounce dried porcini (about $3/4$ cup)

2 tablespoons olive oil

$1/4$ pound shiitake or button (white) mushrooms, stemmed and roughly chopped

2 medium carrots, sliced

$3/4$ cup pearled barley

Salt and freshly ground black pepper

1 bay leaf

1 tablespoon soy sauce

1. Soak the porcini in 1 quart of very hot water. Put the olive oil in a medium saucepan and turn the heat to high. Add the shiitakes and carrots and cook, stirring occasionally, until they begin to brown. Add the barley and continue to cook, stirring frequently, until it begins to brown; sprinkle with a little salt and pepper. Remove the porcini from their soaking liquid (do *not* discard the liquid); sort through and discard any hard bits.

2. Add the porcini to the pot and cook, stirring, for about a minute. Add the bay leaf, the mushroom-soaking water, and 5 cups additional water (or stock if you prefer). Bring to a boil, then lower the heat and simmer until the barley is very tender, 20 to 30 minutes. If the soup is very thick, add a little more water. Add the soy sauce, then taste and add more salt if necessary and plenty of pepper. Serve hot.

SALADS

SIMPLE GREEN SALAD

MAKES 4 SERVINGS   TIME: 10 MINUTES

MANY PEOPLE ARE hooked on premade salad dressing because they believe that homemade dressing is a production, but it need not be. Try this. (And see Basic Vinaigrette, page 304, or Soy or Nut Vinaigrette, page 44.)

About 6 cups torn assorted greens

1/4 cup extra virgin olive oil, more
    or less

2 tablespoons balsamic vinegar or
    sherry vinegar, or fresh lemon
    juice to taste

Salt and freshly ground black
    pepper (pepper optional)

Put the greens in a bowl and drizzle them with oil, vinegar, and a pinch of salt. Toss and taste. Correct the seasoning, add pepper if desired, and serve immediately.

HERBED GREEN SALAD, TWO WAYS

MAKES 4 SERVINGS   TIME: 20 MINUTES

A LOAD OF herbs and a strongly flavored vinaigrette make this salad special. Choose either the soy or the nut vinaigrette depending on what appeals to you, what you're serving the salad with, and what you've got on hand.

1 cup assorted chopped mild fresh
    herbs, like parsley, dill, mint,
    basil, and/or chervil

2 tablespoons minced fresh chives

1/2 teaspoon minced fresh tarragon
    (optional)

6 cups mesclun or other greens

Soy Vinaigrette or Nut Vinaigrette
    (recipes follow)

1. Combine the herbs and greens; cover with a damp towel and refrigerate for up to 24 hours until ready to serve.

2. When you're ready to serve, prepare one of the vinaigrettes and toss with the greens. Add more salt or lemon juice if necessary and serve immediately.

Soy Vinaigrette

Whisk together $1/2$ cup grapeseed or olive oil, $1/4$ cup fresh lemon juice, 2 tablespoons soy sauce, and a large pinch each of salt and pepper. Taste and add more salt if necessary (it may not be).

Nut Vinaigrette

Whisk together $1/4$ cup hazelnut or walnut oil, $1/4$ cup olive oil, $1/4$ cup fresh lemon juice, and a large pinch each of salt and pepper. Taste and add more salt if necessary (it may not be).

====

PEAR AND GORGONZOLA GREEN SALAD WITH WALNUTS

MAKES 4 SERVINGS   TIME: 20 TO 30 MINUTES

AS FAR A cry from iceberg lettuce and bottled dressing as you can imagine, this is a magical combination of powerful flavors made without cooking or any major challenges.

Simple as this salad is, without top-quality ingredients it won't amount to much. So use sherry or good balsamic vinegar to make the dressing, use pears that are tender and very juicy, not crunchy, mushy, or dry, and use real Italian Gorgonzola. It should be creamy; if you can taste it before buying, so much the better.

This rich salad can serve as the centerpiece of a light lunch, accompanied by little more than bread. It makes an equally great starter for a grand dinner—followed by roasted meat or fish, for example—or a simple one, served with soup.

2 large pears (about 1 pound)
1 tablespoon fresh lemon juice
1 cup walnuts
$^1/_4$ pound Gorgonzola or other creamy blue cheese

6 cups mixed greens, torn into bite-sized pieces
About $^1/_2$ cup Basic Vinaigrette (page 304)

1. Peel and core the pears; cut them into $^1/_2$-inch chunks and toss with the lemon juice. Cover and refrigerate for up to 2 hours until needed.

2. Put the walnuts in a dry skillet over medium heat and toast them, shaking the pan frequently, until they are aromatic and beginning to darken in color, 3 to 5 minutes. Set aside to cool.

3. Crumble the Gorgonzola into small bits; cover and refrigerate until needed.

4. When you're ready to serve, toss the pears, cheese, and greens together with as much of the dressing as you like. Crumble the toasted walnuts over the salad and serve immediately.

BIG CHOPPED SALAD WITH VINAIGRETTE

MAKES 8 SERVINGS   TIME: 30 MINUTES

THIS IS A salad for a small crowd, though it can be made as big or as little as you like. But please, see this ingredients list as a series of suggestions rather than dogma—a chopped salad can contain any combination that appeals to you, including raw vegetables like broccoli or cauliflower or crunchy cabbages like bok choy, as well as nuts, seeds, and fruit.

1 big head of romaine lettuce

1 bunch of arugula

1 bunch of watercress

2 medium cucumbers or 1 English
   (seedless) cucumber

1 bunch of radishes

2 yellow or red bell peppers

1 small sweet onion, such as Vidalia

2 carrots

2 celery stalks

1 cup extra virgin olive oil

$1/3$ cup good-quality vinegar, more
   or less

1 shallot, minced

1 tablespoon Dijon mustard

Salt and freshly ground black
   pepper

1. Roughly chop the greens and put them in a big bowl.

2. Peel the cucumber, then cut it in half lengthwise; seed if necessary and chop into $1/2$-inch dice. Trim the radishes and chop into $1/2$-inch dice. Seed and core the peppers and chop into $1/2$-inch dice. Peel and mince the onion. Chop the carrots into $1/2$-inch dice. Chop the celery into $1/2$-inch dice. Toss all the vegetables with the greens.

3. Combine the oil, vinegar, shallot, and mustard and beat with a fork or wire whisk, or emulsify in a blender or with an immersion blender. Season with salt and pepper, then taste and adjust the seasoning as necessary.

4. Just before serving, toss the salad with the dressing.

RAW BEET SALAD

MAKES 4 SERVINGS   TIME: 10 MINUTES

EATEN RAW, BEETS are delicious; even many self-proclaimed beet haters will like them in this salad.

To eat a beet raw, you have to peel it and shred it. The first step is easiest with a regular vegetable peeler. I do the second with the metal blade of a food processor, pulsing the machine on and off until the beets are finely cut. You could use the shredding blade, but it isn't any easier or better. Or you could use a manual grater, but only if you're looking for an upper-body workout.

1 pound beets

1 large shallot

Salt and freshly ground black
    pepper

2 teaspoons Dijon mustard, or to
    taste

1 tablespoon extra virgin olive oil

2 tablespoons sherry vinegar or
    other good-quality strong
    vinegar

Minced fresh parsley, dill, chervil,
    rosemary, or tarragon

1. Peel the beets and the shallot. Combine them in a food processor fitted with the metal blade and pulse carefully until the beets are shredded; do not puree. (Or grate the beets by hand and mince the shallots; combine.) Scrape into a bowl.

2. Toss with the salt, pepper, mustard, oil, and vinegar. Taste and adjust the seasoning. Toss in the herbs and serve.

SIMPLE CUCUMBER SALAD

MAKES 4 SERVINGS   TIME: 1 HOUR, LARGELY UNATTENDED

MANY CUCUMBERS ARE best if they're salted first. The process removes some of their bitterness and makes them extra-crisp—it takes some time but almost no effort. Start with one or two Kirby (pickling) cucumbers per person—or half of a medium cucumber or about a third of a long ("English") cucumber.

For a full-meal cucumber salad with a Southeast Asian flair, try Cucumber Salad with Scallops (page 54).

About 1 1/2 pounds cucumbers,
   peeled and thinly sliced
Salt and freshly ground black
   pepper

1/2 cup coarsely chopped and
   loosely packed fresh mint
   or dill
Juice of 1/2 lemon

1. Put the cucumber slices in a colander and sprinkle with salt, just a little more than if you were planning to eat them right away. Set the colander in the sink.

2. After 30 to 45 minutes, press the cucumbers to extract as much liquid as possible. Toss them with the mint, the lemon juice, and a healthy grinding of black pepper. Serve within a few hours.

SEAWEED SALAD WITH CUCUMBER

MAKES 4 SERVINGS   TIME: 20 MINUTES

THIS IS SIMPLY a kind of sea-based mesclun with a distinctively sesame-flavored dressing. The only challenge in making it lies in the shopping. Few supermarkets carry any seaweed at all, so you need to hit an Asian or health food market for any kind of selection. At most Japanese markets and some health food stores, you can find what amounts to a prepackaged assortment of seaweed salad greens; these are a little more expensive than buying individual seaweeds but will give you a good variety without a big investment.

1 ounce wakame or assorted
   seaweeds
1/2 pound cucumber, preferably thin
   skinned, like Kirby, English, or
   Japanese cucumber
Salt if necessary
1/4 cup minced shallot, scallion, or
   red onion

2 tablespoons soy sauce
1 tablespoon rice wine vinegar or
   other light vinegar
1 tablespoon mirin
1 tablespoon sesame oil
1/4 teaspoon cayenne, or to taste
1 tablespoon toasted sesame seeds
   (optional)

1. Rinse the seaweed once and soak it in at least ten times its volume of water.

2. Wash and dice the cucumber; do not peel unless necessary. (You can salt it if you like; see the preceding recipe.) When the seaweed is tender, 5 minutes later, drain and gently squeeze the mixture to remove excess water. Pick through the seaweed to sort out any hard bits (there may be none) and chop or cut up (you can use scissors, which you may find easier) if the pieces are large. Combine the cucumber and seaweed mixture in a bowl.

3. Toss with the remaining ingredients except the sesame seeds; taste and add salt or other seasonings as necessary and serve garnished with the sesame seeds if you like.

TOMATO SALAD WITH BASIL

MAKES 4 SERVINGS   TIME: 10 MINUTES

SO FEW INGREDIENTS and so much flavor—as long as the ingredients are of high quality! Omit the basil if you can't find any, but where there are good tomatoes there is probably good basil. Add slices of mozzarella to make this more substantial.

4 medium tomatoes, perfectly ripe
Salt and freshly ground black
   pepper

A handful of fresh basil leaves,
   roughly chopped
Extra virgin olive oil

1. Core the tomatoes (cut a cone-shaped wedge out of the stem end) and cut them into slices about $1/4$ inch thick.

2. Lay the tomatoes on a platter or 4 individual plates. Sprinkle with salt, pepper, and basil, drizzle with olive oil, and serve.

WATERMELON, THAI STYLE

MAKES 4 SERVINGS   TIME: 10 MINUTES

A FREQUENTLY SEEN snack in Bangkok and elsewhere in Southeast Asia.

Four 1-inch-thick wedges of
   watermelon
Salt

Finely ground dried red chile
Lime wedges

Put the watermelon on plates and pass the remaining ingredients, allowing guests to season the watermelon to taste.

ASIAN CHICKEN SALAD WITH GREENS

MAKES 4 SERVINGS   TIME: 30 TO 40 MINUTES

THIS SALAD FEATURES grilled chicken; a superflavorful dressing based on soy sauce, peanut or sesame butter, and spices; and cucumber for crunch. Make extra dressing and you can serve the chicken on top of a bed of salad greens.

    Boneless chicken thighs are preferable to breasts, because their flavor and texture are superior, they remain moist during grilling, and they brown perfectly.

VARIATIONS
- Add minced bell pepper (preferably red or yellow), celery, and/or zucchini to the mix.
- Garnish with fresh basil (Thai basil is especially good), mint, or minced scallion in place of or in addition to the cilantro.

$1^1/_2$ pounds skinless, boneless
   chicken thighs or breasts
$^1/_4$ cup soy sauce
3 tablespoons peanut butter or
   tahini (sesame paste)
2 teaspoons sesame oil
2 small garlic cloves, peeled
A few drops of hot sauce, like
   Tabasco

Salt and freshly ground black
   pepper
$^1/_2$ teaspoon sugar
2 tablespoons rice wine vinegar or
   other mild vinegar
1 cucumber
6 cups salad greens
$^1/_2$ cup minced fresh cilantro

1. Start a grill or preheat the broiler. Cut the chicken meat into $1/2$- to 1-inch chunks and thread it onto skewers (if you're broiling, you can forget the skewers and simply use a roasting pan). Put the skewers on a plate and drizzle with 2 tablespoons of the soy sauce.

2. In a blender, combine the remaining soy sauce with the peanut butter, sesame oil, garlic, hot sauce, salt and pepper to taste, sugar, and vinegar. Add $1/3$ cup of warm water and process until the mixture is smooth and creamy. (You can add as much as you like; garlic, vinegar, and sesame oil also can be added to taste.) Put the dressing in the refrigerator to cool.

3. Grill or broil the chicken, turning once or twice. Total cooking time will be 6 to 8 minutes for breasts, 10 to 12 minutes for thighs. Meanwhile, peel the cucumber (if it is waxed), slice it in half the long way, and scoop out the seeds with a spoon. Cut it into $1/2$-inch dice and combine in a bowl with the dressing. When the chicken is done, let it rest and cool on a cutting board for a few minutes, then toss it with a tablespoon or two of the dressing and cucumber.

4. Toss the dressing and cucumbers with the greens, top with the chicken, garnish with the cilantro, and serve.

SOUTHEAST ASIAN SHRIMP AND GRAPEFRUIT SALAD

MAKES 4 SERVINGS   TIME: 30 MINUTES

THIS IS A nearly traditional salad in which the grapefruit plays a leading role, complementing mild shrimp and allowing you to make an almost ridiculously easy dressing, made up of nothing more than fish sauce (called nam pla in Thailand and nuoc mam in Vietnam), or soy, lime, a bit of sugar, and some water. Use good shrimp—Pacific or Gulf whites are the best, though the less expensive and widely available tiger shrimp are acceptable—and buy them big, because you'll have fewer to peel.

1 to 1^1/$_2$ pounds shrimp

Salt

3 tablespoons nam pla (fish sauce) or soy sauce

1 tablespoon sugar

Juice of 2 limes

6 cups lettuce or mesclun

2 grapefruit, peeled and sectioned, tough white pith removed, each section cut in half (see Note)

^{1}/$_4$ cup chopped fresh mint

^{1}/$_4$ cup chopped fresh cilantro or basil, preferably Thai basil

Minced fresh chile or hot red pepper flakes (optional)

^{1}/$_2$ cup chopped dry-roasted peanuts (optional)

1. Put the shrimp in a saucepan with salted water to cover; bring to a boil, then turn off the heat and let sit for 5 minutes, or until opaque in the center. Cool in the refrigerator or under cold running water, then peel (and devein if you like). Cut the shrimp in half if they're large.

2. Meanwhile, make the dressing: Combine the nam pla or soy sauce with 2 tablespoons of water, the sugar, and the lime juice and blend or whisk until smooth.

3. Arrange the lettuce on 4 plates; top each portion with a few grapefruit pieces, some shrimp, and the mint and cilantro; drizzle with the dressing, then sprinkle with a little chile and chopped peanuts if you like, or pass them at the table.

═══════════════

MINTY BROILED SHRIMP SALAD

MAKES 4 SERVINGS   TIME: 20 TO 30 MINUTES

I DEVISED THIS recipe to harness the delicious juices shrimp exude as they're cooking—the shrimp essence. Not wanting to completely overwhelm delicately flavored greens with the powerfully spiced shrimp, I use a mixture of arugula, lettuce, and a high proportion of mint, dressed with olive oil and lemon juice. The result is a nice, juicy, big, flavorful—and easy—salad.

2 pounds shrimp in the 15-to-30-
per-pound range, peeled and, if
you like, deveined

1 teaspoon minced garlic, or more
to taste

1 teaspoon salt

$1/2$ teaspoon cayenne, or to taste

1 teaspoon paprika

$1/4$ cup olive oil

2 tablespoons plus 2 teaspoons
fresh lemon juice

30 to 40 fresh mint leaves

6 cups arugula and/or other greens

1. Preheat the broiler and put the rack as close to the heat source as possible. Put a large ovenproof skillet or heavy-bottomed roasting pan on the stove over low heat.

2. Combine the shrimp with the garlic, salt, cayenne, paprika, half the olive oil, and the 2 teaspoons lemon juice; stir to blend. Turn the heat under the skillet to high.

3. When the skillet smokes, toss in the shrimp. Shake the pan once or twice to distribute them evenly, then immediately put the skillet under the broiler.

4. Mince about one-third of the mint. Tear the remaining leaves and toss them with the arugula. Stir the remaining olive oil and lemon juice together in a bowl.

5. The shrimp are done when opaque; this will take only 3 or 4 minutes. Use a slotted spoon to transfer the shrimp to a plate; it's fine if they cool for a moment. Add the shrimp juices to the olive oil–lemon juice mixture and stir. Dress the greens with this mixture and toss (if the greens seem dry, add a little more olive oil, lemon juice, or both). Put the greens on a platter and arrange the shrimp on top of or around them; garnish the shrimp with the minced mint.

VARIATIONS

Spicy Chicken Salad
This is better with skinless, boneless chicken thighs than breasts. Marinate and cook 1-inch chunks as you would the shrimp; they will take about the same amount of time. Remove the chicken, then put the pan over a burner; turn the heat to high and add $1/2$ cup of water. Stir and scrape to release any of the flavorful bits remaining in the pan (the chicken will not release as much liquid as the shrimp, which is why this step is necessary). When the liquid is reduced to a couple of tablespoons, combine it with the olive oil–lemon mixture and proceed as directed.

Spanish-Style Broiled Shrimp Salad
Substitute sherry vinegar for lemon juice and add a teaspoon of ground cumin along with the paprika. Use chopped parsley or tarragon in place of mint.

Southeast Asian–Style Broiled Shrimp Salad
Use peanut oil in place of olive oil, lime juice in place of lemon juice, and cilantro in place of mint. Add a tablespoon or two of soy sauce or fish sauce (nam pla or nuoc mam) to the salad before tossing it.

• Toss a cup of roughly
chopped watercress,
arugula, or spinach into the
cucumbers before dressing.

• Add a cup of peeled and
minced apple, jícama, or
minced bell pepper—
preferably red, yellow, or a
combination—to the
cucumbers.

• Thinly slice a medium
onion and separate it
into rings. Salt the rings
along with the cucumbers;
their flavor will mellow
considerably.

• Increase the amount of
fresh herbs to 1 cup.

• Toss a cup of bean
sprouts into the salad.

Cucumber Salad
with Chicken

Marinate 1 to 1^1/2 pounds
skinless, boneless chicken
breasts in a mixture of
2 tablespoons nam pla
or soy sauce and
2 tablespoons fresh lime
juice while the cucumbers
drain. Grill or broil the
chicken until it is done,
about 3 minutes per side.
Cut into strips and serve as
you would the scallops.

CUCUMBER SALAD WITH SCALLOPS

MAKES 4 SERVINGS
TIME: ABOUT 1 HOUR (SOMEWHAT UNATTENDED)

SOMETIMES A SIMPLE salad features such powerful flavors that by adding a couple of straightforward ingredients a whole meal appears as if by magic. Here the starting place is a Southeast Asian–style cucumber salad, with a dressing made from lime juice, lemongrass, fish sauce (called *nam pla* in Thailand and *nuoc mam* in Vietnam), and a few other strong seasonings.

This dressing commingles perfectly with the natural juices of the cucumbers to moisten the greens. Top all with grilled scallops—or other fish or meat—and you create an easy one-dish meal whose flavor really jumps off the plate. It looks lovely, too, especially if your cucumbers are good enough to leave unpeeled. And (although not by design, I assure you), this salad is extremely low in fat.

4 medium cucumbers, at least 2 pounds	^{1}/2 teaspoon sugar
Salt	6 cups mixed salad greens
2 tablespoons nam pla (fish sauce)	1 to 1^1/2 pounds sea scallops
Juice of 2 limes	1 tablespoon neutral oil, like corn or grapeseed
1 small garlic clove, very finely minced	^{1}/8 teaspoon cayenne
Hot red pepper flakes or finely minced fresh chiles	^{1}/2 cup chopped fresh mint, cilantro, basil, or a combination
1 tablespoon minced lemongrass	2 teaspoons sesame oil

1. Peel the cucumbers if they have been waxed, then trim their ends and cut them in half the long way. Scoop out the seeds with an ordinary teaspoon. Sprinkle each half with about ^{1}/4 teaspoon salt, then put them all in a colander. Let drain in the sink for about 30 minutes. Rinse lightly and drain again. Cut into ^{1}/8- to ^{1}/4-inch-thick slices and put in a bowl.

2. Mix together the fish sauce, lime juice, garlic, hot pepper to taste, lemongrass, and sugar. Thin with a tablespoon of water. Taste and add more of any flavoring you wish. Toss the dressing with the cucumbers and set aside.

3. Put the greens on a large platter. Put a large nonstick skillet over high heat. Toss the scallops with the oil, then sprinkle them with salt and the cayenne. When the skillet begins to smoke, add the scallops, one at a time and without crowding, until they are all in the pan. Cook for about 2 minutes on the first side, turning as they brown; depending on their size, cook for 1 to 3 minutes on the second side. (Scallops are best when their interior is slightly underdone; cut into one to check it.)

4. Toss the cucumbers with most of the herbs and spoon them and all of their juices over the greens. Top with the scallops. Drizzle with the sesame oil and top with the remaining herbs. Serve immediately.

Cucumber Salad with Shrimp

Treat the shrimp exactly as you do the scallops: Cook about 1^1/2 pounds shrimp (unpeeled are fine if you're willing to let your family or guests use their fingers at the table) the same way, until pink all over. Or peel the shrimp and marinate them for about 30 minutes in a mixture of 1 teaspoon minced garlic, 1 tablespoon coarse salt, ^{1}/2 teaspoon cayenne, 1 teaspoon paprika, 2 tablespoons olive oil, and 2 teaspoons fresh lemon juice. Then cook and serve the shrimp as you would the scallops.

TRIPLE SESAME SALAD WITH SCALLOPS

MAKES 4 SERVINGS   TIME: 20 MINUTES

THE PERFECT WHOLE-MEAL salad features as much flavor, texture, and bulk as any other well-prepared meal, and the fact that the base is a pile of greens makes me feel like I'm getting away with something. This one takes about ten minutes longer than a plain green salad and by changing the topping can be made in different ways every time, always with a minimum of effort.

Use a blender for the dressing; it makes quick work of dispersing the sesame paste or peanut butter throughout the liquid ingredients—something that can be a real hassle with a fork or a whisk—creating a perfect emulsion. And because the blender purees the garlic and ginger, there's no need to mince them; just peel, chop roughly, and drop them into the blender with the other ingredients.

My first choice for topping this salad is grilled scallops—they're almost ludicrously fast and easy, and their texture and flavor complement both greens and dressing—though shrimp, steak, or chicken thighs all could be substituted.

1/4 cup soy sauce

1/4 cup rice wine or other vinegar

2 tablespoons tahini (sesame paste) or smooth peanut butter

1 tablespoon sesame oil

1/4 teaspoon hot red pepper flakes, cayenne, or ground dried chile, or to taste

1 tablespoon honey

1/2 teaspoon chopped garlic

1 teaspoon chopped peeled fresh ginger

1 1/2 to 2 pounds sea scallops

Salt

6 to 8 cups mesclun or other salad greens

1/4 cup torn fresh Thai or other basil (optional)

2 tablespoons toasted sesame seeds

1. Start a grill. Combine the soy sauce, vinegar, tahini, sesame oil, hot pepper, honey, garlic, and ginger in a blender and whiz until smooth. When the grill is hot, sprinkle the scallops with salt and grill them for about 2 minutes per side; they should remain tender and under-cooked in the middle.

2. Combine the greens and basil if you're using it and divide among 4 plates. When the scallops are done, top the greens with them, then drizzle with the dressing; sprinkle with the sesame seeds and serve.

MUSSEL AND POTATO SALAD

MAKES 4 SERVINGS   TIME: 45 MINUTES

FOR POTATO SALADS, my dressing of choice is usually a simple vinai-grette—here no more than oil and vinegar—augmented by a handful each of chopped shallots for crunch and flavor and parsley for color and freshness. The result is a great summer dish, good-looking and good-tasting. As it stands, this is a potato salad with mussels; if you like, you can increase the amount of mussels, by as much as double, giving each component equal weight.

2 pounds mussels, well washed and debearded

2 pounds waxy potatoes, cut into $1/2$-inch cubes

$1/2$ cup dry white wine or water

$1/2$ cup chopped shallot or red onion

$1/2$ cup extra virgin olive oil, or more to taste

$1/2$ cup balsamic or sherry vinegar

Salt and freshly ground black pepper

$1/2$ cup chopped fresh parsley, dill, chives, or a combination

1. Combine the mussels, potatoes, and wine or water in a broad, steep-sided skillet or casserole. Cover and turn the heat to high. When steam arises from the top, shake the pan once or twice and turn the heat to medium. Continue to cook until all the mussels open, checking after 5 minutes or so and then every couple of minutes. When the mussels are done, use tongs or a slotted spoon to transfer them to a plate; leave the potatoes in the skillet and re-cover.

2. Cook until the potatoes are almost tender, then remove the cover and turn the heat to high, cooking until most of the liquid evaporates and the potatoes are done. By this time, the mussels will be cool enough to remove from their shells, do so, putting them in a large bowl.

3. When the potatoes are done, add them to the bowl with the mussels and the shallot, oil, vinegar, salt, and pepper. Taste and adjust the seasoning as necessary. Serve immediately, an hour or two later, or cold, stirring in the herb(s) at the last moment.

RICE SALAD WITH PEAS AND SOY

MAKES 4 TO 6 SERVINGS   TIME: ABOUT 30 MINUTES

YOU CAN USE any short- or medium-grain rice you like for this dish, which is most easily made with leftover rice.

Salt and freshly ground black
   pepper
$1/2$ cup fresh or frozen peas
1 cup Arborio rice
$1/4$ cup minced shallot
$1/4$ cup fresh lime juice, plus more
   as needed

2 tablespoons peanut, grapeseed,
   corn, or other neutral oil
2 tablespoons soy sauce
$1/4$ cup minced fresh cilantro

1. Bring a small pot of water to a boil; salt it. Bring a large pot of water to a boil; salt it. Cook the peas in the small pot for about 2 minutes, or until they lose their raw flavor. Drain and rinse in cold water to stop the cooking. Drain and set aside.

2. When the large pot of water comes to a boil, add the rice and cook, stirring, until it is completely tender, about 15 minutes. Drain the rice and rinse it quickly under cold water to stop the cooking, but don't chill it entirely.

3. Stir the shallot into the rice and mix well. Add the lime juice, oil, and soy and mix well again. Add the cilantro, peas, and pepper and mix. Taste and add more lime juice, soy sauce, or pepper as needed. Serve immediately or refrigerate, well covered, for up to a day. Bring back to room temperature before serving.

GRILLED BREAD SALAD

MAKES 4 SERVINGS

TIME: 45 TO 60 MINUTES (SOMEWHAT UNATTENDED)

EVERYONE LOVES BREAD salad, which—traditionally at least—was most often made with stale bread. You can wait around for bread to get stale, but really the best way to ready bread for salad is to use the grill or broiler to quickly dry the bread while charring the edges slightly, adding another dimension of flavor to the salad. But watch the bread carefully as you grill or broil it; a slight char is good, but it's a short step from toast to burned bread. The time you allow the bread to soften after tossing it with the seasonings varies; keep tasting until the texture pleases you. If your tomatoes are on the dry side, you might add a little extra liquid in the form of more olive oil and lemon juice or a light sprinkling of water.

Because it's juicy, almost saucy, and pleasantly acidic, this salad makes a nice accompaniment to simple grilled meat or poultry and has a special affinity for dark fish such as tuna and swordfish.

1 small baguette (about 8 ounces) or other crusty bread

$1/4$ cup extra virgin olive oil

$1/4$ cup fresh lemon juice or good-quality vinegar

2 tablespoons diced shallot, scallion, or red onion

$1/4$ teaspoon minced garlic (optional)

$1 1/2$ pounds tomatoes, chopped

Salt and freshly ground black pepper

$1/4$ cup or more roughly chopped fresh basil or parsley

1. Start a grill or preheat the broiler; the rack should be 4 to 6 inches from the heat source. Cut the bread lengthwise into quarters. Grill or broil the bread, watching carefully and turning as each side browns and chars slightly; total time will be about 5 minutes.

2. While the bread cools, mix together the olive oil, lemon juice, shallot, garlic (if using), and tomatoes in a large bowl. Mash the tomatoes with the back of a fork to release all of their juices. Season with salt

VARIATIONS

Bread Salad Served with Seafood

If you're serving the salad alongside seafood, consider adding $1/4$ cup chopped olives, 1 tablespoon capers, and/or 2 minced anchovy fillets (or a little less of each) to the salad.

Bread Salad with Shrimp or Chicken

Grill or broil some shrimp or skinless, boneless chicken alongside the bread (you don't need as much as you would if you were serving the shrimp or chicken apart from the salad), then add the chunks to the salad.

Bread Salad with Tuna

Add a goodly amount of tuna (only the Italian kind, packed in olive oil, please) to the mix.

and pepper to taste. Cut the bread into $^1/_2$- to 1-inch cubes (no larger) and toss it with the dressing.

3. Let the bread sit for 20 to 30 minutes, tossing occasionally and tasting a piece every now and then. The salad is at its peak when the bread is fairly soft but some edges remain crisp, but you can serve it before or after it reaches that state. When it's ready, stir in the herb and serve.

SHELLFISH

FENNEL-STEAMED MUSSELS, PROVENCE STYLE

MAKES 4 SERVINGS   TIME: 30 MINUTES

IN A CAFÉ in southern France about thirty years ago, I sat in a bistro and timidly prepared to order salade Niçoise. Just then, a huge bowl of steaming, powerfully fragrant mussels was delivered to a man sitting at the table next to me, and I boldly changed my order. The hot mussels were essentially tossed with fennel and fennel seeds, which I could see, but the licorice bouquet and indeed flavor were far stronger than that combination alone could provide. Later, I realized that there was a secret ingredient: an anise liqueur, either Pernod or Ricard. The combination is alluring.

2 tablespoons extra virgin olive oil

4 garlic cloves, smashed and peeled

1 fennel bulb (about 1 pound), trimmed and thinly sliced

2 tablespoons fennel seeds

1/2 cup Pernod or Ricard or 4 whole star anise

1 cup chopped tomatoes, fresh or drained canned (optional)

1 fresh tarragon sprig (optional)

At least 4 pounds large mussels, well washed and debearded

1. Put the oil in a large pot over medium heat; a minute later, add the garlic, fennel, fennel seeds, liqueur, and tomatoes and tarragon if you're using them. Bring to a boil, cook for about a minute, add the mussels, cover the pot, and turn the heat to high.

2. Cook, shaking the pot occasionally, until the mussels open, 5 to 10 minutes. Use a slotted spoon to transfer the mussels and fennel to a serving bowl, then strain any liquid over them and serve.

VARIATIONS

There are many, many herbs, spices, vegetables, and other seasonings that can lend a licorice flavor, including anise seeds or ground anise; five-spice powder; ouzo or raki, the anise-scented liqueurs of the eastern Mediterranean; and tarragon, chervil, even basil—especially Thai basil. (You could probably throw in a few pieces of Good&Plenty while you're at it.)

Or you can go super-minimal and make plain steamed mussels. The procedure is the same, but omit all ingredients except mussels, oil, and garlic. Shake the pot a couple of times while cooking. These are great with a little melted butter (laced with minced garlic if you like) drizzled over them and a big loaf of crusty bread.

EVERY YEAR, we see more and more cultivated mussels, most often from Prince Edward Island, which is fast becoming the mussel farming capital of North America. These are easy to clean (almost clean enough to eat without washing, but still worth a quick going over), with very few rejects and plump meat. Wild mussels are far tastier but harder to clean.

When cleaning mussels, discard any with broken shells. If the mussels have beards—the hairy vegetative growth that is attached to the shell—trim them off. Those mussels that remain closed after the majority have been steamed open can be pried open with a knife (a butter knife works fine) at the table.

VARIATIONS

Curried Steamed Mussels
Substitute butter for the oil. Substitute shallot for the scallion and omit the ginger and garlic. When the shallot is soft, sprinkle with 1 teaspoon curry powder and cook, stirring, for another 30 seconds. Cook and finish as directed, substituting the juice of 1 lime for the soy sauce.

Thai Steamed Mussels
Use peanut oil. Add 1 lemongrass stalk, roughly chopped; 1 small dried hot red chile; and 2 lime leaves to the scallion, ginger, and garlic. Substitute nam pla (fish sauce) for the soy sauce.

STEAMED MUSSELS, ASIAN STYLE

MAKES 4 SERVINGS   TIME: 30 MINUTES

MOST STEAMED MUSSEL preparations contain parsley, garlic, and white wine, with the occasional addition of tomatoes and herbs. There are, however, other directions to take with no additional effort. Generally, there are two easy changes to make: First, use distinctive Asian seasonings like ginger, soy, or curry powder. And second, omit the cooking liquid. By relying only on the mussels' natural juices, you can add fewer seasonings (and less of each) and still produce a flavorful sauce that is less watery than most. I always serve Asian-style mussels with a bowl of rice on the side.

2 tablespoons peanut or corn oil
$^1/_4$ cup roughly chopped scallion
1 tablespoon roughly chopped peeled fresh ginger

2 garlic cloves, lightly smashed
4 pounds mussels, well washed and debearded
1 tablespoon soy sauce

1. Put the oil in a saucepan large enough to hold all the mussels and turn the heat to medium. A minute later, add the scallion, ginger, and garlic and cook, stirring occasionally, for about 1 minute.

2. Add the mussels, turn the heat to high, and cover the pot. Cook, shaking the pot occasionally, until they all (or nearly all) open, about 10 minutes. Turn off the heat.

3. Scoop the mussels into a serving bowl. Add the soy sauce to the liquid, then pass it through a fine strainer (or a coarse one lined with cheesecloth). Pour the liquid over the mussels and serve.

———————————

BLACK SKILLET MUSSELS

MAKES 2 SERVINGS   TIME: 30 MINUTES

MANY YEARS AGO in Barcelona, I saw mussels and clams cooked *a la plancha*—on a thick slab of hot metal much like the griddles used by short-order cooks. The technique is common in Spain, indeed throughout the Mediterranean. Though the mollusks are usually served unadorned, they're filled with their own flavors as well as a certain smokiness contributed by their juices, which burn on the hot surface. This smokiness sometimes makes people think that mussels cooked this way are cooked over wood, but that is not the case, nor is it necessary. It's best to serve the mussels in the same skillet in which they cooked. To eat, remove a mussel from the shell and dredge it on the dried juices of the pan.

About 1¹/₂ pounds mussels, washed and debearded

Salt and freshly ground black pepper

1. Heat a large cast-iron or heavy steel skillet over high heat for about 5 minutes, or until a few drops of water dance across the surface. Add the mussels to the skillet in one layer (your pan may fit more or less than 1¹/₂ pounds; use only as many as will fit comfortably or use 2 pans).

Steamed Clams with Soy
Most mussel recipes will work for steamers, which are also known as *soft-shell clams*. But steamers must be rinsed after shucking to remove all traces of sand, and you don't want to dilute these delicious broths by dipping clams into them one after the other. The solution is to substitute littlenecks—small hardshell clams, the kind served on the half shell and used for pasta with clam sauce—for the mussels. These contain no sand at all, but because their shells are heavier, use 1¹/₂ to 2 pounds of littlenecks to replace each pound of mussels. Proceed exactly as directed.

VARIATIONS
Black Skillet Clams or Oysters

This dish can be made with hardshell clams—littlenecks, cherrystones, or quahogs— or with oysters. (Softshell clams, or steamers, are too sandy for this treatment.) Be sure to wash the shells of any of these mollusks very well and discard any whose shells are open or cracked. As with the mussels, they are done when their shells open.

To add a slightly different flavor:

• When the mussels begin to open, add 4 cloves of crushed, peeled garlic to the pan, shaking the pan as directed.

• Gently melt 4 tablespoons (1/2 stick) butter in a small saucepan. (If you like, add Tabasco or other hot sauce to taste, along with the juice of a lemon.) Serve it alongside the pan of mussels. To eat, remove a mussel from its shell, dip into the butter, then rub up some of the dried juices from the bottom of the skillet.

2. Cook, shaking the pan occasionally, until the mussels begin to open. The mussels are done when they're all open and their juices have run out and evaporated in the hot pan. Sprinkle with salt and pepper and serve immediately, in the pan.

=====

CRABBY CRAB CAKES

MAKES 4 SERVINGS   TIME: 1 HOUR, LARGELY UNATTENDED

CRAB HAS THE best texture and among the best flavor of all of the crustaceans, and the best crab cakes are those that showcase the crab most fully. So getting the most out of crab cakes often means putting the least into them. When you start loading crab cakes up with white bread, corn, curry, and complicated sauces, you might be making them different, but you're not making them better. I usually serve my crab cakes with nothing more than lemon wedges, but tartar sauce and aïoli (recipes for both are on page 306) are both excellent choices if you choose to make a condiment.

1 pound fresh lump crabmeat

1 egg

1 tablespoon Dijon mustard (optional)

Salt and freshly ground black pepper

2 tablespoons flour, plus flour for dredging

1/4 cup extra virgin olive oil or neutral oil, like corn or grapeseed

Lemon wedges

1. Gently combine the crab, egg, mustard if you're using it, salt and pepper to taste, and 2 tablespoons flour. Cover and put in the freezer for 5 minutes. Shape the mixture into 4 patties. Line a plate with plastic wrap and put the crab cakes on it. Cover with more plastic wrap and refrigerate for about 30 minutes (or up to a day if you like) or freeze for 15 minutes.

2. Put the flour for dredging in a bowl. Put the oil in a 12-inch skillet

over medium heat. When the oil is hot, gently dredge one of the crab cakes in the flour. Gently tap off the excess flour and add the crab cake to the pan; repeat with the remaining crab cakes, then turn the heat to medium-high.

3. Cook, rotating the cakes in the pan as necessary to brown the first side, 5 to 8 minutes. Turn and brown the other side, which will take slightly less time. Serve hot with lemon wedges.

COLD POACHED SHRIMP

MAKES 4 SERVINGS   TIME: 15 TO 20 MINUTES

YOU CAN BUY peeled shrimp, but shrimp poached in their shells have more flavor (as do shrimp poached in salt; the water should taste salty). If you're going to peel the shrimp yourself, as I recommend, it pays to buy larger shrimp and cut down on the work. Go for those in the range of 30 to 40 per pound (sometimes labeled *U-40* as in "under 40"), or even larger if the cost is not prohibitive.

To subtly improve the flavor of the shrimp, add other seasonings to the poaching liquid—the easiest thing is to grab a handful of pickling mix, which usually contains peppercorns, allspice, bay leaf, and coriander and dill seeds. Throw in a couple of cloves of garlic or a piece of onion if you like.

1½ pounds shrimp
Salt

Better Cocktail Sauce (page 306),
Marjoram "Pesto" (page 298),
or other sauce for serving

Put the shrimp in a saucepan with water to cover and a large pinch of salt. Bring to a boil and turn off the heat; let the shrimp cool in the water for about 5 minutes, then rinse in cold water until cool. Peel and devein if you like. Serve with sauce or chill until ready to serve.

ALMOST ALL SHRIMP are frozen before sale. So unless you're in a hurry, you might as well buy them frozen and defrost them yourself; this will guarantee you that they are defrosted just before you cook them, therefore retaining peak quality.

There are no universal standards for shrimp size; *large* and *medium* don't mean much. Therefore, it pays to learn to judge shrimp size by the number per pound, as retailers do. Shrimp labeled *16/20,* for example, contain sixteen to twenty per pound; those labeled *U-20* require fewer (*under*) twenty to make

a pound. Shrimp from fifteen to about thirty per pound usually give the best combination of flavor, ease (peeling tiny shrimp is a nuisance), and value (really big shrimp usually cost more than $15 a pound).

On deveining: I don't. You can, if you like, but it's a thankless task, and there isn't one person in a hundred who could blind-taste the difference between shrimp that have and have not been deveined.

SPANISH-STYLE SHRIMP

MAKES 4 SERVINGS   TIME: ABOUT 20 MINUTES

MUCH OF THE flavor of shrimp can be lost in the cooking, especially when you're grilling or broiling, which allows the juices exuded by the shrimp to escape. Far better at preserving the crustacean's essence is cooking it in liquid, and among the best of those liquids is olive oil. This is not sautéing, but cooking the shrimp slowly in the oil, to tease out its liquids without evaporating them, so these juices combine with the oil to create an irresistible sauce. I usually peel shrimp before cooking, but in this instance the shrimp are better left unpeeled, for the simple reason that the shells contain as much flavor as the meat (maybe more), and you want that flavor in the sauce. The results are a little messier, and certainly more difficult to eat, but they are tastier—and the dish is easier to prepare.

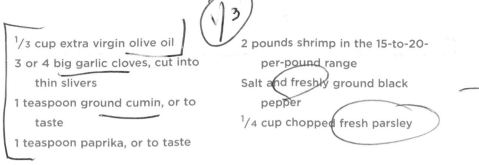

1/3 cup extra virgin olive oil

3 or 4 big garlic cloves, cut into
  thin slivers

1 teaspoon ground cumin, or to
  taste

1 teaspoon paprika, or to taste

2 pounds shrimp in the 15-to-20-
  per-pound range

Salt and freshly ground black
  pepper

1/4 cup chopped fresh parsley

1. Combine the oil and garlic in a 10- or 12-inch skillet. Turn the heat to medium and cook until the garlic begins to sizzle, then add the cumin and paprika. Stir, raise the heat to medium-high, and add the shrimp, along with some salt and pepper.

2. Cook, stirring occasionally, until the shrimp are all pink, no longer; you do not want to evaporate their liquid. Turn off the heat, add the parsley, and serve.

VARIATIONS

Shrimp, Scampi Style
Omit the cumin and paprika; use cayenne in place of black pepper. When the shrimp are cooked, stir in 2 or more tablespoons fresh lemon juice. Garnish with fresh parsley and serve with lemon wedges.

Shrimp with Asian Flavors
Substitute peanut or vegetable oil for the olive oil and cook 1 tablespoon chopped peeled fresh ginger and 2 or 3 small dried red chiles (or to taste) along with the garlic; omit the cumin and paprika. When the shrimp are done, stir in 1 tablespoon soy sauce; garnish with minced scallion or fresh cilantro and serve with lime wedges.

SHRIMP IN MOROCCAN-STYLE TOMATO SAUCE

MAKES 4 SERVINGS   TIME: 40 MINUTES

THE MAIN INGREDIENTS are standard Italian, the technique and appearance are standard, but the seasonings are from the other side of the Mediterranean. And that's the key: by substituting a couple of different spices, most or all of which you have sitting in your kitchen already, you can transform the common into the exotic.

2 tablespoons olive oil

1 tablespoon minced peeled fresh
  ginger

1 tablespoon ground cumin

1 1/2 teaspoons ground coriander

1 lime leaf, minced, or 1 teaspoon
  minced lime zest

One 28-ounce can chopped
  tomatoes, drained, or 2 cups
  chopped fresh tomatoes

Salt and freshly ground black
   pepper
1 1/2 pounds peeled shrimp,
   deveined if you like

Minced fresh cilantro for garnish
Lime wedges

1. Put the olive oil in a deep skillet and over medium-high heat. A minute later, add the ginger and cook, stirring, for about a minute. Add the spices and lime leaf and cook, stirring, for 30 seconds. Add the tomatoes and some salt and pepper, stir, and bring to a boil. Reduce the heat to medium and cook, stirring occasionally, until the mixture is nearly dry, about 15 minutes.

2. Add the shrimp and stir. Cook, stirring occasionally, until the shrimp are cooked through, about 10 minutes.

3. Taste and adjust the seasoning as necessary, then serve over white rice, garnished with the cilantro and accompanied by the lime wedges.

SPICY SHRIMP

MAKES 4 SERVINGS   TIME: 20 MINUTES

DESPITE ITS NAME, this dish isn't fiery hot, but the addition of a fair amount of paprika gives the shrimp a bright red color that makes people think they're eating spicy food. The real key here is fresh paprika, not that tin you inherited from your mother. After you buy it, taste it; if it is hot, use half a teaspoon. You can let the shrimp sit in the spice paste for hours. (In fact, I like to dump both shrimp and paste into a covered plastic container, shake them together to coat the shrimp, then carry the container to a party and grill the shrimp there.) But you can also mix the two together right before cooking.

VARIATION
You can take this dish in a completely different direction by substituting curry powder for the paprika, peanut oil for the olive oil, and lime juice for the lemon juice.

1 large garlic clove
1 tablespoon coarse salt

1/2 teaspoon cayenne
1 teaspoon paprika

2 tablespoons olive oil
2 teaspoons fresh lemon juice

$1^1/_2$ to 2 pounds shrimp in the 15-
   to-18-per-pound range (or
   smaller, if skewered), peeled
   and, if you like, deveined
Lemon wedges

1. Start a grill or preheat the broiler or oven. Make the fire as hot as it will get and put the rack close to the heat source.

2. Mince the garlic with the salt; mix with the cayenne and paprika, then make into a paste with olive oil and lemon juice. Smear the paste on the shrimp. Grill, broil, or roast the shrimp, 2 to 3 minutes per side, turning them once. Serve immediately or at room temperature, with lemon wedges.

SHRIMP, ROMAN STYLE

MAKES 4 SERVINGS   TIME: 30 MINUTES

THIS SHRIMP DISH is based on a combination of ingredients traditionally used to cook tripe in and around Rome. It's a simple tomato sauce spiked with the powerful flavors of browned garlic, chiles, and mint. When you make it with tripe, it must cook a long time for the tripe to become tender; when you use shrimp, the dish is practically done as soon as the shrimp are added.

2 tablespoons extra virgin olive oil
1 tablespoon garlic, slivered or not
   too finely chopped
6 small dried red chiles or hot red
   pepper flakes to taste
One 28-ounce can plum tomatoes,
   chopped, with their juice, or 4
   cups chopped fresh tomatoes

Salt and freshly ground black
   pepper
2 pounds shrimp, peeled and, if you
   like, deveined
1 cup chopped fresh mint or
   1 tablespoon or more dried

VARIATIONS

Shrimp, Roman Style, with Pasta
This consistency makes the dish ideal as a topping for pasta: just cut the amount of shrimp to about a pound—with a pound of pasta as the base, there's no need for more than that. Start the water for the pasta when you start the sauce and begin to cook the pasta at the same time as the shrimp.

Squid or Scallops, Roman Style
The same procedure can be followed to make this dish using squid, which should be cooked just until tender, probably even less time than the shrimp, or scallops, which will take about the same time as shrimp.

1. Put the olive oil in a large, deep skillet over medium heat. Add the garlic and chiles. When the garlic begins to color, cook carefully until it browns just a bit. Turn the heat off for a minute to avoid spattering, then add the tomatoes.

2. Turn the heat to medium-high and bring to a boil, then reduce the heat to medium and simmer, stirring occasionally. Add salt and pepper to taste.

3. Add the shrimp and cook, stirring occasionally, until all are pink, 5 to 10 minutes. Taste and adjust the seasoning; the sauce should be quite strong. Stir in the mint and serve.

========

SHRIMP WITH "BARBECUE" SAUCE

MAKES 4 SERVINGS   TIME: 15 MINUTES

THIS IS AN old New Orleans recipe that has nothing to do with grilling or barbecuing. Its name comes from the spicy, slightly smoky flavor the shrimp gain while being cooked with Worcestershire sauce and lots of black pepper. It's a fine and almost absurdly fast dish—once the shrimp are peeled, you can have it on the table in ten minutes, and that's no exaggeration—with a creamy, rich, savory sauce that completely belies the amount of effort required on your part.

VARIATIONS
- Use 3 tablespoons red wine vinegar in place of the Worcestershire sauce; omit the lemon juice.
- Use 2 tablespoons Dijon mustard and 1 tablespoon of water in place of the Worcestershire sauce.

4 tablespoons ($^1/_2$ stick) unsalted butter

$1^1/_2$ to 2 pounds shrimp, peeled and, if you like, deveined

2 tablespoons Worcestershire or soy sauce

Salt and freshly ground black pepper

Juice of 1 lemon

1. Put the butter in a skillet over high heat; when it melts, add the shrimp and Worcestershire sauce. Cook, stirring occasionally, until the sauce is glossy and thick and the shrimp uniformly pink, about 5

minutes. If at any point the sauce threatens to dry out, add a table-spoon or two of water.

2. When the shrimp are done, add salt to taste and $1/2$ teaspoon or more pepper, then stir in the lemon juice. Serve over rice or with bread.

===

SHRIMP IN YELLOW CURRY

MAKES 4 SERVINGS   TIME: 30 MINUTES

THAI DISHES CALLED *curries* contain curry powder and a combina-tion of herbs and aromatic vegetables. A typical dish might feature a mixture of garlic, shallots, chiles, lime leaf, sugar, and galangal or ginger. This curry, which features coconut milk, is just such a dish. Serve it with white or sticky rice.

2 tablespoons peanut or vegetable oil

1 cup minced onion

1 tablespoon minced garlic

1 tablespoon minced peeled fresh ginger

1 teaspoon minced fresh chiles or hot red pepper flakes to taste

1 tablespoon curry powder, or to taste

1 cup fresh or canned coconut milk

$1^1/2$ to 2 pounds medium to large shrimp, peeled and, if you like, deveined

Salt and freshly ground black pepper

2 tablespoons nam pla or nuoc mam (fish sauce), or to taste

$1/4$ cup chopped fresh cilantro or mint

1. Put the oil in a large, deep skillet over medium heat. Add the onion, garlic, ginger, and chiles and cook, stirring frequently, until the veg-etables are tender and the mixture pasty. Add the curry powder and cook, stirring, for another minute.

2. Add the coconut milk and raise the heat to medium-high. Cook, stirring only occasionally, until the mixture is reduced by about half. (The dish can be prepared to this point a few hours in advance.)

3. Add the shrimp, a few pinches of salt, and a little black pepper and cook, stirring frequently, until the shrimp release their liquid (the mixture will become quite moist again) and turn pink, 5 to 10 minutes. Add 1 tablespoon nam pla, stir, then taste and add the rest if necessary. Garnish with cilantro.

═══════════

STEAMED SHRIMP WITH LEMONGRASS-COCONUT SAUCE

MAKES 4 SERVINGS   TIME: 30 MINUTES, PLUS TIME TO CHILL

DEALING WITH THE lemongrass is the sole challenge of this dish, and only if you've never done it before. Maximum flavor is released from whole lemongrass stalks when they are beaten up a bit; bruising the length of each stalk with the blunt edge of a knife takes care of this in seconds. But to include lemongrass in a sauce you must first remove the tough outer layers—this is not unlike peeling a woody scallion—and then carefully and finely mince the inner core.

2 lemongrass stalks

1 tablespoon nam pla (fish sauce)

2 limes

1 pound shrimp, peeled and, if you like, deveined

1 small dried chile

$1/2$ cup fresh or canned coconut milk

$1^1/2$ teaspoons sugar

Pinch of saffron threads or
    $1/2$ teaspoon ground turmeric or curry powder

Salt

1. Trim the ends from the lemongrass, then bruise one of the stalks all over with the back of a knife. Cut it in half and put the halves in the bottom of a saucepan with the nam pla. Squeeze the juice of one of the limes into the pot, then throw the lime halves in there. Top with the shrimp, cover tightly, and turn the heat to medium-high. Cook for 5 to 10 minutes, or until the shrimp are pink and firm. Remove the shrimp and chill.

2. Remove the hard outer layers from the remaining lemongrass stalk and mince the tender core; you won't get much more than a teaspoon or two. Combine this with the chile, coconut milk, sugar, and saffron in a small saucepan over low heat. Cook, stirring occasionally, until the mixture is a uniform yellow. Remove the chile and chill. Cut the remaining lime into wedges.

3. Taste the sauce and add a little salt if necessary. Serve the cold shrimp topped with the cold sauce and accompanied by lime wedges.

COCONUT MILK

ALTHOUGH CANNED COCONUT milk is perfectly convenient, making coconut milk at home is easy and will contain no preservatives: Combine 2 cups of water and 2 cups dried unsweetened shredded or grated coconut in a blender. Use a towel to hold the lid on tightly and turn the switch on and off a few times quickly to get the mixture going. Then blend for about 30 seconds. Let rest for 10 minutes. Pour the milk through a strainer. This will be fairly thick. If you need more milk, just pour additional water through the coconut, up to another cup or two. Press the coconut to extract as much liquid as possible. Use immediately or freeze indefinitely.

SHRIMP OR SCALLOP SEVICHE

MAKES 4 SERVINGS   TIME: 30 MINUTES

IN SEVICHE, the scallops are "cooked" by the acidity of the citrus.

1/2 pound perfectly fresh sea
    scallops, cut into 1/4-inch dice
1 1/2 tablespoons peeled and minced
    bell pepper, preferably a
    combination of red, yellow, and
    green
1/2 teaspoon minced lemon zest

1 1/2 teaspoons fresh orange juice
1 1/2 teaspoons fresh lemon juice
Salt to taste
Cayenne to taste
1 tablespoon minced fresh cilantro
    (optional)

1. Toss together all the ingredients, except the cilantro, and let sit at room temperature for 15 minutes.
2. Taste, adjust the seasoning, and serve, garnished with the cilantro if you like.

SHRIMP COOKED IN LIME JUICE

MAKES 4 SERVINGS   TIME: 20 TO 30 MINUTES

THIS IS A Southeast Asian–style preparation, mildly sweet and mouth-puckeringly sour. It's also ridiculously fast; if you start some rice before tackling the shrimp, they will both be done at about the same time, twenty minutes later. (This assumes your shrimp are already peeled, a task that will take you about ten minutes and one that should be undertaken before cooking the rice.)

For best flavor, see if you can find head-on shrimp; they make for a more impressive presentation, and it's fun to suck the juices out of the heads themselves (which, I realize, is not something that everyone enjoys). But none of these assets is worth making head-on shrimp a sticking point. Note that this technique will work with scallops or cut-up squid; each will take slightly less time to cook than the shrimp.

About $^{1}/_{2}$ cup lime juice (3 or 4 limes)

$^{1}/_{4}$ cup sugar

1 tablespoon nam pla (fish sauce) or salt to taste

2 tablespoons neutral oil, like corn or grapeseed

1 teaspoon minced garlic

$^{1}/_{2}$ teaspoon hot red pepper flakes, or to taste

$1^{1}/_{2}$ pounds shrimp, peeled and, if you like, deveined, or 3 pounds head-on shrimp, unpeeled

Minced fresh cilantro for garnish

1. Combine the lime juice, sugar, and nam pla. Put the oil in a 10- or 12-inch skillet over high heat. A minute later, add the garlic and hot pepper and cook just until the garlic begins to brown. Immediately add the lime juice mixture all at once and cook until it reduces by half, or even more, 3 to 5 minutes; there should be only about $^{1}/_{4}$ cup of liquid in the skillet, and it should be syrupy.

2. Add the shrimp and cook, still over high heat. The shrimp will give off liquid of their own and begin to turn pink almost immediately. After about 2 minutes of cooking, stir. Continue cooking and stirring occasionally until all the shrimp are pink, about 2 minutes later. Taste and adjust the seasoning, then garnish with cilantro.

STIR-FRIED LEEKS WITH GINGER AND SHRIMP

MAKES 4 SERVINGS   TIME: 30 MINUTES

LEEKS, ONE OF the first legitimate spring vegetables, are the highlight here (in fact this recipe is great without the shrimp; see page 230). In place of the shrimp, you could use scallops, tofu, chunks of chicken or pork, or slices of beef.

2 tablespoons peanut or olive oil

2 large leeks, about 1^1/2 pounds, washed and chopped

^{3}/4 to 1^1/2 pounds shrimp, peeled and, if you like, deveined

2 tablespoons minced peeled fresh ginger

Salt and freshly ground black pepper

1^1/2 teaspoons good-quality stock, dry sherry, or soy sauce (optional)

1. Put half the oil in a large skillet, preferably nonstick, over high heat. When a bit of smoke appears, add the leeks all at once. Let sit for a couple of minutes, then cook, stirring only occasionally, for about 10 minutes. When the leeks dry out and begin to brown, remove them from the pan and set aside.

2. With the heat still on high, add the remaining oil to the pan, immediately followed by the shrimp; sprinkle with the ginger. Cook for about a minute and stir. Cook, stirring every minute or so, until the shrimp are almost all pink. Add the leeks, along with some salt and pepper. When the shrimp are done (no traces of gray will remain), stir in the liquid if desired, taste and adjust the seasoning, and serve.

===========

SOY-DIPPED SHRIMP

MAKES 4 SERVINGS   TIME: 20 MINUTES

MANY PEOPLE WILL find this their idea of paradise: simply grilled shrimp in a strong-flavored soy dipping sauce.

1 tablespoon medium-hot paprika

2 tablespoons peanut oil

Salt and freshly ground black pepper

1^1/2 pounds shrimp, peeled and, if you like, deveined

^{1}/2 cup good-quality soy sauce

1^1/2 teaspoons minced garlic

1^1/2 teaspoons minced peeled fresh ginger

2 tablespoons fresh lemon juice

^{1}/8 teaspoon cayenne, or to taste

1. Preheat a grill to moderately hot. Mix the paprika, peanut oil, and salt and pepper to taste and rub all over the shrimp. Grill the shrimp, turning once, until done, about 5 minutes. Meanwhile, mix the soy sauce with the garlic, ginger, lemon juice, and cayenne; taste and adjust the seasoning.

2. Serve the shrimp hot, with the soy mixture as a dipping sauce.

STUFFED SCALLOPS

MAKES 4 SERVINGS   TIME: 30 MINUTES

THE SEA SCALLOP is one of the most perfect of nature's convenience foods—almost nothing cooks faster. This is especially true if you opt to heat the mollusk until it remains rare in the center, as do most scallop admirers.

Sea scallops are also large enough to stuff, not with bread crumbs or other fish, as is common with clams or lobsters, but with herbs, garlic, and other flavorings. As long as a scallop is a good inch across and roughly three-quarters of an inch thick, you can make an equatorial slit in it and fill it with any number of stuffings.

20 large fresh basil leaves
1 small garlic clove, peeled
1/2 teaspoon coarse salt
1/4 teaspoon freshly ground black
   pepper

3 tablespoons extra virgin olive oil
1 1/4 to 1 1/2 pounds large sea
   scallops of fairly uniform size

1. Mince the basil, garlic, salt, and pepper together until very fine, almost a puree (use a small food processor if you like). Mix in a small bowl with 1 tablespoon of the olive oil to produce a thick paste.

2. Cut most but not all of the way through the equator of each scallop, then smear a bit of the basil mixture on the exposed center; close the scallop.

VARIATIONS

Sautéed Scallops with Herb Paste
Substitute prepared pesto for the basil mixture. Alternatively, substitute fresh parsley, cilantro, or dill for the basil.

Stuffed Scallops with Greens
When the scallops are done, put them on a bed of greens (about 6 cups is right for this amount of scallops). Turn the heat under the skillet to low and add 3 tablespoons fresh lemon juice. Cook, stirring, for about 10 seconds, then pour the pan juices over the scallops and greens and serve, drizzled with more olive oil if you like.

(continued)

3. Put a large nonstick skillet over high heat for a minute; add the remaining oil, then the scallops, one at a time. As each scallop browns—it should take no longer than 1 or 2 minutes—turn it and brown the other side. Serve hot, drizzled with the pan juices.

(Variations, continued)
Sautéed Scallops Stuffed with Peanut Sauce
Cream 2 tablespoons chunky natural peanut butter with $^1/_4$ teaspoon minced garlic, minced fresh chiles or cayenne to taste, 1 teaspoon sugar, and sufficient soy sauce to make a thin paste. Use this paste as you would the basil paste and use peanut oil to sauté the scallops.
When the scallops are done, put them on a bed of lightly steamed or sautéed bitter greens, such as dandelion or mustard. Turn the heat under the skillet to low and add 3 tablespoons fresh lime juice. Cook, stirring, for about 10 seconds, then pour the pan juices over the scallops and greens and serve, drizzled with a little more peanut oil if you like.

<hr>

MISO-BROILED SCALLOPS

MAKES 4 APPETIZER SERVINGS   TIME: 20 MINUTES

A DISH THAT harnesses the complexity of miso to make a simple, quick, and highly flavored appetizer.

$^1/_3$ cup miso	Salt
$1^1/_2$ tablespoons mirin, fruity white wine, or dry white wine	Cayenne
$^1/_2$ cup minced onion	1 pound sea scallops
	Juice of 1 lime

1. Preheat the broiler or start a grill, setting the rack as close as possible to the heat source. Put the miso in a bowl, add the mirin or wine, and whisk until smooth. Stir in the onion, a little bit of salt, and a pinch of cayenne. Add the scallops and marinate while the broiler or grill preheats; or refrigerate for up to a day.
2. Broil until lightly browned, without turning, 2 to 3 minutes, or grill, turning once after a minute or two. Sprinkle with the lime juice and serve with toothpicks.

A WORD ABOUT buying scallops: Many are dipped in a chemical solution to prolong their shelf life. Not coincidentally, this soaking causes them to absorb water, which increases their weight and—water being cheaper than scallops—decreases their value. Furthermore, the added water makes browning more difficult. You can recognize processed scallops by their stark white color; in addition, they are usually sitting in liquid at the store. Buy dry, beige (or slightly pink or orange) scallops from a reliable fishmonger and you won't have a problem.

Many cooks remove the tough little hinge present on one side of most scallops before cooking. But when you're stuffing scallops, leave it on and cut from the side directly opposite. The hinge will then serve the purpose of holding the scallop together and can be removed at the table or eaten; it's slightly tough, but not unpleasant.

SCALLOPS *A LA PLANCHA*

MAKES 4 SERVINGS   TIME: 20 MINUTES

THE SCALLOP IS ideal for fast cooking, because even a large scallop needs only to be browned on both sides to complete its cooking. A good sear on the outside caramelizes the shellfish's natural sugars and leaves the interior cool, creamy, and delicious.

$1^1/_2$ pounds sea or bay scallops

1 garlic clove, peeled and lightly crushed

2 tablespoons extra virgin olive oil

1 tablespoon sherry vinegar

Salt and freshly ground black pepper

Minced fresh parsley for garnish

1. Toss the scallops and the garlic on a plate and drizzle with the oil and vinegar; sprinkle with salt and pepper and turn over a couple of times. Go about your business for 5 minutes.

2. Preheat a large skillet, preferably nonstick, over high heat. When the skillet smokes—this will take a couple of minutes—add the scallops (leave the liquid behind), not all at once. By the time you've added the last scallop, the first one will probably be browned on one

VARIATIONS

Shrimp or Squid *a la Plancha*
This technique works perfectly with both shrimp and squid. Keep the cooking time especially short for squid or it will get tough.

• Another option is to vary the kind of oil, vinegar, seasoning, and garnish as you like. For example, use peanut oil with scallions and peeled fresh ginger, then garnish with a drizzle of soy sauce or fresh cilantro for a completely different take.

side, so begin turning them. Cook until brown on both sides but still rare in the center. (You must work more quickly with bay scallops—add them a few at a time and turn them quickly; you may even have to work in batches to keep them from overcooking.)

3. Serve, drizzled with the juices from the plate and garnished with the parsley.

CURRIED SCALLOPS WITH TOMATOES

MAKES 4 SERVINGS   TIME: 20 MINUTES

YOU CAN NEVER go wrong by adding a little crunch to scallops when you sauté them (see the following recipe for another example). Usually, you dredge them in flour, cornmeal, or bread crumbs before adding them to the hot pan, and it's something that most everyone seems to like. But you can take that crunch and give it an intense flavor by dredging the scallops directly in a spice mix. Although you can't do this with everything—dried herbs don't get crisp, and some spices are far too strong to use in this quantity—it works perfectly with curry powder, which not only seasons the scallops and their accompanying sauce but gives them the crunch we all crave.

3 medium tomatoes

1 tablespoon peanut or vegetable oil

1 1/2 to 2 pounds large sea scallops

Salt and freshly ground black pepper

2 tablespoons curry powder, or to taste

1/2 cup heavy or sour cream or yogurt (optional)

Juice of 1 lime

1/2 cup chopped fresh cilantro or Thai basil

1. Core the tomatoes (cut a cone-shaped wedge out of the stem end), then squeeze and shake out their seeds. Chop their flesh into

1/2-inch pieces and set aside. Put the oil in a 12-inch nonstick skillet over medium heat for about 3 minutes. While it is heating, sprinkle the scallops with salt and pepper and spread the curry powder on a plate.

2. When the oil is hot, work quickly to dredge the scallops lightly in the curry powder and add them to the pan. About 2 minutes after you added the first scallop, turn it—it should be nicely browned (if it is not, raise the heat a bit). When the scallops are all browned and turned, cook for another minute, then add the tomatoes and the cream if you're using it (if you are using yogurt, lower the heat immediately; it must not boil).

3. Heat the tomatoes through, then taste and add more salt and pepper if necessary. Sprinkle with the lime juice, stir in the cilantro, and serve.

SEA SCALLOPS WITH NUTS

MAKES 4 SERVINGS   TIME: 15 MINUTES

IF YOU CAN find the rare (and shockingly expensive) true bay scallops from Nantucket or Long Island, by all means use them in this dish, but reduce the cooking time. Do not, however, try this dish with the tiny calico scallops (sometimes mislabeled as bays), which, despite your best efforts, will overcook before they brown.

1 tablespoon olive oil
2 tablespoons butter
About 1 1/2 pounds sea scallops
Salt
Pinch of cayenne

1/3 cup roughly chopped skin-on
    almonds, pecans, or walnuts
3/4 cup dry white or red wine
Chopped fresh parsley for garnish
    (optional)

1. Put the oil and half the butter in a large skillet, preferably nonstick, over medium-high heat. Sprinkle the scallops with salt and a bit of

cayenne. When the butter foam subsides, add the scallops to the skillet, one at a time (or all at once if you're using bay scallops), and turn the heat to high. Cook for about 2 minutes or until brown on one side, then turn and brown the other side for another minute or two. (Scallops are best when rare in the center; if you like them more well done, cook for another couple of minutes.)

2. Transfer the scallops to a plate and keep warm. Add the nuts to the skillet and, still over high heat, cook, stirring, until dark brown, just a minute or two. Add the wine and cook, stirring occasionally, until reduced to a syrup, about 5 minutes. Add the remaining butter; when it has thickened the sauce, pour over the scallops, garnish if you like, and serve.

ROASTED BAY SCALLOPS WITH BROWN BUTTER AND SHALLOTS

MAKES 4 SERVINGS   TIME: 20 MINUTES

REAL BAY SCALLOPS—which come from the waters between Cape Cod and Long Island—are in season through the winter and are an amazing treat (they're also amazingly expensive). Though you can eat them raw, they're also good cooked, but simply . . . very simply.

4 tablespoons ($^1/_2$ stick) butter
$1^1/_2$ pounds bay scallops
3 tablespoons minced shallot
Salt and freshly ground black
    pepper

Chopped fresh basil or snipped
    chives for garnish

1. Preheat the oven to the maximum, at least 500°F. As it preheats, put a roasting pan large enough to hold the scallops in one layer in there. When the oven is hot, add the butter and return the pan to the

oven. Cook, shaking the pan once or twice, until the butter has melted and begun to turn brown.

2. Immediately add the scallops and cook, undisturbed, for about 3 minutes. Remove the pan, add the shallot, and stir. Return to the oven for about 2 minutes, or until the scallops are done (they should be tender and not at all rubbery; do not overcook). Season with salt and pepper, stir in the herb, and serve.

SQUID IN RED WINE SAUCE
MAKES 4 SERVINGS
TIME: 1 HOUR, LARGELY UNATTENDED

THIS IS AMONG my favorite dishes using this plentiful but still under-appreciated cephalopod. (The term, which is also used for octopus and cuttlefish, describes sea creatures whose "feet" grow from their heads.) Like many people, I'm a fan of fried "calamari," but that dish is best suited to restaurants because of squid's tendency to spatter when deep-fried. Although sautéing and stir-frying are good, fast techniques for squid, they, too, tend to be messy. A gentle braise in flavorful liquid and seasonings is the perfect alternative, and this one, with its Provençal spirit, is delicious and warming.

3 tablespoons extra virgin olive oil

5 garlic cloves, crushed

2 pounds cleaned squid, the bodies cut up if large

1 cup fruity red wine, like Côtes-du-Rhône

Several fresh thyme sprigs or 1 teaspoon dried

Salt and freshly ground black pepper

Chopped fresh parsley for garnish (optional)

1. Put 2 tablespoons of the olive oil in a large skillet that can later be covered and turn the heat to medium-high. Add the garlic and cook,

VARIATIONS

Add fennel seeds or crushed red chiles to alter the flavor entirely, or try one of these additions:

Squid in Red Wine Sauce with Potatoes

Add some crisp-sautéed potatoes or croutons of bread to the finished dish for a contrasting texture.

Squid in Red Wine Sauce with Tomatoes

Add a few chopped tomatoes (canned are fine) to make the sauce a bit thicker and more plentiful. In this case, you might as well serve the dish over pasta.

ALMOST ALL SQUID is sold so clean it just needs a quick rinse to be ready for cutting up and cooking; some of it is even sold cut into rings. To make it even more convenient, squid, like shrimp, is one of those rare seafoods whose quality barely suffers when frozen, so you can safely tuck a two-pound bag in the freezer and let it sit for a month or two, defrosting it the day you're ready to cook. (Like shrimp, it will defrost quickly and safely when covered with cold water.)

stirring, until lightly browned. Add the squid and stir, then lower the heat and add the wine. Stir, add the thyme, and cover.

2. Cook at a slow simmer until the squid is tender, about 45 minutes. Uncover, season to taste, raise the heat, and cook until most but not all of the liquid has evaporated. Stir in the remaining olive oil, garnish if you like, and serve.

BROILED OR GRILLED SOFTSHELL CRABS

MAKES 4 SERVINGS   TIME: 15 MINUTES

THOUGH YOU CAN just shove the crabs under the broiler in this recipe, this slightly more complicated procedure works best: Preheat a large roasting pan in the broiler for ten minutes or so. When you're ready to cook, put the crabs in the pan, adjusting the broiler rack so that it's two or three inches from the heat source or as close as you can get it (in my oven, this means propping the roasting pan on top of another pan). The crabs will be done in less than 5 minutes. Remember that some oven broilers work best if the door is ajar, which will keep the element from cycling off and make cooking time faster, not slower.

| 8 softshell crabs | Salt |
| 2 tablespoons extra virgin olive oil (optional) | 2 lemons, quartered |

1. Preheat the broiler, adjusting the rack so that it is just beneath the heat source; put a large nonstick roasting pan or skillet in there to heat up for about 10 minutes. Or start a grill, adjusting the rack so that it is about 4 inches from the coals.

2. To broil, place the crabs, top shell up, in the pan. Broil until they are firm and their tops lightly browned, 3 to 5 minutes. Brush lightly with olive oil if you like, sprinkle with salt, and serve with lemon wedges.

To grill, brush the crabs with a little olive oil and sprinkle with salt. Grill, turning once or twice, until browned and firm, 5 to 10 minutes. Brush with olive oil and serve with lemon or, if you like, melted butter.

GRILLED OR BROILED LOBSTER

MAKES 4 SERVINGS   TIME: 40 MINUTES

BOILING OR STEAMING lobster is the simplest cooking method, and it may seem like the best when you consider that plopping a lobster into a pot of boiling water is also the easiest way to kill it. Fortunately, there is a way to "parboil" lobster to kill it that will then allow you to grill or broil it without overcooking. The technique outlined here is easy, foolproof, and perhaps even humane.

Make sure you boil plenty of water for the first step. You want to cook the lobsters barely but quickly. And have an ice-water bath ready to stop the cooking.

| Salt and freshly ground black pepper | $3/4$ cup melted butter, Mayonnaise (page 305), or Basic Vinaigrette (page 304) |
| Four $1^1/4$- to $1^1/2$-pound live lobsters | |

1. Start a grill if you're using one. Bring a large pot of water to a boil and salt it. Plunge the lobsters into the water (one or two at a time if necessary) and cook just until they turn red, about 2 minutes. Remove the lobsters and plunge them into an ice-water bath to stop the cooking. (You can do this several hours in advance and refrigerate the lobsters until you're ready to proceed.) Split the tails down the middle of their soft sides so they will lie flat.

2. Preheat the broiler if you're using it. With either broiler or grill, adjust the rack so that there will be about 3 inches between the lobsters and the heat source. Broil or grill the lobsters with their flesh side facing the heat until they are hot and their shells just begin to char, about 10 minutes. Sprinkle with salt and pepper and serve hot, warm, at room temperature, or cold, with the melted butter, mayonnaise, or a basic vinaigrette.

PAELLA, FAST AND EASY

MAKES 4 SERVINGS   TIME: 30 MINUTES

SOME PEOPLE ARGUE that a true paella must contain only meat or seafood, never both, that a true paella can be prepared only in a paellera, or that true paella must be cooked outdoors over wood. Perhaps they're all right. What's clear to me is that you can produce a fabulous rice dish I call paella in just over half an hour, which makes it a great option for weeknights.

1 quart chicken stock

Pinch of saffron threads (optional)

3 tablespoons olive oil

1 medium onion, minced

2 cups medium-grain rice

Salt and freshly ground black
  pepper

2 cups peeled and, if you like,
  deveined shrimp, cut into
  $1/2$-inch chunks

Minced fresh parsley for garnish

1. Preheat the oven to 500°F or as near that temperature as you can get it. Warm the stock in a saucepan along with the saffron if you're using it. Put an ovenproof 10- or 12-inch skillet over medium-high heat and add the oil. A minute later, add the onion and cook, stirring occasionally, until translucent, about 5 minutes.

2. Add the rice and cook, stirring occasionally, until glossy, just a minute or two. Season liberally with salt and pepper and add the warmed stock, taking care to avoid the rising steam. Stir in the shrimp and transfer the skillet to the oven.

3. Bake for about 25 minutes, or until all the liquid is absorbed and the rice is dry on top. Garnish with parsley and serve immediately.

CLAMBAKE IN A POT

MAKES 4 SERVINGS   TIME. 40 MINUTES

THREE OR FOUR ingredients are traditional in a clambake: clams (which should be littlenecks, not steamers, to minimize sandiness and make eating easier); lobster, of which you don't need much, about half per person; corn, an ear (or two, if it's good) per person; sausage, which you can certainly do without if you prefer; and melted butter, which is entirely optional (and I find entirely unnecessary). If you have those things, all you need to do to mimic a real outdoor clambake, basically, is dump them in a pot, cover it, and turn on the heat. No kidding.

$^1/_2$ to 1 pound kielbasa (optional)

$^1/_2$ to 1 pound good slab bacon in 2 pieces (optional)

3 pounds hardshell clams, washed

3 pounds mussels, well washed and debearded

About 1 pound tiny new potatoes or larger waxy potatoes cut into chunks of less than 1 inch

Two $1^1/_4$- to $1^1/_2$-pound lobsters

4 ears corn, shucked

Melted butter (optional)

VARIATIONS
Shrimp is my first choice for this dish, but the alternatives are numerous. As long as the pieces are less than $^1/_2$ inch thick, anything will cook through in the time it takes for the liquid to evaporate. Try any combination:
• Sausage, (especially chorizo), cut into bits
• Peas and/or other vegetables, cut up if necessary
• Scallops, treated exactly like the shrimp
• Boneless pork or chicken, cut into $^1/_2$-inch or smaller cubes
• Tofu, stirred into the rice during the last 5 minutes of baking
• Clams and/or mussels, well scrubbed, placed on top of the rice when you put the pan in the oven

1. Put the meat if you're using it in the bottom of a very large pot, like a lobster pot (or divide the ingredients between 2 large pots). Add the clams and mussels, then the potatoes. Top with the lobster and corn and add $^1/_2$ cup of water. Cover and turn the heat to high.

2. Cook, shaking the pot a little every few minutes, for about 20 minutes. Remove the lid and carefully (there is a danger of scalding) check one of the potatoes to see whether it is done. If not, re-cover and cook for another 10 minutes or so.

3. Put the corn, meat, and lobsters on one or more platters. Put the mollusks in a large bowl and ladle some of the cooking juices over them. Serve, if you like, with melted butter.

BOUILLABAISSE

MAKES 4 SERVINGS   TIME: 1 HOUR

BOUILLABAISSE, THE MEDITERRANEAN fish stew that is more difficult to spell than to prepare, is traditionally neither an idée fixe nor the centerpiece of a grand bouffe, but a spur-of-the-moment combination of the day's catch. The key to bouillabaisse is a variety of good fish of different types, so use this recipe as a set of guidelines rather than strict dogma and don't worry about duplicating the exact types or quantities of fish.

1 tablespoon olive oil

1 medium onion, roughly chopped

Strips of zest from 1 navel or other orange

1 teaspoon fennel seeds

Pinch of saffron threads (optional)

1 small dried chile, or a pinch of cayenne, or to taste

2 cups chopped tomatoes

$^1/_2$ to $^3/_4$ pound monkfish, catfish, or blackfish, cut into 1-inch cubes

$1^1/_2$ pounds hardshell (littleneck) clams, cockles, or mussels, well washed

$^1/_2$ to $^3/_4$ pound shrimp, peeled
    and, if you like, deveined, or
    scallops, cut into bite-sized
    pieces if necessary
$^1/_2$ to $^3/_4$ pound cod or other
    delicate white-fleshed fish, cut
    into 6 large chunks

$1^1/_2$ teaspoons minced garlic
$^1/_2$ cup roughly chopped fresh
    parsley

1. Put the olive oil in a casserole or large saucepan over medium heat. Add the onion and cook, stirring occasionally, until softened, about 5 minutes. Add the zest, fennel, saffron if you're using it, and chile and cook for about a minute. Add the tomatoes and turn the heat to medium-high. When the mixture boils, reduce the heat to medium and cook, stirring occasionally, until the mixture becomes saucelike, 10 to 15 minutes. (You can prepare the dish several hours in advance up to this point; cover and set aside until you're ready to eat.)

2. Add the monkfish and raise the heat to medium-high. When the mixture begins to boil, reduce the heat to medium-low and cook, stirring occasionally, until it is just about tender, 10 minutes or so.

3. Add the clams, raise the heat to high, and stir. When the mixture boils, reduce the heat to low, cover, and cook until the clams begin to open, 5 to 10 minutes. Add the shrimp and white fish, stir, and cover; cook, stirring gently once or twice, until the white fish is just about done (a thin-bladed knife will pierce it with little resistance), about 5 minutes. (If the mixture is very thick—there should be some broth—add a cup or so of hot water.) Stir in the garlic and cook for 1 minute more. Stir in the parsley and serve, with crusty bread.

FISH

SIMPLEST STEAMED FISH

MAKES 4 SERVINGS   TIME: 10 MINUTES

IF YOU HAVE forgotten how delicious a fillet of fish can be, do this: Steam it, with nothing. Drizzle it with olive oil and lemon. Sprinkle it with salt. Eat it. If the number of ingredients and technique are minimal, the challenge is not. You need a high-quality and uniformly thick piece of fish to begin with, your timing must be precise—which is all a matter of attention and judgment, really—and your olive oil flavorful. That taken care of, there is no better or easier preparation.

1¹/2 pounds cod, red snapper, grouper, striped bass, sea bass, or halibut in 2 pieces or 1 large halibut steak	2 tablespoons extra virgin olive oil Juice of ¹/2 lemon Coarse salt

1. Put at least 1 inch of water in the bottom of a steamer (see Note), cover, and bring to a boil. Put the fish on the steamer's rack—making sure the rack is elevated above the water—cover again, and steam for 4 to 8 minutes, or until the fish is done. You must check often—taking care not to scald yourself when removing the steamer's lid—and stop the cooking the instant a thin-bladed knife meets no resistance when poking the fillet. (A good-sized halibut fillet may require 10 or even 12 minutes.)

2. Transfer the fish to a warm platter and drizzle with olive oil and lemon juice. Sprinkle with coarse salt and serve.

NOTE

To jerry-rig a steaming vessel, I use a large oval casserole with a rack that fits in it; it was designed for roasting meat. Since the rack sits only about a quarter of an inch above the bottom, though, I have to elevate it, which I do by resting it on a couple of glass ramekins. As long as you have a large rack that fits inside of a larger pot, you will figure something out.

VARIATION

Simplest Steamed Fish with Soy

You can drizzle the fish with anything you like in place of the olive oil and lemon. Try, for example, a drizzle of soy sauce and a little minced peeled fresh ginger and/or chopped scallion.

FLOUNDER POACHED IN BROTH

MAKES 4 SERVINGS   TIME: 20 MINUTES

THIN FISH FILLETS can be tricky to prepare, mostly because they fall apart the instant they're overcooked. But the fact that quarter-inch-thick fillets of flounder, sole, and other flatfish take so little time to cook can be an advantage. By poaching them in barely hot liquid, you slow the cooking and gain control. By flavoring the liquid first with a quick-cooking aromatic vegetable, you create a dish that needs only bread or rice to become a meal. Unlike with broiling or sautéing, the fish never dries out.

The traditional liquid for poaching fish is court bouillon, a stock made from scratch using fish bones, onions, carrots, and celery enhanced with white wine and herbs. Assuming you don't have any court bouillon on hand—and who does?—my poaching liquid of choice is chicken stock, and the canned variety is fine, because you're going to add flavor to it, and quickly, in the form of leeks and fish.

2 cups chicken stock or one 14- or 15-ounce can

Three 1-inch-thick leeks

Salt and freshly ground black pepper

$1\frac{1}{2}$ pounds flounder or other thin fish fillets

1. Put the stock in a large skillet that can be covered and turn the heat to high. Let it boil and reduce by about half while you prepare the leeks. Trim the leeks of the root and green end; cut the white part in half the long way and rinse thoroughly. Chop each half into $1/8$- to $1/4$-inch-thick semicircles, adding them to the boiling broth as you cut them.

2. When all the leeks are added, cook for another minute. Add salt and pepper to taste and stir, then add the fish. Cover and turn off the heat or keep the heat at an absolute minimum. Uncover and check the fish after 3 minutes; it is done when a thin-bladed knife encounters no resistance. Continue to check every minute until the fish is done.

3. Serve the fish with the leeks and some broth spooned over it; top all with a sprinkling of coarse salt.

SPARKLING CIDER–POACHED FISH

MAKES 4 SERVINGS   TIME: 15 MINUTES

THIS IS A simple marriage of butter, shallots, and mushrooms, splashed in a dose of hard cider (the dry, sparkling kind from France or England, sold nearly everywhere you can buy beer and wine) and used to poach fish in a hot oven. The fish may be haddock, cod, monkfish, halibut, red snapper, or any other white-fleshed fish. The cider provides a distinctively sour fruitiness, not at all like white wine, and the completed dish has complementary textures: crunchy shallots, meaty mushrooms (portobellos are good here), and tender fish.

1 tablespoon butter

$1/2$ cup sliced or minced shallot

1 cup roughly chopped portobello or other mushrooms

$1^1/2$ pounds white-fleshed fish fillet, like cod or red snapper, about 1 inch thick, in 1 or 2 pieces

Salt and freshly ground black pepper

1 cup dry sparkling cider

1. Preheat the oven to 500°F. Smear the bottom of an ovenproof skillet with the butter; sprinkle the shallot and mushrooms around the sides of the skillet. Season the fish with salt and pepper to taste and lay it in the center of the skillet. Pour the cider around the fish.

2. Bring to a boil on top of the stove, then transfer to the oven. Bake for about 8 minutes; it's highly unlikely the fish will need more time than this unless it is very thick (or you like it very well done). Baste with the pan juices and serve.

VARIATIONS

• The lone improvement you can make to the main recipe is to add more butter. Although I stopped at 4 tablespoons—$1/2$ stick—I realized that there really was almost no upper limit as far as my taste buds were concerned. But the dish is awfully nice when made on the lean side, too.

• Substitute any aromatic vegetable, or a combination, for the shallot: onion, leek, carrot (cut very small), celery, fennel, scallion.

• Use a mixture of mushrooms, or fresh mushrooms combined with reconstituted dried mushrooms. A little of the strained mushroom-soaking liquid added to the poaching liquid is nice, too.

• A teaspoon of thyme leaves added to the poaching liquid is great; also good is parsley (a small handful of stalks), chervil (a small bunch), or dill (a few stalks). Garnish with chopped fresh leaves of the same herb.

• Some seeds are good in the poaching liquid, too—try caraway, coriander, or fennel.

Broiled Fish on Fennel or Dill

Preheat the broiler and put the rack as close to the heat source as possible. Put about $1/2$ inch of water in the bottom of a roasting pan and lay the fennel or dill stalks in it. Sprinkle the fish lightly with salt and pepper and lay it (skin side down, if there is a skin side) directly onto the fennel or dill. Broil until the fish is lightly browned on top and opaque throughout, about 10 minutes. (If at any time the fish is browning too quickly, move the broiler rack down a notch.) Finish as directed.

Grilled or Broiled Fish on Fennel or Dill with Butter Sauce

In a small saucepan, cook 2 tablespoons minced shallot with $1/3$ cup each white wine and white wine vinegar, along with a little salt and pepper, until the liquid is almost evaporated. Over the lowest possible heat, stir in 4 to 8 tablespoons ($1/2$ to 1 stick) butter, a bit at a time, adding the next bit only when each has been absorbed, until the sauce is smooth and creamy. Serve immediately.

GRILLED FISH THE MEDITERRANEAN WAY

MAKES 4 SERVINGS   TIME: 30 MINUTES

THIS IS ONE of those recipes in which the shopping may take you longer than the cooking, because fennel stalks—or those from dill, which are nearly as good—are often discarded by grocers. When you buy a bulb of fennel, you're buying the bottom, trimmed of its long stalks; when you buy a bunch of dill, you're buying the feathery tops, trimmed of the stalks that support them. Because this recipe requires some of those stalks, you will probably have to speak directly to a produce manager, visit a farmstand or a friend's garden, or simply get lucky.

The technique of grilling fish on top of fennel or dill stalks solves a couple of problems at once: it seasons the fish subtly and without effort, and it helps prevent the fish from sticking to the grill and falling apart. In fact, this method allows you to grill even relatively delicate fillets like cod, usually one of the most challenging fishes to grill because of its tendency to fall apart as it nears doneness.

4 to 6 fennel or dill stalks, each at least 6 inches long	Salt and cayenne
	1 teaspoon fennel or dill seeds
Four 6-ounce halibut fillets, or $1^1/2$ pounds other white-fleshed fish fillet, like striped bass, monkfish, or cod	1 lemon
	2 teaspoons extra virgin olive oil

1. Preheat a grill (for broiling instructions, see the variations) until quite hot and put the grill rack about 4 inches from the heat source.

2. When the grill is ready, make a bed of the fennel or dill stalks. Sprinkle the fish lightly with salt and cayenne to taste and lay it (skin side down, if there is a skin side) directly onto the fennel or dill. Close the grill if possible and cook, without turning, until the fish is done— it will be just about opaque all the way through and offer no resistance to a thin-bladed knife—about 10 minutes.

3. While the fish is cooking, mince or grind the fennel or dill seeds.

Cut about 1 inch off each end of the lemon and juice those pieces; slice the remaining lemon as thinly as you can.

4. When the fish is done, remove it from the grill, leaving as much of the stalks behind as possible (some of the burned fronds will adhere to the fish; this is fine). Sprinkle the fish with the fennel or dill seeds, then decorate it with the lemon slices. Drizzle with the lemon juice and olive oil and serve.

FISH BAKED WITH LEEKS

MAKES 4 SERVINGS   TIME: 30 MINUTES

THIS IS A dish that is almost too simple to believe, one that combines wonderful textures and flavors with a minimum of ingredients, no added fat, and almost no preparation or cooking time. Like the best minimalist dishes, everything counts here: the fish, the leeks—which remain crisp and assertive thanks to the quick cooking time—and even the wine or stock. The Dijon mustard provides a bit of a kick.

You need a tightly covered container to preserve all the liquid and flavors inherent in this dish, but that can be as simple as a pot with a good-fitting lid or a heatproof glass casserole—anything that prevents moisture from escaping.

$1^1/_2$ pounds leeks

$^1/_2$ cup dry white wine or chicken or
   fish stock

Salt and freshly ground black pepper

1 tablespoon Dijon mustard

About $1^1/_2$ pounds cod, salmon, or
   other fish fillet, about 1 inch
   thick

1. Preheat the oven to 400°F. Trim about $^1/_2$ inch from the root ends of the leeks, then trim off all the tough green leaves. Cut the rest in half lengthwise and chop; then wash well in a colander, being sure to rinse between all the layers.

2. Scatter the washed leeks over the bottom of an ovenproof casserole. Mix with the wine or stock, salt, pepper, and mustard. Top with the fish; sprinkle the fish with salt and pepper. Cover the casserole and put it in the oven.

3. Bake for 10 to 15 minutes, or until a thin-bladed knife meets little or no resistance when inserted into the thickest part of the fish. Uncover and serve the fish with the leeks and pan juices spooned over it.

───────────

COD CAKES WITH GINGER AND SCALLIONS

MAKES 4 SERVINGS   TIME: 1 HOUR

BETWEEN YOUR FAVORITE crab cake and a box of frozen fish sticks lies a world of crisp, easily produced fish cakes that make for great weeknight eating. In addition to fish, they all have two elements in common: something to "bind" the cake as it cooks and a fair amount of seasoning.

My favorite way to hold fish cakes together is to mix the flaked meat with mashed potatoes, about three parts fish to one part potato. If you begin with a mild fish, like cod, the flavorings can be as adventuresome as you like. My preferred combination is a hefty dose of ginger and cilantro, spiked with a bit of hot red chile. The result is a zingy cake that needs nothing more than a squeeze of lime.

1 baking potato (about $^1/_2$ pound)	$^1/_2$ cup minced fresh cilantro, plus more for garnish
Salt and freshly ground black pepper	1 small fresh or dried hot red chile, minced, or $^1/_4$ teaspoon cayenne, or to taste
$1^1/_2$ pounds cod or other mild, delicate white-fleshed fish fillet	2 teaspoons peanut or vegetable oil
1 tablespoon minced peeled fresh ginger	Lime wedges for serving

1. Boil the potato in salted water to cover until it is tender but not mushy, 30 to 40 minutes.

VARIATIONS

Panfried Fish Cakes

Increase the oil to $^1/_3$ cup, or more if necessary. Heat about $^1/_{16}$ inch oil in a large skillet over medium-high heat. When it is hot (a pinch of the fish mixture will sizzle immediately), add the cakes. Cook, turning once, until brown on both sides, about 10 minutes total.

• Substitute minced garlic, shallot, scallion, or onion for the ginger and parsley for the cilantro.

• Season with a grating of nutmeg or a teaspoon or more of curry powder (in place of the seasonings in the original recipe).

• Add $^1/_4$ cup or more sour cream and a little butter to the potato as you mash it.

• Add minced yellow or red bell pepper to the mix.

• Serve with Mayonnaise (page 305) or tartar sauce (page 306), Worcestershire sauce, or any other condiment.

2. Meanwhile, put the fish in a skillet that can later be covered. Add water to cover, salt the water, and bring to a boil over high heat. Cover, turn off the heat, and set a timer for 10 minutes. Use a slotted spoon to transfer the fish to a bowl.

3. When the potato is done, peel it and mash it with the fish. Add the ginger, cilantro, and chile along with some salt and pepper to taste and work the mixture with your hands until it is well blended. Shape into 8 equal burger-shaped patties.

4. Preheat the broiler and set the rack about 4 inches from the heat source. Brush the patties on both sides with the oil, then place on a nonstick baking sheet. Broil carefully until nicely browned on top, then turn and brown on the other side. Sprinkle with more cilantro and serve hot, with lime wedges.

COD WITH CHICKPEAS AND SHERRY

MAKES 4 SERVINGS   TIME: 30 MINUTES

AN ANDALUSIAN DISH with a sweet, aromatic sauce. Do not use canned chickpeas here.

3 tablespoons olive oil

2 cod fillets, each about 1 inch thick (about 1^1/$_2$ pounds total)

Salt and freshly ground black pepper

4 cups cooked chickpeas, with their liquid (see page 36)

^{3}/$_4$ cup sherry, preferably amontillado

2 tablespoons minced garlic

Chopped fresh parsley for garnish (optional)

1. Preheat the oven to 300°F. Put 1 tablespoon of the oil in a nonstick skillet large enough to hold the cod in one layer (cook in batches if necessary, but undercook the first batch by about a minute, as it will remain in the oven longer); turn the heat to medium-high. When the oil is hot, add the fish, shiny side (where the skin was) up. Cook, undisturbed, for about 5 minutes, or until the cooked side is evenly browned. Turn the fish onto an ovenproof plate, browned side up, sprinkle with salt and pepper, and put it in the oven.

2. Immediately add the chickpeas (with about 1 cup of their cooking liquid) to the skillet and cook, stirring, for about a minute. Add all but 2 tablespoons of the sherry and raise the heat to high. Cook, shaking the pan now and then, until the liquid is all but evaporated and the chickpeas are beginning to brown. Stir in the garlic along with some salt and pepper and cook for 1 minute, stirring occasionally; stir in the remaining olive oil and sherry.

3. By this time the fish will be done. (If it is not, hold the chickpeas over low heat until it is.) Serve it on top of the chickpeas, garnished with the parsley if you like.

EMMA'S COD AND POTATOES

MAKES 4 SERVINGS   TIME: 1 HOUR

ONCE, FOR A special occasion, I produced potatoes Anna—a dish in which potatoes are thinly sliced, drenched in butter, and roasted until golden, the ultimate in crisp potato dishes—for my daughter Emma. This was a fatal error, because potatoes Anna are a pain to make, contain about a week's allotment of butter, and were forever in demand thereafter. So I set about shortcutting the process, creating something approaching an entire meal. I cut back on the butter (when attacks of conscience strike, I substitute olive oil) and enlisted the broiler to speed the browning process. I figured that it would be just as easy to broil something on top of the potatoes during the last few minutes of cooking and, after a few tries, I found a thick fillet of fish to be ideal. The result is this simple weeknight dish that I now make routinely and one that even impresses guests.

4 to 5 medium potatoes (2 pounds
    or more)
6 tablespoons extra virgin olive oil
    or melted butter
Salt and freshly ground black
    pepper

1 1/2 pounds cod or other white-
    fleshed fish fillets, about 1 inch
    thick (skinned), in 2 or more
    pieces

1. Preheat the oven to 400°F. Peel the potatoes and cut them into slices about 1/8 inch thick (a mandoline comes in handy here). Toss the potatoes in an 8 X 11-inch or similar-size baking pan with 4 tablespoons of the oil or butter. Season the potatoes liberally with salt and pepper, spread them evenly, and put the pan in the oven.

2. Cook for about 40 minutes, checking once or twice, until the potatoes are tender when pierced with a thin-bladed knife and have begun to brown on top. Turn on the broiler and adjust the rack so that it is 4 to 6 inches from the heat source.

3. Top the potatoes with the fish, drizzle with the remaining oil or butter, and sprinkle with some more salt and pepper. Broil until the fish is done, 6 to 10 minutes depending on its thickness (a thin-bladed knife will pass through it easily). If at any point the top of the potatoes begins to burn, move the pan a couple of inches farther away from the heat source.

VARIATIONS

• Toss 1 teaspoon or more of minced garlic with the potatoes.
• Mix up to 1/2 cup chopped fresh parsley, dill, basil, or chervil or 1 or 2 teaspoons of stronger herbs like thyme or rosemary with the potatoes.
• Season the potatoes with a tablespoon or so of curry, chili powder, or paprika or a few pinches of cayenne or hot red pepper flakes.
• Top the fish with thinly sliced tomatoes and drizzle them with olive oil or dot them with butter before broiling.
• Add other vegetables to the potatoes—a cup or more of chopped spinach, for example—but be aware that their moisture may keep the potatoes from browning well.

ROAST MONKFISH WITH CRISP POTATOES, OLIVES, AND BAY LEAVES

MAKES 4 SERVINGS   TIME: 40 MINUTES

THE STURDY TEXTURE of monkfish is ideal for roasting, but certain other fillets will give similar results: red snapper, sea bass, pollock, wolffish, even catfish.

- You can mix sliced onion or other root vegetables in with the potatoes, and the results will be delicious, but the juices of the vegetables will reduce the potatoes' browning; it's a trade-off, and there's nothing to be done about it.
- Substitute about 10 fresh sprigs thyme for the bay or about 2 teaspoons fresh (or 1 dried) rosemary.
- Other possibilities: 1 tablespoon ground cumin or cumin seeds; 1 tablespoon fennel seeds; 3 teaspoons curry powder (sprinkle 1 teaspoon on the fish itself); a few saffron threads; or 1 tablespoon good-quality, medium-hot paprika.

2 large baking potatoes (about 1 pound)
$1/2$ cup extra virgin olive oil
Salt and freshly ground black pepper

15 bay leaves
1 cup good-quality black olives, like Kalamata
$1^1/2$ pounds monkfish or other fillets

1. Preheat the oven to 400°F. Peel and thinly slice the potatoes (use a mandoline if you have one). Spread the bottom of a 9 X 12-inch baking pan with half the olive oil; top with a single layer of the potatoes (it's okay if they overlap a little). Season with salt and pepper and top with the bay leaves and remaining oil.
2. Roast for 10 minutes. Check and turn the pan from back to front, shaking it a little to bathe the potatoes in oil. Roast for 10 minutes more. If the potatoes aren't browning, roast for 5 minutes more.
3. Top the potatoes with the olives and the fish; sprinkle the fish with salt and pepper. Roast for 10 minutes more, or until the fish is tender but not overcooked. Serve immediately.

═══════════════

ROAST MONKFISH WITH MEAT SAUCE

MAKES 4 SERVINGS   TIME: 40 MINUTES

I USED TO make an understated but impressive dish of monkfish with a meat sauce that was simple in appearance but tiresome in preparation, because the sauce was a reduction that began with meat bones, continued with roasted vegetables, and required four or five steps over a two-day period. The result was delicious, but so ordinary looking that only the best-trained palates ever picked up on how complex it was.

Now I make the same sauce with pan-roasted vegetables, a simple combination of onion, carrot, and celery, darkly browned in a little bit of butter, and a can of beef stock. It takes a half hour or less, and although it doesn't have the richness of my original work of art, no one to whom I served both could tell the difference with certainty.

Four 6- to 8-ounce pieces monkfish

1 tablespoon butter

1 small carrot, roughly chopped

1 celery stalk, roughly chopped

1 small onion, roughly chopped

1 tablespoon tomato paste
(optional)

1 can (about 13 ounces) beef broth
or 1 $^1/_2$ cups meat or chicken
stock

Salt and freshly ground black pepper

1 teaspoon extra virgin olive oil

VARIATION

Roast Monkfish with Asian Meat Sauce

To season the stock with Asian aromatic vegetables rather than traditional European ones, substitute 10 slices peeled fresh ginger, a lemongrass stalk, and 5 scallions for the carrot, celery, and onion. Omit the tomato paste.

1. Preheat the oven to 500°F or as close to that as it will get. It's best to remove the thin membrane clinging to the monkfish before cooking. Just pull and tug on it while cutting through it with a paring knife and it will come off, you don't have to be too compulsive about this task, but try to get most of it off.

2. Put a cast-iron or other ovenproof skillet or roasting pan in the oven while it is heating. Put half the butter in a small saucepan and turn the heat to medium-high. Add the carrot and celery and stir; a minute later, add the onion. Cook, stirring occasionally, until the vegetables brown—be careful not to let them burn—less than 10 minutes. Stir in the tomato paste if you're using it, then the broth or stock. Bring to a boil, then adjust the heat so the mixture simmers for about 10 minutes.

3. Strain the broth, pressing on the vegetables to extract their liquid. Return to medium-high heat and bring to a boil; let boil until reduced by about three-quarters, or until less than $^1/_2$ cup of thick liquid remains. Season the fish with salt and pepper.

4. Meanwhile, once you've strained the broth and begun reducing it, carefully remove the hot pan from the oven and add the olive oil to it; swirl to coat the bottom of the pan. Add the fish and roast for 5 minutes. Remove from the oven and carefully pour the liquid that has accumulated around the fish into the simmering sauce; once again, bring it to a boil and reduce until thick, syrupy, and about $^1/_2$ cup. Turn the fish and roast it for another 5 minutes, or until a thin-bladed knife inserted into its thickest part meets little resistance.

5. Stir the remaining butter into the sauce, then serve the fish with the sauce spooned over it.

GRAVLAX

MAKES AT LEAST 12 SERVINGS

TIME: ABOUT 24 HOURS, LARGELY UNATTENDED

THE INTENSE ORANGE color, meltingly tender texture, and wonderful flavor of gravlax give it an allure shared by few fish preparations—not bad for a dish whose name means "buried salmon" in Swedish. The curing process intensifies the color, tenderizes the texture, and enhances the flavor. Although most chefs jazz up gravlax with sauces and side dishes, it is brilliant on its own or with just a few drops of lemon or mild vinegar. And the rankest kitchen novice can make it at home.

Be sure to check your salmon fillet for pinbones, the long bones that run down the center of the fillet; these are not always removed by routine filleting. Press your finger down the center of the flesh and you will feel them; remove them, one at a time, with needle-nose pliers or similar tool.

VARIATIONS

Low-Salt Gravlax

Use $1/2$ cup salt and $1/4$ cup sugar. Combine a couple of chopped bay leaves, $1/4$ cup minced shallot, and 1 teaspoon cracked black pepper with the dill. Refrigerate for 48 hours and proceed as directed.

Citrus Gravlax

Use 1 cup each salt and sugar, combined with the grated zests of 2 oranges, 2 lemons, 2 limes, and 2 grapefruit, 2 tablespoons juniper berries; 1 tablespoon cracked coriander seeds; and 1 bunch of dill, stems and all. Marinate for 12 to 24 hours.

1 cup salt

2 cups sugar

1 bunch of dill, stems and all, chopped

One 2- to 3-pound salmon fillet, pinbones removed

1. Mix together the salt, sugar, and dill. Put the salmon, skin side down, on a large sheet of plastic wrap. Cover the flesh side of the salmon with the salt mixture, being sure to coat it completely (there will be lots of salt mix; just pile it in there).

2. Wrap the fish well. If the air temperature is below 70°F and it is not too inconvenient, let it rest outside the refrigerator for about 6 hours, then refrigerate for 18 to 24 hours more. Otherwise, refrigerate immediately for about 36 hours.

3. Unwrap the salmon and rinse off the cure. Dry, then slice on the bias. Serve plain or with lemon wedges, crème fraîche, sour cream, or a light vinaigrette.

SALMON BURGERS

MAKES 4 SERVINGS   TIME: 30 MINUTES

THE PROCESS FOR making these salmon burgers is simple as long as you have a food processor. A portion of the salmon is finely ground, almost pureed; the machine takes care of that in about thirty seconds. Then the rest of the fish is chopped, by pulsing the machine on and off a few times. The two-step grinding process means that those flavorings that you want finely minced, like garlic or ginger, can go in with the first batch of salmon; those that should be left coarse, like onion or fresh herbs, can go in with the second batch. The only other trick is to avoid overcooking; this burger, which can be sautéed, broiled, or grilled, is best when the center remains pink (or is it orange?)—two or three minutes per side does the trick.

1^1/$_2$ pounds skinless, boneless salmon	1 tablespoon drained capers
2 teaspoons Dijon mustard	Salt and freshly ground black pepper
2 shallots, cut into chunks	2 tablespoons butter or olive oil
^{1}/$_2$ cup coarse bread crumbs	Lemon wedges
	Tabasco sauce

1. Cut the salmon into large chunks and put about a quarter of it into the container of a food processor, along with the mustard. Turn the machine on and let it run—stopping to scrape down the sides if necessary—until the mixture has become pasty.

2. Add the shallots and the remaining salmon and pulse the machine on and off until the fish is chopped and well combined with the puree. No piece should be larger than ^{1}/$_4$ inch or so in diameter, but be careful not to make the mixture too fine.

3. Scrape the mixture into a bowl and, by hand, stir in the bread crumbs, capers, and some salt and pepper. Shape into 4 burgers. (You can cover and refrigerate the burgers for a few hours at this point if you like.)

4. Put the butter or oil in a 12-inch nonstick skillet and turn the heat to medium-high. When the butter foam subsides or the oil is hot,

VARIATIONS

Though I am partial to the formula in the main recipe for salmon burgers, the mustard, shallots, and capers can be considered optional, so you can combine them or omit them as you like when experimenting.

• Use any fresh herbs, like parsley, chervil, dill, or cilantro. Add 2 tablespoons or more with the second batch of salmon.

• Use a combination of soy sauce (about a tablespoon), sesame oil (a teaspoon), and ginger (a teaspoon, added with the first batch of salmon). Use peanut oil for sautéing if you have it.

• Add a small garlic clove along with the first batch of salmon. (Don't overdo it, because the garlic will remain nearly raw.)

• Add ^{1}/$_4$ cup onion or scallion chunks in addition to or instead of the shallots.

• Add spice mixtures like curry or chili powder to the mixture—a teaspoon to a tablespoon, to taste.

• Add roughly chopped red or yellow bell pepper (about ^{1}/$_2$ cup) with the second batch of salmon.

• Add ^{1}/$_4$ cup or more lightly toasted pine nuts or about 1 tablespoon sesame seeds along with the bread crumbs.

cook the burgers for 2 to 3 minutes per side, turning once. Alternatively, you can grill them; let them firm up on the first side, cooking for about 4 minutes, before turning them over and finishing the cooking for just another minute or two. On no account should the burgers be overcooked. Serve the burgers on a bed of greens, or buns, or simply plates, with lemon wedges and Tabasco or any dressing you like.

HERB-RUBBED SALMON

MAKES 4 SERVINGS   TIME: 30 MINUTES

ALTHOUGH THIS MINIMALIST but infinitely variable technique of herb-coating salmon is about as straightforward as can be, allowing the fillets to sit for a while after coating will encourage the fragrant seasonings to permeate the flesh of the fish; try fifteen minutes or so at room temperature or up to 24 hours in the refrigerator.

Four 6-ounce skinned salmon fillets

Salt and freshly ground black pepper

1 tablespoon fennel seeds

1 tablespoon minced fresh rosemary

1 tablespoon minced orange zest

2 tablespoons olive oil or butter

1. Season the fillets on both sides with salt and pepper to taste. Grind the fennel seeds coarsely and mix them with the rosemary and orange zest. Press this mixture into the top (nonskin side) of each fillet. Let sit, refrigerated and covered, for up to 24 hours.

2. When you're ready to cook, preheat the oven to 450°F. Preheat a large nonstick ovenproof skillet over medium-high heat for 3 or 4 minutes. Add the oil or butter and, when it shimmers, place the fillets, coated side down, in the pan. Cook for about 1 minute, or until the herb mixture forms a nicely browned crust.

3. Turn the fillets and cook for about a minute more, then transfer to the oven. Cook for about 4 minutes for rare salmon, 5 to 6 minutes for medium-rare, and 8 minutes for well done.

VARIATIONS

Seed-Rubbed Salmon
Combine 2 tablespoons shelled raw pumpkin seeds and about 2 tablespoons dried porcini pieces in a coffee or spice grinder and grind to a coarse powder. Press some of the mixture into the top (nonskin side) of each of the fillets and cook as directed.

Spice-Rubbed Salmon
Combine 1 tablespoon coriander seeds or ground coriander, $1/4$ teaspoon whole or ground cloves, $1^1/2$ teaspoons cumin seeds or ground cumin, and 1 teaspoon freshly grated nutmeg (grind all together if necessary). Press some of the mixture into the top (nonskin side) of each of the fillets and cook as directed.

ROAST SALMON STEAKS
WITH PINOT NOIR SYRUP

MAKES 4 SERVINGS   TIME: 30 MINUTES

THIS MYSTERIOUS, DARK extraordinarily delicious sauce is a kind of *gastrique*, a relatively simple sauce based on caramelized sugar.

Note that if the sugar turns black and begins to smoke, you have burned rather than caramelized it. Throw it out and start again, with lower heat and more patience this time. And if the caramel sticks to your pan and utensils when you're done, boil some water in the pan, with the utensils in there if necessary. The caramel will loosen right away.

$^1/_2$ cup sugar

2 cups Pinot Noir

1 fresh rosemary sprig, plus
   1 teaspoon chopped

4 salmon steaks (about $^1/_2$ pound
   each)

Salt and freshly ground black
   pepper

1 tablespoon balsamic vinegar

1 tablespoon butter

1. Preheat the oven to 450°F. Put the sugar in a heavy saucepan, preferably nonstick and with rounded sides, and turn the heat to medium. Cook, without stirring (just shake the pan occasionally to redistribute the sugar) until the sugar liquefies and begins to turn brown, about 10 minutes. Turn off the heat and carefully add the wine. Turn the heat to high and cook, stirring, until the caramel dissolves again. Then add the rosemary sprig and reduce over high heat, stirring occasionally, until the mixture is syrupy and reduced to just over $^1/_2$ cup, 10 to 15 minutes.

2. Heat a nonstick ovenproof skillet over high heat until it begins to smoke. Season the salmon on both sides with salt and pepper, then put it in the pan; immediately put the pan in the oven. Cook for 3 minutes, then turn the salmon and cook for another 3 minutes. Check to see that the salmon is medium-rare or thereabouts (it should be) and remove it and keep it warm, or cook for another minute or two if you like.

3. When the sauce is reduced, stir in the balsamic vinegar and butter and turn the heat to medium-low. Cook until the butter melts, add some salt and pepper, and remove the rosemary sprig. Taste and adjust the seasoning, then serve over the fish, garnished with the chopped rosemary.

VARIATIONS

Salmon with Spicy Sherry Vinegar Oil

Use a total of 3 tablespoons olive oil in place of the peanut and sesame oils. Combine the remaining 2 tablespoons olive oil in a small saucepan with the garlic, chiles, and some salt. Cook, gently shaking the pan occasionally, until the garlic and chiles sizzle and the garlic colors lightly, about 5 minutes. Turn off the heat and remove the chiles. (This step may be done in advance.) When the oil cools a bit, add 1 tablespoon sherry vinegar. Garnish with $1/4$ cup roughly chopped fresh parsley or 2 teaspoons minced fresh tarragon.

Salmon with Soy and Black Beans

Before cooking the fish, soak 1 tablespoon preserved (Chinese) black beans in 1 tablespoon dry sherry or water. Drain the beans and add them to the oil along with the garlic and chiles.

ROAST SALMON WITH SPICY SOY OIL

MAKES 4 SERVINGS　　　TIME: 20 MINUTES

IT DOESN'T TAKE much to cook salmon or to dress it up, and there's no way simpler than this: cook fillets by any of a number of methods, then finish them with flavored oil. Here I focus on a spicy soy oil that contains slivered garlic, peanut and sesame oils, and soy sauce, but it's easy enough to change the spirit from Asian to European. Although oil is the basis for this sauce, the quantity is minimal because heating the oil thins it, enabling even a small amount to coat and flavor the fish.

2 tablespoons peanut oil
$1^1/2$ to 2 pounds salmon fillets in
　　4 pieces
Salt and freshly ground black
　　pepper
1 tablespoon sesame oil

1 tablespoon slivered garlic
2 small dried red chiles
1 tablespoon soy sauce
$1/2$ cup chopped scallion, or
　　$1/4$ cup roughly chopped
　　fresh cilantro for garnish
　　(optional)

1. Preheat the oven to 500°F. Heat a 12-inch nonstick ovenproof skillet over medium-high heat, then add 1 tablespoon of the peanut oil and swirl it around. Season the salmon with salt and pepper and put it, skin side up, in the skillet. A minute later, when the salmon has browned, turn and immediately transfer it to the oven.

2. Combine the remaining peanut oil in a small saucepan with the sesame oil, garlic, and chiles and turn the heat to medium. Cook, gently shaking the pan occasionally, until the garlic and chiles sizzle and the garlic colors lightly, about 5 minutes. Turn off the heat and remove the chiles. (This step may be done in advance.) When the oil cools a bit, add the soy sauce.

3. The salmon will be medium-rare after about 6 minutes in the oven. Transfer it to a plate. Drizzle it with the oil, garnish if you like, and serve.

ROSSI

excellent

MAY 24, 2015
MAY 31 2013!

SALMON ROASTED IN BUTTER
MAKES 4 SERVINGS   TIME: 20 MINUTES

ALTHOUGH AQUACULTURE HAS made fresh salmon a year-round product, wild salmon does have a season, from spring through fall. At those times it's vastly preferable to the farm-raised fish, because the best salmon—king, sockeye, and coho—has so much flavor of its own that it needs nothing but a sprinkling of salt. But a simple formula of salmon, oil or butter, and a single herb, combined with a near-foolproof oven-roasting technique, gives you many more options and makes even farm-raised salmon taste special. Be sure to preheat the pan in the oven—this allows the fish to brown before it overcooks. (If you start the same fillet in a cold pan, it will simply turn a dull pink and will not brown until it is as dry as chalk.)

1/3

4 tablespoons (^{1}/2 stick) butter

^{1}/4 cup minced fresh chervil, parsley, or dill

1 salmon fillet (1 ^{1}/2 to 2 pounds)

Salt and freshly ground black pepper

Lemon wedges for serving

1. Preheat the oven to 475°F. Put the butter and half the herb in a roasting pan just large enough to hold the salmon (you may have to cut the fillet in half) and put it in the oven. Cook for about 5 minutes, until the butter melts and the herb begins to sizzle.

VARIATIONS

Salmon Roasted in Olive Oil
Substitute extra virgin olive oil for the butter and fresh basil, thyme leaves (2 teaspoons total), or marjoram (2 tablespoons total) for the herb.

• Substitute peanut oil for the butter (adding a teaspoon of sesame oil for extra flavor if you like) and fresh cilantro or mint for the herb. Use lime instead of lemon.

FISH   111

2. Add the salmon to the pan, skin side up. Roast for 4 minutes. Remove from the oven, then remove the skin from the salmon (it should peel right off; if it does not, cook for another 2 minutes). Sprinkle with salt and pepper and turn the fillet. Sprinkle with salt and pepper again.

3. Roast for another 3 to 5 minutes, depending on the thickness of the fillet. Spoon a little of the butter over each serving, garnish with the remaining herb, and serve with lemon wedges.

SALMON AND TOMATOES COOKED IN FOIL

MAKES 4 SERVINGS   TIME: 40 MINUTES

COOKING IN PACKAGES requires a small leap of faith to determine that the food is done, because once you open the packages you want to serve them. This method works well.

$^1/_4$ cup extra virgin olive oil

$1^1/_2$ to 2 pounds salmon fillet, cut crosswise into 4 pieces

12 cherry tomatoes, sliced in half

Salt and freshly ground black pepper

16 fresh basil leaves

1. Take 2 sheets of aluminum foil, each about 18 inches long, and place one piece on top of the other; repeat with 2 more sheets (you will make 2 packages). Smear the top sheet of each pair with 1 tablespoon of the olive oil, then cover with 2 pieces of salmon, 12 tomato halves, some salt and pepper, 8 basil leaves, and another tablespoon of oil. Fold the foil onto itself and crimp the edges as tightly as possible. Repeat the process. (You can refrigerate the packages until you're ready to cook, no more than 6 hours later.) Put a baking pan in the oven and preheat it to 450°F shortly before cooking.

2. Put the packages in the baking pan and bake for about 15 minutes (or about 8 minutes from the time it starts sizzling). Let sit for a couple of minutes before carefully slitting open the package—spoon out (the tomato will have liquefied) and serve.

TUNA OR SWORDFISH WITH ONION CONFIT

MAKES 4 SERVINGS   TIME: 45 MINUTES

SLOW-COOKED ONIONS are good enough by themselves, but when you combine them with the liquid exuded by olives and tomatoes you have a gloriously juicy bed on which to serve any fish fillet or steak. This combination, I think, is best with grilled tuna or swordfish—their meatiness gives them the presence to stand up to the richly flavored mass of onions, creating an easy dish that is strikingly Provençal and perfect for summer.

3 tablespoons extra virgin olive oil

3 large or 4 or 5 medium onions, thinly sliced

Salt and freshly ground black pepper

1 large fresh thyme sprig or a large pinch of dried

2 medium tomatoes

1^1/2 to 2 pounds tuna or swordfish

About ^{1}/2 cup pitted and roughly chopped black olives

VARIATIONS

Chicken with Onion Confit
Serve the onions with grilled skinless, boneless chicken breasts.

• Omit the thyme and use a bay leaf instead, or finish the dish with a handful of chopped fresh basil, chervil, or parsley.

• Cook some finely chopped aromatic vegetables, like carrots, celery or fennel, and garlic, along with the onions.

1. Put the olive oil in a 10- or 12-inch skillet over medium heat. Add the onions, a healthy pinch of salt, some pepper, and the thyme. Cook, stirring occasionally, until the mixture starts to sizzle, a minute or two. Adjust the heat so that you have to stir only every 5 minutes at most to keep the onions from browning. They will become progressively softer; do not allow them to brown. Figure at least 30 minutes total for the onions to cook.

2. Core the tomatoes, then cut them in half horizontally. Squeeze and shake out the seeds, then cut the tomatoes into ^{1}/2-inch dice. Preheat a grill to moderately hot.

3. When the onions are very soft, almost a shapeless mass, season the fish and grill it, turning once, for a total of about 6 minutes for tuna, 8 to 10 minutes for swordfish; check for doneness by making a small cut in the center of the fish and peeking inside. (Tuna can be quite rare; swordfish is best cooked to medium, when its interior is still slightly pearly rather than completely opaque.) While the fish is

grilling, stir the olives and tomatoes into the onions and raise the heat a bit; cook, stirring occasionally, until the tomatoes liquefy and the mixture becomes juicy. Taste and adjust the seasoning. Serve the fish on a bed of the onion confit.

===

TUNA AU POIVRE

MAKES 4 SERVINGS   TIME: 15 MINUTES

NOWADAYS MOST EXPERIENCED home cooks grill tuna, but there are alternatives. Top of my list is tuna au poivre, yet another recipe that plays on tuna's similarity to beef steaks. How finely to grind the pepper turns out to be a matter of taste. Mine dictates "coarsely ground" as opposed to "cracked." That is, ground to the point where there are no large pieces left, but not to the point of powder. The coarser you make the grind, the more powerful the result will taste.

2 tablespoons coarsely ground
    black pepper
1 tablespoon extra virgin olive oil
Two 8 to 10-ounce tuna steaks,
    each at least 1 inch thick

Salt
2 tablespoons butter (or more oil)
1/4 cup minced shallot
3/4 cup dry red wine

1. Preheat the oven to 500°F. Put the pepper on a flat plate. Put the olive oil in a large skillet, preferably nonstick, over medium-high heat. Dredge both sides of each piece of tuna lightly in the pepper; it will adhere nicely, forming a thin coat. (Use a bit more pepper if necessary.) As they're dredged, add the steaks to the pan (if you must use 2 pans, double the amount of oil); when they are all in, turn the heat to high. Cook for about 2 minutes, then turn; add salt, then cook for another 1 minute. Turn the heat to low, transfer the steaks to an ovenproof plate, and place in the oven.

2. Add half the butter to the pan (if you used 2 pans to brown the

tuna, use just one to make the sauce), followed by the shallot. Turn the heat to medium and cook, stirring, until the shallot softens, about 2 minutes. Turn the heat to medium-high and add the wine; let it bubble away for a minute or so and add the remaining butter. Cook, stirring occasionally, until the butter melts and the sauce is thickened.

3. By this time the tuna steaks will be medium-rare (cut into one to make certain and roast a little longer if you like). Put each of them on a plate and spoon a little of the sauce over it. Serve immediately.

GRILLED SWORDFISH "SANDWICH" WITH GREEN SAUCE

MAKES 4 SERVINGS   TIME: 30 MINUTES

BECAUSE THE SAUCE is so moist, swordfish treated in this way will take a little longer to grill than usual; the interior, after all, has what amounts to a thick liquid cooling it off. So instead of cooking a one-and-a-half-inch-thick steak—about the right size for this procedure—for eight to ten minutes, I'd estimate twelve to fourteen. The actual time will vary depending on the heat of your grill or broiler, but you can assume a little bit longer than what you're used to. Check by cutting into the fish when you think it's done; the interior can be pearly but should not look raw.

10 anchovy fillets

1 1/2 cups fresh parsley leaves, washed and left wet

2 garlic cloves

Zest and juice of 1 lemon

1/4 cup extra virgin olive oil

2 tablespoons capers with their liquid

1 1/2 to 2 pounds swordfish steak, skin on

Salt and freshly ground black pepper

1. Preheat a grill or broiler to moderately hot and put the rack 4 to 6 inches from the heat source. Combine the anchovies, parsley, garlic,

lemon juice and zest, and 2 tablespoons of the oil in a small food processor or blender. Process until pureed, adding a little bit of hot water (or more olive oil) if necessary to allow the machine to do its work. Combine the puree with the capers.

2. Cut the swordfish in half horizontally, leaving the skin attached as a hinge. Spread about half of the mixture on the inside of the "sandwich," then close the steak with a couple of toothpicks. Brush with the remaining oil, then sprinkle with salt and pepper.

3. Grill for at least 5 minutes per side, or until the swordfish is done (it should remain slightly translucent in the center). Serve with the remaining green sauce.

SHAD ROE WITH MUSTARD

MAKES 2 SERVINGS   TIME: 15 MINUTES

SHAD, THE LARGEST member of the herring family, migrates to the rivers of the East Coast every spring. It's a big, bony fish (filleting it properly is an increasingly rare skill) with moist flesh that is not unlike that of salmon. But its huge egg sacs, which come in pairs held together by a thin membrane, are the real attraction. They're filled with millions of eggs, which, if they are not overcooked, remain creamy and rich in a way that is reminiscent of fine organ meat—not quite foie gras, but not that far away either. As a bonus, the exterior membrane becomes slightly crisp.

Most shad roe is sadly overcooked, but this need not be the case. Keep the cooking time for shad roe short, just long enough to firm up the roe and cook it to the equivalent of medium-rare. (It's okay to cut into it for a look-see the first couple of times you try this, but it's also pretty easy to get the hang of it, because the change in texture is rather dramatic.) Note that this recipe serves two; it's easy enough to double, however; just use two skillets instead of one to avoid crowding the roe.

2 tablespoons butter

1 large pair shad roe (about ³/4 pound)

Salt and freshly ground black pepper

2 tablespoons Dijon mustard

Minced fresh parsley for garnish (optional)

1. Heat an 8- or 10-inch nonstick skillet over medium heat for a minute or two, then add the butter. When it melts, gently lay the shad roe in the pan and sprinkle it with salt and pepper. Cook for about 3 minutes, or until the underside is lightly browned.

2. Turn very gently—a large spatula is best for this—and season the cooked side. Cook for another 3 minutes or so, again until the underside is lightly browned. By this time the roe should be quite firm to the touch; if it is still soft, cover the pan and cook for another minute or two, then cut into it to check. When done, the center will be red and the area surrounding it pink.

3. Transfer the roe to a warm plate. Add the mustard and ¹/4 cup of water to the pan; stir. Raise the heat to high and stir the sauce with a wooden spoon until smooth and thick. Spoon over the roe, garnish if you like, and serve immediately.

VARIATIONS

Shad Roe with Capers and Vinegar

In step 3, omit the mustard. Instead, stir in 2 tablespoons capers, 1 tablespoon vinegar, and 2 tablespoons of water. Stir until blended and the liquid is reduced by about half. Spoon over the roe, garnish, and serve.

Shad Roe with Bacon

Omit the butter. Begin by cooking 4 thick slices good-quality bacon over medium heat until the fat is rendered and the bacon is done; remove the bacon and keep warm. Cook the shad roe in the bacon fat, exactly as directed. Serve the shad roe and bacon with lemon wedges, garnished with fresh parsley.

FISH TACOS WITH FRESH SALSA

MAKES 4 SERVINGS   TIME: 20 MINUTES

FISH BREATHES NEW life into the "sandwich" of Mexico and the Southwest, replacing mystery meat with an identifiable fillet of delicate white fish like cod to make fish tacos, a rarity on the East Coast. Instead of frying, as is common in tacquerias, I like to steam the fish in its own juices, which can be done on top of the stove or in a microwave oven (in fact, this is one of the few cooking tasks at which the microwave excels).

1 medium onion, roughly chopped

1 jalapeño chile, stemmed and
  roughly chopped

$1^1/2$ pounds cod or other thick
  white-fleshed fish fillet

Salt and freshly ground black
  pepper

Twelve 6-inch corn tortillas or eight
  12-inch corn or flour tortillas

Salsa

Hot sauce or chile paste (optional)

Sour cream or grated cheese
  (optional)

Chopped lettuce, tomatoes,
  cucumbers, and fresh cilantro
  sprigs for serving (optional)

Lime wedges for serving

1. Put the onion and jalapeño in the bottom of a nonstick skillet (or, if you prefer, a microwave-safe casserole). Add a tablespoon of water and top with the fish; sprinkle with salt and pepper. Cover the skillet (or casserole) and put the pan over medium heat (or the casserole in the microwave). Cook for about 6 minutes (3 for the microwave), or until the fish is done.

2. While the fish is cooking, heat the tortillas. You can dry-toast them in a skillet, one at a time; just flip once or twice over medium heat until hot, a minute or so. Or heat them in a microwave: wrap half a dozen in a just slightly damp towel and nuke for about a minute.

3. To serve, put a portion of fish (along with a bit of its onion and jalapeño), salsa, and, if you like, hot sauce, sour cream or cheese, and/or vegetables in a warm tortilla. Squeeze a bit of lime juice over all.

POULTRY

FASTEST ROAST CHICKEN

MAKES 4 SERVINGS   TIME: 45 MINUTES

ROAST CHICKEN IS one of the most basic dishes of home cooking, but there are a couple of challenges: You need high heat to brown the skin, but ultra-high heat may burn it. You need to cook the legs through before the more delicate breast dries out. And, if you're interested in minimalist cooking, you must accomplish these things without a lot of fuss, such as turning the chicken over three times, searing it on top of the stove before roasting, or constantly adjusting the oven temperature. Plus, you want to do it all as fast as possible.

Well, here it is: fast, nearly foolproof roast chicken.

1 3- to 4-pound chicken   Salt and freshly ground black pepper

1. Preheat the oven to 450°F. Five minutes after turning on the oven, put a cast-iron or other heavy, ovenproof skillet on a rack set low in the oven. (Alternatively, put the skillet over high heat about 3 minutes before the oven is hot.) Season the chicken with salt and pepper to taste.

2. When the oven is hot, about 10 minutes later, carefully put the chicken, breast side up, in the hot skillet. Roast, undisturbed, for 30 minutes, or until an instant-read thermometer inserted in the meaty part of the thigh registers 155°F. Remove from the oven, let rest a minute or two, then carve and serve.

VARIATIONS

• To make a quick gravy while the chicken is resting: Pour out most of the fat, put the skillet over high heat, and add about a cup of water, wine, or stock. Cook, stirring and scraping, until just about $1/2$ cup of liquid is left. Season with salt and pepper and, if you're feeling extravagant, a tablespoon or two of butter.

• Rub the chicken with olive oil and/or any fresh herbs you like about halfway through the cooking—especially good is a bit of tarragon or a mixture of chopped rosemary and garlic.

- Follow the general rules for making a reduction sauce (page 126) and you can sauce this duck however you like. Chicken stock and green peppercorns are always good; orange juice is classic. Just be sure to drain nearly all of the fat first.
- Or flavor the duck in a variety of ways while it's roasting: Put a whole lemon, cut in half, in the cavity while the bird roasts, then squeeze the juice from that lemon over the bird after you carve it. Or stuff the bird with a few sprigs of fresh thyme or parsley. Or keep the pan juices moist with water or stock and cook, along with the duck, a few chopped leeks, carrots, celery stalks, and/or onions.
- Another method for roasting duck is more work but gives somewhat better results: First, steam the duck on a rack over simmering water until it is nearly cooked, about 45 minutes. Then chill it for up to a day; finally, roast it on a rack in a roasting pan at 400°F for about 30 minutes, or until the skin is crisp.

ROAST DUCK IN ONE HOUR

MAKES 2 TO 4 SERVINGS   TIME: ABOUT AN HOUR

WHAT TURNS PEOPLE off to roasting duck—its thick layer of subcutaneous fat—is actually its best feature, one that makes it a nearly foolproof dish. The fat keeps the meat juicy even when it's well done—a distinct advantage because the breast is best medium-rare, but the legs must be cooked through, or nearly so, to be palatable.

In fact, duck is so difficult to roast badly that all experienced cooks seem to claim their procedure is the best. Having tried many methods, I can say that the results are all about the same. So I usually rely on the one presented here, which I believe is the easiest way to guarantee a succulent but beautifully browned bird.

One challenge: a roast duck can easily be finished by two people. If you want to serve four, roast two or plan on a lot of side dishes.

One 4- to 5-pound duck
Freshly ground black pepper
$^1/_4$ cup soy sauce, more or less

1. Preheat the oven to 450°F. Discard the neck and giblets or keep them for another use; remove excess fat from the duck's cavity.
2. Put the duck, breast side down (wings up), on a rack in a roasting pan; add water to come to just below the rack. Sprinkle with pepper and brush with a little soy sauce.
3. Roast for 30 minutes, undisturbed. Prick the back all over with the point of a sharp knife, then flip the bird onto its back. Sprinkle with pepper and brush with soy sauce again. Add a little more water to the bottom of the pan if the juices are spattering (carefully—you don't want to get water on the duck).
4. Roast for 20 minutes, prick the breast all over with the point of a knife, and brush with soy sauce. Roast for 10 minutes; brush with soy sauce. Roast for another 5 or 10 minutes if necessary, or until the duck is a glorious brown all over and an instant-read thermometer inserted into the thigh measures at least 155°F. Let rest for 5 minutes before carving and serving.

ROAST TURKEY BREAST

MAKES 6 TO 10 SERVINGS   TIME: ABOUT 1 HOUR

SMALLER TURKEY BREASTS of about three pounds are perfectly adequate for a party of four or so, and larger ones—they're available in sizes of six pounds and even more—can be counted on to serve about ten, especially if you make a few side dishes.

The greatest advantage of roasting a turkey breast in lieu of a whole bird is that you can produce white meat that is truly moist—as opposed to the dried-out white meat that is the nearly inevitable result of roasting a whole turkey until the legs are cooked through. Perfectly cooked white meat (all you need is an instant-read thermometer) does not require tons of gravy to become edible, although you may like to serve it with a light sauce.

One 3- to 6-pound turkey breast

2 tablespoons olive oil, melted
   butter, or chicken stock
   (optional)

Salt and freshly ground black
   pepper

1. Preheat the oven to 450°F. Put the turkey in a roasting pan; you can place stuffing under its breastbone if you like; if you want crisp stuffing, however, add it to the pan (or bake it separately) when about 30 minutes of cooking time remain.

2. Brush the turkey with oil, butter, or stock if you like and season it with salt and pepper to taste. Put it in the oven. Roast for 40 to 60 minutes, depending on size, basting with the pan juices (or a little more chicken stock) every 15 minutes or so, then begin checking for doneness every few minutes with an instant-read thermometer. The turkey is ready when the thermometer reads 155°F. Let the turkey rest for 5 to 10 minutes (during which time its internal temperature will rise to about 160°F) before carving and serving.

VARIATION

Herb-Roasted Turkey Breast

Increase the melted butter, oil, or stock to $1/4$ cup and combine with $1/4$ cup chopped fresh parsley, along with a mixture of other fresh herbs, like tarragon (about a teaspoon), dill (about a tablespoon), or celery or fennel leaves (a tablespoon or more). Baste and roast as directed.

FOR SAFETY, the USDA recommends roasting white-meat poultry to 170°F, at which point it will be unpalatably dry (especially when you consider that the internal temperature typically rises at least five degrees during the resting period). Should you choose to do this, I strongly recommend that you serve the turkey with plenty of gravy. I stop the cooking at a lower temperature and have never regretted it.

THE MINIMALIST'S THANKSGIVING TURKEY

MAKES AT LEAST 12 SERVINGS (WITH LEFTOVERS)

TIME: 2 1/2 HOURS

ONE THANKSGIVING, I vowed to minimize everything: time, number of ingredients, and, most of all, work. My goal was to buy all the food with one trip to the store and prepare the entire feast in the time it took to roast my twelve-pound turkey—less than three hours. The results are close to a traditional Thanksgiving dinner: Without using convenience foods—I made both the stuffing and the cranberry sauce from scratch, each in less than ten minutes—I prepared a full-fledged feast for twelve with more food than anyone could possibly finish.

The stuffing was inspired by a clever recipe from the late great chef Pierre Franey; you can make it and stuff the bird in less time than it takes to preheat the oven. The gravy relies on pan drippings but is finished with nothing more than water, good-quality sherry, and butter; it's made in ten minutes or so, while the turkey rests before carving.

One 12-pound turkey

Fastest Bread Stuffing (recipe follows)

1. Preheat the oven to 500°F. Rinse the turkey and remove the giblets; save the liver to make the stuffing. Loosely pack the turkey cavity with the stuffing, then tie the legs together to close the vent.

2. Put the turkey on a rack in a large roasting pan. Add $1/2$ cup of water to the bottom of the pan along with the turkey neck, gizzard, and any other trimmings. Put in the oven, legs first.

3. Roast for 20 to 30 minutes, or until the top begins to brown, then turn the heat down to 350°F. Continue to roast, checking every 30 minutes or so; if the top threatens to brown too much, lay a piece of aluminum foil directly onto it. If the bottom dries out, add water, about $1/2$ cup at a time. The turkey is done when an instant-read thermometer inserted into the thickest part of the thigh measures 165°F. If, when the turkey is nearly done, the top is not browned enough, turn the heat back up to 425°F for the last 20 to 30 minutes of cooking.

4. Remove the turkey from the oven. Take the bird off the rack and make Sherry Reduction Gravy (page 126) while the bird rests (let it sit for about 20 minutes before carving).

Fastest Bread Stuffing

MAKES 12 SERVINGS   TIME: 2 $1/2$ HOURS

6 tablespoons butter

3 chicken livers or an equal amount of turkey liver (about $1/4$ pound)

1 cup chopped fresh parsley

Salt and freshly ground black pepper

8 slices good-quality one- or two-day-old white bread, crusts trimmed

1. Chop together (by hand or in a small food processor) the butter, livers, and parsley; season to taste.

2. Spread half of the mixture on 4 of the bread slices; use the remaining bread to make 4 sandwiches. Spread the remaining mixture on the outside of the sandwiches. Cut each of the sandwiches into 6 pieces.

3. Stuff the turkey and roast as described in the preceding recipe.

Sherry Reduction Gravy

MAKES 4 SERVINGS   TIME: 15 MINUTES

1½ cups amontillado or oloroso
    sherry

3 tablespoons butter (optional)

Salt and freshly ground black
    pepper

1. Remove the giblets and pour off all but a tablespoon of the fat from the turkey's roasting pan; leave as many of the solids and as much of the dark liquid behind as possible. Put the roasting pan over 2 burners and turn the heat to high.

2. Add the sherry and cook, stirring and scraping all the brown bits off the bottom of the pan, until the liquid has reduced by about half, 5 minutes or so.

3. Add 3 cups of water (or stock if you have it) and bring to a boil, stirring all the while. Turn the heat to medium and simmer for about 5 minutes.

4. Stir in the butter if you like and, when it melts, salt and pepper to taste. Keep warm until ready to serve. Strain before serving if desired.

DEVILED CHICKEN THIGHS

MAKES 4 SERVINGS   TIME: 30 MINUTES

PREPARED MUSTARD IS about as underappreciated as a staple could be. After all, it's fat-free, low in calories, and high in flavor. Despite these assets, its main role in most households is as a condiment for meat and, perhaps, as an occasional ingredient in vinaigrette. In this chicken dish, however—essentially broiled chicken smeared with a spicy mustard paste—it plays a leading role.

    You can make this dish with chicken breasts if you prefer, but I recommend starting with bone-in breasts and following the same procedure. If you want to use skinless, boneless breasts (forget about crispness), smear the meat all over with the mustard mixture, then broil for just about six minutes, turning two or three times to prevent burning.

8 chicken thighs or a mixture of thighs and drumsticks, about 2 pounds

Salt and freshly ground black pepper

$^1/_3$ cup Dijon mustard

$^1/_3$ cup minced shallot, onion, or scallion

$^1/_4$ teaspoon cayenne or Tabasco sauce, or to taste

Minced fresh parsley for garnish (optional)

1 Preheat the broiler to its maximum and set the rack about 4 inches from the heat. Season the chicken on both sides and place it in a pan, skin side up. Broil, watching carefully, until the skin is golden brown, about 5 minutes.

2. Meanwhile, combine the mustard, shallot, and cayenne. (If you have a small food processor, just throw them in there and pulse the machine on and off a few times.)

3. When the chicken has browned, remove it from the oven and turn it. Spread just a teaspoon or so of the mustard mixture on the underside of the chicken and broil for about 5 minutes. Turn the chicken and spread the remaining mixture on the skin side. Broil until the mustard begins to brown, about 5 minutes.

4. At this point the chicken may be done (there will be only the barest trace of pink near the bone, and an instant-read thermometer inserted into the meat will read 160°F). If it is not, turn off the broiler and let the chicken remain in the oven for another 5 minutes or so. Garnish with the parsley if you like and serve.

VARIATIONS

• For extra crunch, combine the mustard and shallot with about 1 cup bread crumbs. Be especially careful in broiling, for the bread crumbs will burn very soon after they brown.

• For extra flavor, combine the mustard and shallot with about $^1/_2$ cup chopped fresh parsley (or basil, cilantro, dill, or chervil). Proceed as directed.

• You can use the same coating with pork or veal chops; they should be at least 1 inch thick. Cooking time will be about the same.

CHICKEN WITH SWEET-AND-SOUR SHERRY SAUCE

MAKES 4 SERVINGS   TIME: 25 MINUTES

CHICKEN BREASTS ARE so bland that they demand something—a spice rub, a salsa, or a strong reduction sauce. If you start with strong-tasting solids and add a variety of bold liquids, reducing each one to a syrupy consistency, you end up with an intense and complex reduction sauce. The process can involve esoteric ingredients and procedures, or it can be quite straightforward, like this one, which is direct, quick, and easy, especially considering that the result is a dark, complex sauce that can be used in many ways (see the variations).

1 tablespoon plus 1 teaspoon olive oil

1/2 cup oyster or shiitake mushrooms, trimmed and roughly chopped (shiitake stems discarded or reserved for stock)

1/4 cup sliced shallot

2 teaspoons honey

2 tablespoons sherry vinegar or good-quality wine vinegar

1/3 cup dry (fino) sherry

1 cup meat, chicken, or vegetable stock

4 skinless, boneless chicken breast halves (1 to 1 1/2 pounds)

Salt and freshly ground black pepper

1. Preheat the broiler or start a grill. Put a 10-inch skillet over medium-high heat for a minute or two. Add the tablespoon of olive oil, then the mushrooms and shallot, and turn the heat to high. Cook, stirring occasionally, until the mushrooms brown nicely on the edges, about 5 minutes.

2. Add the honey and stir until it evaporates, less than a minute. Add the vinegar and cook, stirring occasionally, until the mixture is dry, about 2 minutes. Add the sherry and cook, stirring once or twice, until the mixture is syrupy and nearly dry, about 5 minutes. Add the stock and cook, stirring once or twice, until the mixture thickens slightly, about 5 minutes. Reduce the heat to medium-low and keep warm.

VARIATIONS

Mushrooms and Shallots with Sweet-and-Sour Sherry Sauce

Sauté about 1 pound fresh mushrooms, sliced (a combination of different mushrooms is best, but you can use all shiitakes or all button if you like), in 2 tablespoons olive oil over medium-high heat. The mushrooms will first give up their liquid, then begin to brown. When they start to crisp up, add 1/4 cup minced shallot. Cook for another 3 or 4 minutes, then serve with the sauce.
• Sauté the chicken breasts, using the recipe for Chicken Cutlets Meunière (page 141), and serve with the sauce.
• Serve the sauce with poached, grilled, or sautéed shrimp.

3. Sprinkle the chicken breasts with salt and pepper and broil or grill them for about 6 minutes, or until cooked through.

4. When the chicken is done, season the sauce to taste with salt and pepper and strain it if you like; stir in the remaining olive oil. Serve the chicken with the sauce spooned over it.

GRILLED CHICKEN THIGHS WITH SAUCE AU CHIEN

MAKES 4 SERVINGS   TIME: 30 MINUTES

ONCE IN MARTINIQUE I ate at a restaurant that was so simple that almost all of the food—chicken, tuna, quail, pork, and veal kidneys—was grilled. Not only that; it was all served with the same thin, powerful sauce, made of lime, scallion, chile, and garlic, with loads of allspice. It was the allspice that made the sauce unusual, but there was more to it than that: the garlic and scallion looked uncooked but had lost their harshness and become easily digestible. Furthermore, the base of the sauce was not oil, but water. With the help of a friend who was born on Martinique, I was able to duplicate the sauce at home. It's called *sauce au chien,* which means "dog sauce" (a fact I chose not to research too aggressively). And it's great with almost anything grilled.

VARIATIONS
- Serve the sauce with grilled fish or shellfish, especially shrimp; grilled ribs (or in fact grilled pork of any kind); or any grilled poultry.
- Add some chopped capers to the finished sauce to vary the flavor.

1 tablespoon slivered or minced garlic

6 scallions, trimmed and minced

1 jalapeño, habanero, or scotch bonnet chile, seeded, stemmed, and minced, or chile paste (see Notes) or hot red pepper flakes to taste (start with about $1/2$ teaspoon)

Salt and freshly ground black pepper

$1/2$ teaspoon ground allspice, or to taste (see Notes)

1 tablespoon peanut, grapeseed, corn, or other neutral oil

8 chicken thighs (about 2 pounds)

Juice of 1 lime

• *Scotch bonnet pepper, with its fierce heat and distinctive flavor, makes this sauce more authentic. But a small amount of Asian chile paste is fine, as is any other source of heat.*
• *If you have the patience to mince or grind allspice berries, the sauce will taste brighter; preground allspice will do the trick as long as it is reasonably fresh.*

1. Start a grill or preheat the broiler. Meanwhile, prepare the sauce: Combine the garlic, scallions, chile, $1/2$ teaspoon each of salt and pepper, the allspice, and oil in a small bowl. Add $1/2$ cup of boiling water; stir and let sit.

2. Sprinkle the chicken with salt and pepper and grill or broil it, turning 2 or 3 times, until it is cooked through, about 15 minutes. Taste the sauce and add more chile, salt, pepper, or allspice if needed. Stir in the lime juice (which must be added at the last moment to retain its freshness). Serve the chicken hot or at room temperature, passing the sauce at the table.

GRILLED CHICKEN BREASTS WITH EGGPLANT, SHALLOTS, AND GINGER SAUCE

MAKES 4 SERVINGS   TIME: 30 MINUTES

EGGPLANT IS SO strongly associated with the cooking of Italy and southern France that it is almost always prepared with olive oil and garlic. This need not be the case, of course, and with a few ingredient changes—like the addition of ginger—you can make a novel kind of "ratatouille," which readily converts an ordinary boneless chicken breast into an unusual and appealing dish. Be sure to spend a few minutes thoroughly cooking the shallots before adding the eggplant, allowing them to brown and begin to soften; and don't overcook the ginger.

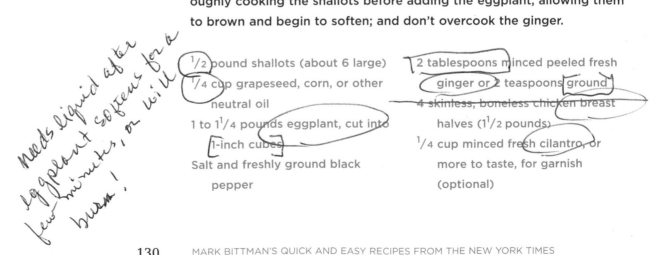

needs liquid after eggplant softens for a few minutes, or will burn!

$1/2$ pound shallots (about 6 large)

$1/4$ cup grapeseed, corn, or other neutral oil

1 to $1/4$ pounds eggplant, cut into 1-inch cubes

Salt and freshly ground black pepper

2 tablespoons minced peeled fresh ginger or 2 teaspoons ground

4 skinless, boneless chicken breast halves ($1/2$ pounds)

$1/4$ cup minced fresh cilantro, or more to taste, for garnish (optional)

1. Peel the shallots and cut them in half the long way (most large shallots have two lobes anyway and will naturally divide in half as you peel them). If they are small, peel them and leave them whole. Start a grill or preheat the broiler.

2. Put the oil in a large nonstick skillet over medium-high heat. Add the shallots and cook for about 5 minutes, stirring occasionally, until they begin to brown. Add the eggplant, salt, and pepper and lower the heat to medium. Cook, stirring occasionally, until the eggplant softens, about 15 minutes.

3. When the eggplant begins to brown, add half the ginger and cook for another 3 minutes or so, until the eggplant is very tender and the mixture fragrant. Meanwhile, rub the chicken breasts with salt, pepper, and the remaining ginger. Grill or broil, about 4 inches from the heat source, for 3 minutes per side, or until done.

4. If you're using the cilantro, stir half into the eggplant mixture. Serve the chicken breasts on a bed of the eggplant and garnish with the remaining herb.

VARIATIONS

• For a more traditional dish, substitute garlic for the ginger (or use half of each to make the total) and revert to olive oil. Use fresh parsley in place of cilantro.

• Stir in a cup or more of seeded and chopped tomatoes at the last minute; these boost color as well as flavor, and the combination of tomatoes and ginger is another unexpectedly pleasant one. (Peel the tomatoes if you like, but I don't think it's worth the effort in this case.)

CHICKEN THIGHS WITH MEXICAN FLAVORS

MAKES 4 SERVINGS   TIME: 30 TO 60 MINUTES

THE DARK, RICH meat of a chicken thigh responds brilliantly to the strong, equatorial flavors associated most closely with grilling. This Mexican-style treatment packs plenty of punch, even if you use the minimum amount of cayenne (as I do) or omit it entirely.

4 garlic cloves, peeled

1 medium onion, quartered

1 tablespoon fresh oregano leaves
    or 1/2 teaspoon dried

1 1/2 teaspoons ground cumin

1/2 teaspoon cayenne, or to taste

Pinch of ground cloves

Salt and freshly ground black
    pepper

2 tablespoons peanut or other oil

2 tablespoons orange juice,
    preferably fresh

2 tablespoons fresh lime juice
About 1 1/2 pounds boneless
    chicken thighs or 2 pounds
    bone-in

Minced fresh cilantro for garnish

1. Preheat a grill or broiler to moderately hot and put the rack at least 4 inches from the heat source. Combine the garlic, onion, oregano, cumin, cayenne, cloves, salt, pepper, and oil in a blender or small food processor and blend until fairly smooth. Add the juices, then taste and adjust the seasoning; the blend should be powerful.

2. Smear this mixture all over the chicken; if time allows, marinate the chicken for 30 minutes or so. Grill or broil for 6 to 8 minutes per side, watching carefully, until the meat is nicely browned on the outside and cooked through on the inside (bone-in thighs will take longer, about 20 minutes total). Serve hot or at room temperature, garnished with the cilantro.

GRILLED CHICKEN, SAUSAGE, AND VEGETABLE SKEWERS

MAKES 4 SERVINGS   TIME: 40 MINUTES

BRANCHES OF ROSEMARY are ideal for this dish, especially if you live in a Mediterranean climate where rosemary grows in shrubs. You can slide the food right onto them (in the direction of the needles, so as not to dislodge them), and they flavor it brilliantly; but so does some rosemary tucked in among the chunks of food. If you skewer on wood or metal skewers, turning will be made easier if you use two sticks in parallel for each skewer, separating them by about a half inch; you can also buy two-pronged metal skewers that do the trick nicely.

4 skinless, boneless chicken thighs, small thighs cut in half, larger ones in thirds or quarters

1/2 pound sweet or hot Italian sausage, cut into 1- to 2-inch lengths

1 pound eggplant, zucchini, or baby pattypan squash, cut into 1-inch pieces

2 bell peppers, preferably one red and one yellow, cut into 2-inch sections

1 lemon, cut into eighths

Salt and freshly ground black pepper

Several fresh rosemary sprigs or 4 large branches

1. Preheat a grill or broiler to moderately hot. If you're using wooden skewers, soak them in water to cover while you prepare the food. Make 4 skewers, alternating the different ingredients but generally surrounding both chicken and sausage with the moister lemon and eggplant. Pack the food fairly tightly together on each skewer and sprinkle with salt and pepper. If you are not using rosemary skewers, tuck some rosemary in among the cubes of food.

2. Grill over moderate heat, covered or not, turning the skewers 3 or 4 times to brown evenly. Total cooking time will be 10 to 15 minutes, depending on the heat of the grill and the distance from the heat source. By the time the chicken and sausage are browned, the eggplant will be tender; do not overcook.

3. Serve, squeezing hot lemon juice from the cooked lemons over all.

CHICKEN UNDER A BRICK

MAKES 4 SERVINGS   TIME: 45 MINUTES

CHICKEN AL MATTONE, as it's rightfully called, is the simplest and best method for producing crisp, delicious skin and wonderfully moist meat. All you need is a split chicken and two ovenproof skillets or a skillet and a couple of bricks or rocks. (The weight serves two purposes: it partially covers the chicken, which helps it retain moisture, and it ensures that the flesh of the chicken remains in contact with the skillet, which encourages browning.) Once covered, the chicken is transferred to a very hot oven to finish cooking. Handling the hot, heavy pan takes two hands—be careful.

One 3- to 4-pound chicken, trimmed of excess fat and split, backbone removed

1 tablespoon minced fresh rosemary or 1 teaspoon dried

Salt and freshly ground black pepper

1 tablespoon coarsely chopped garlic

2 tablespoons extra virgin olive oil

2 fresh rosemary sprigs, if available

1 lemon, quartered

1. Put the chicken on a cutting board, skin side down, and press down as hard as you can with your hands to make it as flat as possible. Mix together the minced or dried rosemary, salt and pepper, garlic, and 1 tablespoon of the olive oil and rub this all over the chicken. Tuck some of the mixture under the skin as well. If time permits, cover and marinate in the refrigerator for up to a day (even 20 minutes helps).

2. When you are ready to cook, preheat the oven to 500°F. Preheat an ovenproof 12-inch skillet (preferably nonstick) over medium-high heat for about 3 minutes. Press the rosemary sprigs into the skin side of the chicken. Put the remaining olive oil in the pan and wait about 30 seconds for it to heat up.

3. Put the chicken in the skillet, skin side down, along with any remaining pieces of rosemary and garlic; weight it with another skillet or one or two bricks or rocks wrapped in aluminum foil. The basic idea is to flatten the chicken by applying a fair amount of weight evenly over its surface.

4. Cook over medium-high to high heat for 5 minutes, then transfer to the oven. Roast for 15 minutes. Remove from the oven and remove the weights; turn the chicken over (it will now be skin side up) and roast for 10 minutes more, or until done (large chickens may take an additional 5 minutes or so). Serve hot or at room temperature, with lemon wedges.

GRILLED CHICKEN WINGS
WITH ANCHOVY DIPPING SAUCE

MAKES 4 SERVINGS   TIME: 30 MINUTES

PROPERLY GRILLED CHICKEN is a pleasure, even when you dress it with nothing but lemon juice—or even salt. But if you make this Ligurian-inspired full-flavored dipping sauce based on anchovies, you can turn the simple grilled chicken into something really special. And the sauce can be used for whatever else you're serving at the same time.

When you're grilling the chicken, don't build too hot a fire and keep part of the grill cool—don't put any fuel under it at all—so you can move the pieces over to it in the (likely) event of flare-ups. And you can broil it if you prefer: adjust the broiling rack so that it is about four to six inches from the heat source and turn the meat as it browns.

3 pounds chicken wings

Salt and freshly ground black
    pepper

3 tablespoons extra virgin olive oil

3 tablespoons butter (or more oil)

2 garlic cloves, roughly chopped

10 oil-packed anchovy fillets, or to
    taste, plus some of their oil

VARIATIONS

• This sauce makes a great dressing for grilled fish as well. It's also good with raw or lightly cooked vegetables.

• Chicken thighs, or leg-thigh pieces, are just as good as wings here; the cooking time will be a little longer.

1. Preheat a grill or broiler to moderately hot and put the rack about 4 to 6 inches from the heat source. If you like, cut the chicken wings at each of their 2 joints to make 3 pieces and discard the tips (or save for stock); you can also cook the wings whole.

2. Grill or broil the wings, turning frequently, until thoroughly cooked and nicely browned. As they are cooking, sprinkle them with a little salt and a lot of pepper.

3. Meanwhile, combine the oil and butter in a small saucepan and turn the heat to low. When the butter melts, add the garlic and anchovies. Cook, stirring occasionally, until the anchovies break up and the sauce bubbles. Add salt if necessary and a good sprinkling of pepper.

4. Serve the chicken hot or at room temperature, with the hot sauce for dipping or drizzling.

BROILED CORNISH HENS WITH SPICY SALT

MAKES 4 SERVINGS   TIME: 30 MINUTES

CORNISH HENS ARE better looking, faster to cook, and easier to handle than chickens. With a minimalist spice mix and a broiling technique that involves no turning, they're perfect for a speedy menu. You can find Szechwan peppercorns (which are not really peppercorns) at many supermarkets and any Asian food market.

1 tablespoon Szechwan
    peppercorns
2 Cornish hens, split in half

Salt
Juice of 1 lime

1. Preheat the oven to its maximum and put a roasting or broiling pan large enough to hold the birds in it. Adjust the broiler rack so that it is about 6 inches from the heating element.

2. Toast the peppercorns in a dry pan over medium heat, shaking occasionally, until fragrant, about 5 minutes. Grind to a powder in a spice mill, coffee grinder, or mortar and pestle. Sprinkle about 1 teaspoon of the powder over the skin side of the hens; sprinkle with a bit of salt as well. Combine the remaining powder with an equal amount of salt and set aside.

3. Turn off the oven and turn on the broiler; carefully remove the pan and put the hens in it, skin side up. Broil without turning, moving the pieces as necessary to brown evenly, for about 20 minutes, or until nicely browned and cooked through.

4. Transfer the birds to a plate and drizzle with a little of their pan juices and the lime juice. Serve, passing the spicy salt at the table.

Rossi *May 23, 2013*

lovely

BROILED CORNISH HENS WITH LEMON AND BALSAMIC VINEGAR

MAKES 4 SERVINGS　　　TIME: 30 MINUTES

ALL SOURNESS IS not the same, as this simple preparation of broiled Cornish hens with lemon and vinegar demonstrates. I love the taste of lemon and sometimes grill or broil poultry completely unadorned, finishing it with nothing but fresh lemon juice. But I wanted to develop a dish that would take advantage of the complex flavor of the entire lemon, rind and all, and offset it with another, equally gentle sourness.

The result is a crisp-skinned Cornish hen (you could use chicken, of course), topped with nicely browned lemon slices (sweet and tender enough to eat) and drizzled with just enough balsamic vinegar to make you wonder where the extra flavor is coming from. There are no other ingredients, though a garnish of parsley or a hint of rosemary and garlic make nice additions.

VARIATION

In step 3, spread 1 teaspoon finely minced garlic combined with 1 tablespoon minced fresh rosemary (or 1 teaspoon dried) on the birds' skin after it browns but before covering with the lemon slices. //

2 Cornish hens or 1 chicken
Salt and freshly ground black
　pepper
2 lemons

2 teaspoons balsamic vinegar, or to
　taste
Chopped fresh parsley for garnish
　(optional)

1. Preheat the broiler and put the rack about 4 inches from the heat source, a little lower for a chicken, which will take longer to cook. Use a sharp, sturdy knife to split the hens through their backbones; it will cut through without too much effort. Flatten the hens in a broiling or roasting pan, skin side down, and liberally sprinkle the exposed surfaces with salt and pepper. Slice one of the lemons as thinly as you can and lay the slices on the birds.

2. Broil for about 10 minutes, or until the lemon is browned and the birds appear cooked on this side; rotate the pan in the oven if necessary. Turn the birds, sprinkle with salt and pepper, and return to the broiler. Cook for another 10 minutes, or until the skin of the birds is nicely browned. Meanwhile, slice the remaining lemon as you did the first.

3. Lay the lemon slices on the birds' skin side and return to the broiler; broil for another 5 minutes, by which time the lemons will be slightly browned and the meat cooked through; if it isn't, cook for an additional couple of minutes. Drizzle with the balsamic vinegar, garnish if you like, and serve.

VARIATIONS

• Substitute any vegetable, or combination, for the peppers and onions. Try cut-up and parboiled (simmered in boiling water just until slightly tender) broccoli, asparagus, green beans, or dark leafy greens; shredded raw cabbage; raw snow peas; or chopped tomatoes.
• Use any boneless meat in place of the chicken, or shrimp or scallops. Cooking time will remain the same.
• Sprinkle the meat with about 1 tablespoon curry powder as it cooks.
• Along with the hoisin, add ground bean paste (about 1 tablespoon), plum sauce (about 1 tablespoon), or chili-garlic paste (about $1/2$ teaspoon, or to taste) during the last minute of cooking.
• Replace the hoisin with 3 or 4 small dried hot red chiles (optional), 1 tablespoon minced garlic, 1 tablespoon soy sauce, and $1/2$ cup chopped scallion, all added along with the nuts.

TEN-MINUTE STIR-FRIED CHICKEN WITH NUTS

MAKES 4 SERVINGS   TIME: 10 MINUTES

STIR-FRYING—the fastest cooking method there is—can change your life. You can use it for almost anything, and it can be so fast that the first thing you need to do is start a batch of white rice. In the fifteen or twenty minutes it takes for that to cook, you can not only prepare the stir-fry but set the table and have a drink.

For many stir-fries made at home, it's necessary to parboil—essentially precook—"hard" vegetables like broccoli or asparagus. So in this fastest possible stir-fry, I use red bell peppers, onions, or both; they need no parboiling and become tender and sweet in three or four minutes. If you cut the meat into small cubes or thin slices, the cooking time is even shorter.

I include nuts here for three reasons: I love their flavor, their chunkiness adds great texture (I don't chop them at all), and the preparation time is zero.

1 tablespoon peanut or vegetable oil

2 cups red bell pepper strips, onion slices, or a combination

1 pound skinless, boneless chicken breasts, cut into $1/2$- to $3/4$-inch-thick chunks

1 cup halved walnuts, whole cashews, or other nuts

3 tablespoons hoisin sauce (see Note)

- A flat-bottomed skillet—the larger the better and preferably nonstick—is better than a wok for stir-fries made at home. Keep the heat high and don't stir too much to ensure nicely browned, even slightly charred meat and vegetables.

- Keep it simple; too many ingredients slow you down and eventually overload the skillet so that browning becomes impossible.

1. Put the oil in a large nonstick skillet (12 inches is best) over high heat; a minute later, add the vegetables in a single layer and cook, undisturbed, until they begin to char a little on the bottom, about 1 minute. Stir and cook for 1 minute more.

2. Add the chicken and stir once or twice. Again, cook until the bottom begins to blacken a bit, about a minute. Stir and cook for another minute; by this time the vegetables will have softened and the chicken will be done, or nearly so (cut into a piece to check). Lower the heat to medium.

3. Stir in the nuts and the hoisin sauce. Cook for about 15 seconds, then add 2 tablespoons water. Cook, stirring, until the sauce is bubbly and glazes all the chicken and vegetables. Serve immediately, with white rice.

NOTE
Look for a brand of hoisin sauce whose first ingredient is fermented soybeans rather than sugar or water; the flavor will be more intense.

SIMPLEST SAUTÉED CHICKEN WITH GARLIC

MAKES 4 SERVINGS   TIME: 30 MINUTES

SAUTÉED CHICKEN SHOULD be crisp, moist, and flavorful, and you can accomplish this easily. Use a large skillet, or two smaller ones, because crowding the chicken pieces prevents them from browning. There should be sufficient room in the skillet so that the pieces barely touch each other, and they should certainly not overlap. This recipe contains no added fat—the bird provides plenty of its own—so the skillet should be nonstick, or at least well seasoned.

1 2- to 3-pound chicken, cut into
   serving pieces
Salt and freshly ground black
   pepper
$1/2$ teaspoon paprika

1 teaspoon minced garlic
Chopped fresh parsley for garnish
   (optional)
Lemon wedges for serving
   (optional)

1. Put the chicken, skin side down, in a nonstick skillet large enough to accommodate it without crowding; use 2 skillets if necessary. Turn the heat to medium and season with salt and pepper. Cook, adjusting the heat and moving chicken pieces around as needed to brown them evenly. As they become evenly golden brown on the first side—not very dark, but crisp looking—after about 10 minutes, turn them. Season the skin with salt, pepper, and paprika and brown on the other side. When nearly done, add the garlic to the skillet. When browned, turn the pieces skin side down again.

2. Continue to cook, turning once or twice more if necessary, until no traces of red blood remain when you cut into a piece or two. Garnish if you like and serve.

CHICKEN CUTLETS MEUNIÈRE

MAKES 4 SERVINGS   TIME: 20 MINUTES

MEUNIÈRE **ONCE REFERRED** to fillets of sole that were floured and quickly sautéed in clarified butter, then finished with parsley, lemon juice, and a little melted butter. Over the years its definition has expanded, to the point where it describes a series of flexible techniques that can be applied to just about any thin cut of meat, poultry, or fish, all of which makes it more useful.

You must preheat the skillet before adding the oil (or clarified butter, if you're feeling extravagant) and you must use a large, flat-bottomed skillet, preferably nonstick, with deep, sloping sides, which makes turning the cutlets easier and keeps the inevitable spattering to a minimum.

4 skinless, boneless chicken breast halves (1 to 1 1/2 pounds)	1 to 2 tablespoons butter (optional)
Salt and freshly ground black pepper	1 tablespoon fresh lemon juice
Flour or cornmeal for dredging	2 tablespoons minced fresh parsley
Olive or other oil (or clarified butter) as needed	

1. Heat a 12-inch skillet, preferably nonstick, over medium-high heat for about 2 minutes. While it is heating, sprinkle the chicken with salt and pepper to taste and put the flour or cornmeal on a plate.

2. Put the oil or clarified butter in the skillet—it should coat the bottom well—and turn the heat to high. When the oil is hot, dredge a piece of the chicken in the coating, turning it over a few times and pressing it down so that it is well covered. Add the piece to the pan, then repeat with the rest of the chicken.

3. Cook until the chicken is nicely browned on the first side, 3 to 5 minutes, then turn. Cook on the second side for 2 to 4 minutes—lower the heat a bit if the coating begins to scorch—until the chicken is firm

VARIATIONS
• For the chicken, you can substitute similarly shaped cutlets of pork, turkey, or veal, all of which will cook through in 6 to 8 minutes, just like the chicken. Shrimp, scallops, and calf's liver can also be cooked this way, all for somewhat less time—generally 4 to 6 minutes.
• Chicken breasts made this way can be prepared in advance and served at room temperature; don't hold them for more than a couple of hours, however.
• Substitute bread crumbs (season them with finely minced garlic and fresh parsley if you like), ground nuts, or sesame seeds for the flour or cornmeal.
• Stir a tablespoon or more of any spice mixture, like chili powder or curry powder, into the coating.
• Add a garlic clove and/or a small handful of chopped fresh herbs to the browning butter.
• Add a teaspoon of balsamic vinegar and/or a tablespoon of capers to the browning butter (omit the lemon juice).

to the touch. As the chicken is cooking, melt the butter if you're using it over medium heat until it is nut-brown.

4. When the chicken is done, drain it briefly on a paper towel, then transfer to a warm platter. Drizzle with lemon juice and top with half the parsley. At the last minute, pour the browned butter over all, add the remaining parsley, and serve.

PANFRIED DUCK

MAKES 4 SERVINGS   TIME: 1 HOUR

HERE'S A METHOD that takes less than an hour and results in a crisp bird from which nearly all of the fat has been rendered. It's accomplished by the simple procedure of cutting up the duck, then cooking it, covered, on top of the stove. Served hot or at room temperature, the bird is crisp, tender, and far more flavorful than any chicken.

VARIATION

Soy Duck

Rub the duck with salt, pepper, 1 tablespoon soy sauce, and 1 tablespoon dry sherry before putting it in the pan. When it is done, garnish with minced peeled fresh ginger or minced fresh cilantro.

One 5- to 6-pound duck
Salt and freshly ground black
     pepper

3 garlic cloves (optional)
Several fresh thyme sprigs
     (optional)

1. Cut the duck into 6 or 8 serving pieces. Reserve the wing tips, back, and neck for stock. (Cut the gizzard into slices and cook along with the duck if you like; reserve the liver for another use.) Put the duck, skin side down, in a 12-inch skillet. Sprinkle it with salt and pepper, add the garlic and a few thyme sprigs, and turn the heat to medium-high. When the duck begins to sizzle, cover and turn the heat to medium.

2. After 15 minutes, turn the duck and season the skin side. After 15 more minutes, uncover the skillet and turn the heat back to medium-high. Cook the duck, turning as necessary, so that it browns nicely on both sides; this will take another 15 minutes.

3. Serve hot or at room temperature. Strip some of the leaves from the remaining thyme sprigs and use them as a garnish if you want.

CHICKEN WITH RIESLING

MAKES 4 TO 6 SERVINGS   TIME: 1 HOUR OR MORE

THE WINE PLAYS such a major role here that it's worth buying the right one. Finding a good off-dry white is not difficult: Almost any German wine made with Riesling (the grape name will be on the label) will do, except for those labeled *trocken,* which means dry.

Although the cooking time for Chicken with Riesling is not short, it is largely unattended, and the dish can be made well in advance. In fact, as with many meat-and-liquid preparations, this may be more delicious on the second day. And this is a preparation that you can take in many directions, as you'll see in the variations.

2 tablespoons butter or neutral oil, like corn or grapeseed

4 medium to large onions (about $1^1/2$ pounds), sliced

Salt and freshly ground black pepper

$1^1/2$ to 2 cups off-dry Riesling

One 3- to 4-pound chicken, cut into 8 or 10 serving pieces

1. Put the butter in a skillet large enough to hold the chicken and turn the heat to medium. Add the onions, a large pinch of salt, and some pepper and cook, stirring occasionally, until the onions soften completely and begin to melt into a soft mass, about 20 minutes.

2. Add $1^1/2$ cups of the wine and let it bubble away for a minute, then tuck the chicken pieces among the onions; sprinkle the chicken with salt and pepper. Turn the heat to low and cover the pan.

3. Cook, turning the chicken pieces once or twice, for 40 to 60 minutes, or until the chicken is very tender (the meat on the drumsticks will begin to loosen from the bone). If the dish appears to be drying out at any point, add the remaining wine.

4. Serve the chicken, spooning the onions and their liquid over it.

VARIATIONS

• Cook the onions for 10 minutes or so longer before adding the wine, until they darken in color and become even softer.

• While the onions are cooking, brown the chicken by putting it, skin side up, in a 500°F oven for about 20 minutes. When you add the chicken to the onions, include some of its juice.

• Tuck a couple of bay leaves and/or a few sprigs of fresh thyme in among the onions after they've begun to soften.

• Sauté about $1/4$ pound of bacon or salt pork cut into $1/2$-inch chunks in the pan before adding the onions.

• Cook about $1/2$ pound of sliced mushrooms (or an ounce or two of dried porcini mushrooms, reconstituted) along with the onions.

• Cook 1 tablespoon or more of chopped garlic with the onions.

• After cooking, puree the onions and their liquid in a blender for a creamlike sauce; use it to top the chicken.

(handwritten: 12/29/12 and MANY times before)

CHICKEN WITH VINEGAR

MAKES 4 SERVINGS   TIME: 40 MINUTES

THIS IS JUST one of several great poultry dishes from the area around Lyon, a region whose famous poulet de Bresse was long considered by many to be the best chicken in the world. Chef Paul Bocuse learned poulet au vinaigre as a youth and, some years later, showed considerable audacity by putting what is essentially a peasant dish on the menu of his Michelin three-star restaurant just outside of Lyon. He insisted that it was neither how much work nor the cost of ingredients that determined the worthiness of a dish, but how it tasted. Bravo.

2 tablespoons olive oil

One 3-pound chicken, cut up for sautéing

Salt and freshly ground black pepper

¼ cup minced shallot or scallion

1 cup good-quality red-wine vinegar

1 tablespoon butter (optional)

1. Preheat the oven to 450°F. Heat the oil in a large, deep skillet over medium-high heat until it is good and hot. Put the chicken in the skillet, skin side down, and cook for about 5 minutes, or until the chicken is nicely browned. Turn and cook for 3 minutes on the other side. Season with salt and pepper to taste.

2. Put the chicken in the oven. Cook for 15 to 20 minutes, or until it is just about done (the juices will run clear, and there will be just the barest trace of pink near the bone). Transfer the chicken to an ovenproof platter and place the platter in the oven; turn off the oven and leave the door slightly ajar.

3. Pour most but not all of the cooking juices out of the skillet. Put the skillet over medium-high heat and add the shallot; sprinkle with a little salt and pepper and cook, stirring, until the shallot is tender, about 2 minutes. Add the vinegar and raise the heat to high. Cook for a minute or two, or until the powerful smell has subsided somewhat. Add ½ cup water and cook for another 2 minutes, stirring, until the

VARIATIONS

Paul Bocuse's Poulet au Vinaigre

In step 1, brown the chicken in 7 tablespoons butter. In step 3, add 3 tablespoons butter to the reduced vinegar sauce.

• Substitute chopped garlic or onion for the shallot.

• Add an herb to the chicken as it's browning: a sprig of fresh tarragon (or a big pinch of dried tarragon), a few fresh thyme sprigs (or 1 teaspoon dried), or 5 or 6 bay leaves.

• Use champagne, rice, or white wine vinegar.

• Add about 2 tablespoons capers to the vinegar as it reduces.

• Stir a tablespoon or more of Dijon mustard into the sauce just before serving.

mixture is slightly reduced and somewhat thickened. Stir in the butter if you like.

4. Return the chicken and any accumulated juices to the skillet and turn the chicken in the sauce. Serve immediately.

CHICKEN WITH APRICOTS

MAKES 4 SERVINGS   TIME: 40 MINUTES

CHICKEN WITH DRIED apricots is hardly a new idea, but it's almost always too sweet, and the routine addition of cinnamon and cloves makes the whole thing taste more like dessert than dinner. Take them away, add a little vinegar to counter the fruit's sweetness, improve and simplify the cooking technique, and you have a beautiful dish for a winter meal.

1 cup dried apricots or other fruit

$1/4$ cup red wine vinegar

$1/2$ cup red wine

1 chicken, cut into serving pieces

Salt and freshly ground black pepper

1 medium onion, chopped

1. Put the apricots in a small bowl (or a 2-cup measure) and add the vinegar, wine, and about $1/4$ cup water to cover. Let soak while you brown the chicken.

2. Turn the heat to medium-high under a 12-inch nonstick skillet and add the chicken, skin side down. Cook, rotating the pieces (not turning them) so they brown evenly. When they are nicely browned—take your time—turn them so they are skin side up and season with salt and pepper. Make a little space in which you can add the onion and cook, stirring the onion occasionally, until it has softened a bit, a minute or two.

3. Add the apricots and their liquid and bring to a boil; cook for a

VARIATIONS

• A few fresh thyme sprigs, added at the beginning of step 2 and discarded before you serve the chicken, add another dimension to this dish.

• A tablespoon or two of butter, stirred in at the end, will make the sauce considerably richer. Or you might render some bacon, remove it, and brown the chicken in the bacon fat; crumble the bacon and stir it in at the end of cooking.

minute, then turn the heat to low and cover. Cook until the chicken is done, 15 to 20 minutes; do not turn while it is cooking. Remove the lid, raise the heat, and season the chicken well with salt and pepper. Boil out any excess liquid; you do not want the sauce to be too watery. Taste and adjust the seasoning if necessary and serve.

===========

COQ AU VIN WITH PRUNES

MAKES 4 SERVINGS   TIME: 1 HOUR

THE CHICKEN MUST be well browned before the rest of the dish is cooked, and in this instance there is no hurrying the process. Take your time and brown each piece of chicken well; especially if you're cooking for eight or more, this will take a while, as you'll have to brown in batches.

2 tablespoons olive oil

1 chicken, cut into serving pieces

Salt and freshly ground black pepper

1 large onion, chopped

$1/4$ cup minced salt pork or bacon (optional)

$1^1/2$ teaspoons minced garlic

$3/4$ pound pitted prunes

$1/2$ to $3/4$ bottle Burgundy, Pinot Noir, or other fruity red wine

4 tablespoons ($1/2$ stick) butter (optional)

Minced fresh parsley for garnish

1. Put the oil in a large skillet, preferably nonstick, over medium-high heat. When hot, add as many of the chicken pieces as will fit without crowding, skin side down. Cook, rotating the pieces and adjusting the heat as necessary to brown them evenly, about 5 minutes; turn and brown on the other side(s). As the pieces are done, sprinkle them with salt and pepper and transfer them to a large casserole.

2. Add the onion to the fat remaining in the skillet and cook over medium-high heat, stirring occasionally, until softened, 5 minutes or so. Transfer it to the casserole, add the salt pork or bacon if you're using it, and cook, stirring occasionally, until brown and crisp, about 5

minutes; transfer to the casserole and drain all but 1 tablespoon of the fat. Turn the heat under the skillet to medium and add the garlic and, 30 seconds later, the prunes. Cook for a minute, stirring once or twice, then add to the casserole.

3. Turn the heat under the skillet to high and add half the wine. Cook, stirring and scraping the bottom of the pan to release any solid particles there, until the wine is reduced by half. Pour into the casserole along with the remaining wine. Turn the heat under the casserole to high and bring to a boil; stir, then reduce the heat to low and cover. Simmer, stirring once or twice, until the chicken is done, about 30 minutes. Remove the top, stir in the butter if you like, and raise the heat to high; cook until the sauce thickens a bit. Taste and adjust the seasoning if necessary, garnish with parsley, and serve.

CHICKEN CURRY IN A HURRY

MAKES 4 SERVINGS   TIME: 20 MINUTES

THIS DISH IS so fast that you must begin cooking white rice, the natural accompaniment, before even chopping the onion. That's because it uses preblended curry powder, one of the original convenience foods, a venerable spice rub and all-purpose flavor booster. I like to use it in tandem with a twentieth-century convenience food, the skinless, boneless chicken breast. Even a breast from a good chicken is about as bland as meat can get, and one from the supermarket is not much more flavorful than unsauced pasta. Curry changes that quickly.

1 tablespoon corn, grapeseed, or
    other neutral oil

1 medium onion, sliced

Salt and freshly ground black pepper

1^1/$_2$ teaspoons curry powder, or to
    taste

4 skinless, boneless chicken breast
    halves (1 to 1^1/$_2$ pounds)

1 cup sour cream

Minced fresh cilantro or parsley
    for garnish

VARIATIONS

Chicken Curry with Yogurt
Because yogurt will curdle if it boils, some extra care must be taken here: In step 3, turn the heat to very low and wait a minute before adding the yogurt. Stir the yogurt into the onion and cook, stirring constantly, until the yogurt is hot. Return the chicken to the skillet and cook for 2 more minutes, turning once. At no point should the sauce boil.

(continued)

(Variations, continued)

• Add nuts (slivered almonds are best), raisins, and/or dried coconut pieces to the onion as it cooks.

• Add a couple of small dried hot red chiles or hot red pepper flakes to taste, along with the onion; add more at the end of cooking if you like.

• Substitute peeled shrimp or thinly sliced beef or pork for the chicken; in each case, cooking time will be marginally shorter.

1. Put the oil in a large skillet over medium-high heat. When hot, add the onion, sprinkle with some salt and pepper, and cook, stirring occasionally, until translucent, about 5 minutes. Turn the heat down to medium, sprinkle with about half the curry powder, and continue to cook for a minute or two.

2. Meanwhile, season the chicken with salt and pepper to taste and sprinkle it with the remaining curry powder. Move the onion to one side of the skillet and add the chicken in one layer. Cook for about 2 minutes per side; transfer to a plate.

3. Add the sour cream and stir constantly over medium-low heat until the mixture is nice and thick. Return the chicken to the skillet and cook for 2 more minutes, turning once. Garnish and serve with plenty of white rice.

═══════════════

CHICKEN WITH COCONUT AND LIME

MAKES 4 SERVINGS   TIME: 20 MINUTES

I HAD SOMETHING like this on a visit to Bangkok, chicken with a creamy but spicy lime sauce. At first I thought the rich texture had come from a pan reduction or even a béchamel-like sauce, but I detected the faint taste of coconut and realized it was little more than coconut milk spiked with lime. With canned coconut milk, it can be made in less than a half hour.

4 skinless, boneless chicken breast halves (1 to 1$^{1}/_{2}$ pounds)

Minced zest and juice of 2 limes

$^{1}/_{2}$ cup canned or fresh coconut milk (see page 75)

Salt and cayenne

1 teaspoon nam pla (fish sauce; optional)

4 scallions, minced, for garnish

$^{1}/_{4}$ cup minced fresh cilantro for garnish

1. Marinate the chicken in half the lime juice while you start a grill or preheat the broiler; put the rack about 4 inches from the heat source.

2. Warm the coconut milk over low heat; season it with salt (hold off on salt if you use the nam pla) and a pinch of cayenne. Add the lime zest.

3. Put the chicken, smooth (skin) side up, on an ungreased baking sheet lined with aluminum foil and place in the broiler. Add half the remaining lime juice to the coconut milk mixture.

4. When the chicken is nicely browned on top, about 6 minutes later, it is done (make a small cut in the thickest part and peek inside if you want to be sure). Transfer it to a warm platter. Add the nam pla, if you're using it, to the coconut milk; taste and adjust the seasoning as necessary. Spoon a little of the sauce over and around the breasts, then garnish with the scallions and cilantro and sprinkle with the remaining lime juice. Serve with white rice, passing the remaining sauce.

VARIATIONS

• Add a teaspoon of curry powder.

• Add a tablespoon of minced shallot to the coconut milk as it warms.

This sauce can also be used with many different foods:

• Grilled or broiled shrimp or scallops, with the cooking time reduced by a minute or two

• Boneless pork cutlets, treated like the chicken, with the cooking time increased by a couple of minutes (turn it once during cooking)

• Almost any white-fleshed fillet of fish, especially firmer ones like grouper, red snapper, or monkfish

---

SPICY CHICKEN
WITH LEMONGRASS AND LIME

MAKES 4 SERVINGS   TIME: 45 MINUTES

IT MAY SEEM absurd, even insulting, to attempt to reduce an entire cuisine to a few flavors, but with just a handful of Thai ingredients—nearly all of which are available at most supermarkets—you can duplicate or even improve on many of the dishes found in your typical neighborhood Thai restaurant. A few ingredients will be unfamiliar to most American cooks, but no complicated techniques are involved in either preparation or cooking. This chicken dish, which can be taken in many directions, is a good example.

USED Boneless Tues 8/24/07 (handwritten)

VARIATIONS

This type of preparation is used with many different foods in both Thailand and Vietnam, and most of them not only adapt perfectly to this recipe but are faster to prepare.

• Use boneless chicken, cut into chunks. Cook for only about 5 minutes after adding the chicken and bringing the liquid back to a boil. Or leave boneless breasts or thighs whole; cooking time will be about 10 minutes for breasts to 15 minutes for thighs.

• Use whole shrimp or scallops or a combination. Cooking time will be about 5 minutes from the time the liquid returns to a boil.

• Use chunks of boneless or bone-in pork like lean pork chops. Boneless pork will cook in about 10 minutes (from the time the liquid returns to a boil), bone-in in about 20 minutes.

• Use chunks of firm tofu, which will cook through in 3 to 5 minutes.

• Use vegetables in the dish: quartered peeled onions, roughly chopped bell pepper, or chunks of zucchini; add them along with the shallots and other seasonings.

2 tablespoons peanut or vegetable oil

1/2 cup minced shallot *1/2* (handwritten)

1 tablespoon minced garlic

1 tablespoon minced peeled fresh galangal or ginger

1 teaspoon minced fresh hot chile or hot red pepper flakes, or to taste

1 teaspoon ground turmeric

1 teaspoon ground coriander

1 teaspoon sugar

2 lemongrass stalks

One 3-pound chicken, cut into serving pieces

Salt and freshly ground black pepper

1 tablespoon minced lime leaves or zest

2 tablespoons nam pla (fish sauce)

1/4 cup minced fresh cilantro for garnish

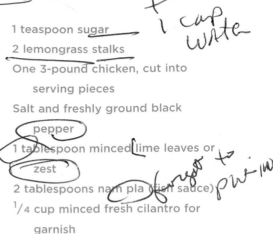

+ 1 cup water (handwritten)

1. Put the oil in a large, deep skillet over medium heat. Add the shallot, garlic, galangal, and chile and cook, stirring frequently, until the vegetables are tender and the mixture pasty. Add the turmeric, coriander, and sugar and cook, stirring, for another minute. Trim the lemongrass stalks of their toughest outer layers, then bruise them with the back of a knife; cut them into sections and add them to the mixture along with 1 cup of water.

2. Add the chicken and turn it once or twice in the sauce, then nestle it in the sauce; season with a little salt and pepper to taste. Turn the heat to low and cover the skillet. Cook, turning once or twice, until the chicken is cooked through, 20 to 30 minutes. (You can prepare the recipe in advance up to this point; cover and refrigerate for up to a day, then reheat before proceeding.)

3. Uncover the skillet and raise the heat to medium-high; turn the chicken skin side down. Let most (but not all) of the liquid evaporate and brown the chicken just a little on the bottom. Stir in the lime leaves or zest and nam pla; taste and adjust the seasoning as necessary, then garnish and serve, with white rice.

SLOW-COOKED DUCK LEGS WITH OLIVES

MAKES 4 SERVINGS   TIME: 2 HOURS, LARGELY UNATTENDED

UNLESS YOU'VE MADE your own duck confit, you may never have cooked duck legs by themselves; but in many ways they're superior to both duck breasts and whole birds. They're quite lean, and just a quick trimming of the excess fat is all that's necessary. And, given proper cooking—that is, long, slow cooking—they become fork-tender and richly flavorful, reminiscent of some of the "lesser" cuts of beef and pork, like brisket and cheek. Finally, it's easy enough to cook enough legs for eight—which is hardly the case with whole duck!

4 duck legs

5 or more garlic cloves

1 cup olives, preferably a
    combination of green and black

Several fresh thyme sprigs

One 14-ounce can tomatoes with
    juice

1 medium onion, roughly chopped
    (optional)

1 carrot, roughly chopped (optional)

1 celery stalk, roughly chopped
    (optional)

Salt and freshly ground black
    pepper

Chopped fresh parsley for garnish

1. Trim all visible fat from the duck legs, then lay them in a large, broad skillet; they can overlap if necessary. Turn the heat to medium and add all the remaining ingredients except the parsley. When the mixture reaches a lively simmer, turn the heat to low and cover.

2. Cook, checking occasionally—the mixture should be bubbling gently when you remove the cover—until the duck is very tender, about 1^1/$_2$ hours. Transfer the duck to a warm plate and cover (or put in a very low oven), then turn the heat to medium-high under the remaining sauce. Cook, stirring occasionally, until the mixture is reduced to a thick, saucelike consistency, about 10 minutes. Spoon over the duck legs, garnish, and serve.

BRAISED GOOSE WITH PEARS OR APPLES

MAKES 6 SERVINGS
TIME: ABOUT 3 HOURS, LARGELY UNATTENDED

THERE IS NO more celebratory food than goose, but when it is roasted it is difficult to carve and can be disappointing. Braising it, especially with fruit, is a different approach that works brilliantly.

Any dried fruit can be used in this preparation, but dried pears hold their shape better and are a little less sweet than prunes and apricots; there's no reason you can't substitute, however, or combine.

1 goose, cut into serving pieces, excess fat removed

Salt and freshly ground black pepper

1/2 cup diced bacon or pancetta (optional)

2 large onions, roughly chopped

4 bay leaves

A few fresh thyme sprigs

1/2 pound dried pears or apples

2 cups dry white wine

1 tablespoon vinegar: white wine, champagne, or sherry

About 2 pounds pears or apples, peeled, cored, and sliced

1. Turn the heat to medium-high under a casserole or deep skillet at least 12 inches across; a minute later, add the goose pieces, skin side down. Cook, rearranging the pieces now and then so that they brown evenly, until nicely browned and rendered of fat, 10 to 15 minutes. Sprinkle with salt and pepper and turn; brown for 2 or 3 minutes on the meat side. Remove the goose and pour off all but a tablespoon of the fat.

2. If you're using it, cook the bacon in the same skillet over medium-high heat until brown and crisp all over, about 10 minutes. Add the onions, bay leaves, and thyme and cook, stirring occasionally and seasoning with salt and pepper, until the onions are softened, about 10 minutes. Add the dried fruit and cook for another minute or two, stirring occasionally. Add the wine and raise the heat to high; cook until the wine is reduced by about half, 5 minutes or so.

3. Return the goose pieces to the skillet and turn the heat to very low.

Cover and cook (the mixture should be bubbling, but barely) for at least 2 hours, turning only once or twice, until the goose is very tender. Add the vinegar, sliced fruit, and a good grinding of black pepper and cook, stirring occasionally, until the fruit is tender, 10 to 15 minutes. Taste and adjust the seasoning.

SEARED AND STEAMED CHICKEN BREASTS

MAKES 4 SERVINGS   TIME: 20 MINUTES

HERE'S HOW TO keep a skinless, boneless chicken breast moist while giving it a crust, without using a lot of fat. This technique relies on two properties of the chicken breast that make it more like fish than like other meat: it cooks quickly, and it contains a fair amount of moisture. This enables you to start cooking the breasts with just a bit of fat over fairly high heat to begin browning, then lower the heat and cover the pan, which not only allows the meat to steam in its own juices but maintains the nicely browned exterior (on one side anyway). If you use mass-produced commercial chicken, the results will be somewhat cottony. Free-range or kosher chickens are usually considerably better.

2 tablespoons extra virgin olive oil, butter, or a combination

4 plump skinless, boneless chicken breast halves, ($1^1/2$ to 2 pounds)

Salt and freshly ground black pepper

$1/3$ cup dry white wine, chicken stock, or water

1 cup peeled, seeded, and diced tomato (canned is fine; drain first)

2 tablespoons drained capers

2 tablespoons chopped pitted black olives, preferably imported

$1/2$ cup chopped fresh parsley

1. Preheat the oven to 200°F. Heat the oil or butter in a 12-inch skillet over medium-high heat. When the oil is hot or the butter foam has subsided, season the chicken breasts well with salt and pepper and put them in the skillet, smooth (skin) side down. Turn the heat to

• Before adding the liquid in step 3, sauté a bit of onion, shallot, mushroom, or other chopped vegetable in the pan; proceed as directed, with or without the tomatoes, capers, and olives.
• For the stock or wine, substitute cream.
• Use chopped fresh basil or a few thyme leaves in place of the parsley.

high, then cook for about a minute until the chicken begins to brown. Turn the heat to medium and cover the pan.

2. Cook, undisturbed, until the chicken is firm and nearly cooked through, 6 to 8 minutes. Uncover the skillet and transfer the chicken to an ovenproof plate; put the plate in the oven.

3. Over high heat, add the wine and stir and scrape the pan to release any bits of chicken that have stuck to the bottom; when the liquid has reduced by about half, add the tomato and cook, stirring occasionally, for about a minute. Add the capers, olives, and all but 1 tablespoon of the parsley and cook for a minute more, stirring occasionally. Return the chicken to the sauce and turn once or twice. Sprinkle with the remaining parsley and serve.

SOY-POACHED CHICKEN

MAKES 4 SERVINGS TIME: 40 MINUTES

THIS TRADITIONAL CHINESE dish is simple to make: You boil the soy and wine along with some water, ginger, and crushed sugar and add star anise and scallion for flavor. The chicken is boiled too—not simmered, really boiled—but only for ten minutes; it finishes cooking in the liquid with the heat turned off.

There are unusual but inexpensive ingredients that make this dish slightly better: mushroom-flavored soy sauce, which is dark and heavy; yellow rock sugar, a not-especially-sweet, lumpy sugar that must be broken up with a hammer before use; and mei kuei lu chiew, or "rose wine," a floral wine that smells like rose water and costs two bucks a bottle. But don't knock yourself out looking for any of these—I give substitutions in the recipe.

But if you can easily acquire them, do, because this sauce can be used time and again, as long as you freeze it between uses (or refrigerate it and bring it to a rolling boil every few days) and top up the liquids now and then.

3 cups mushroom-flavored soy
    sauce or any dark soy sauce
3 cups (1 bottle) mei kuei lu chiew
    wine, or any floral, off-dry white
    wine, like Gewürztraminer or
    Muscat
2 whole star anise
14 ounces (1 box) yellow rock sugar
    or 1 cup granulated sugar

3 ounces (about a 5-inch knob)
    fresh ginger, peeled, cut into
    thick slices, and bruised with the
    side of a knife
10 medium scallions, untrimmed
One $2^1/2$- to 3-pound chicken

1. In a narrow pot with about a 6-quart capacity, combine the soy sauce, wine, 2 cups of water, and the star anise over high heat. While the sugar is still in its box (or wrapped in a towel), smack it several times with a hammer or rolling pin to break it up; it need not be too fine. Add the sugar and ginger to the liquid and bring it to a rolling boil.

2. Add 6 of the scallions, then gently and slowly lower the chicken into the liquid, breast side down. (In a narrow pot, the liquid will easily cover the chicken; if it is close, just dunk the chicken under the liquid as it cooks. If it is not close, add a mixture of soy sauce and water to raise the level.) Bring the liquid back to a boil and boil steadily for 10 minutes. Turn off the heat and turn the chicken over so the breast side is up. Let it sit in the hot liquid for 15 minutes. Meanwhile, trim and mince the remaining scallions and preheat the oven to 500°F, if you like.

3. Carefully remove the chicken from the liquid and serve it hot or at room temperature. Or place it in an ovenproof skillet or roasting pan. Roast for 5 minutes, or until nicely browned; keep an eye on it, because it can burn easily. In either case, reheat the sauce and, when the chicken is ready, carve it. Serve the chicken with a few spoonfuls of sauce on it. Put another cup or so of the sauce in a bowl and add the remaining scallions; pass this at the table.

VARIATIONS
• Poach other vegetables in the soy sauce for added flavor and to serve along with the chicken. Root vegetables, like carrots, turnips, and parsnips, are best.
• Cook cut-up chicken or Cornish hens in the same way; the cooking time will be somewhat less.

As everyone knows from
sad experience, a single
duck provides skimpy
servings for four people.
You can make up for this
with side dishes, but there
are other solutions as well:
• Braise a piece of slab
bacon and/or smoked or
fresh pork along with
the duck, after adding
the sauerkraut; you'll have
to increase the cooking
time a bit.
• Peel and cut up some
potatoes (or carrots,
parsnips, or turnips) and
cook them along with the
duck and sauerkraut.
• Finally, you can simply
cook more duck—start with
2 ducks or use a couple of
duck legs or, best of all,
sear a duck breast and
serve the slices separately.

*The best sauerkraut is sold
in bulk, but you can buy
perfectly good sauerkraut in
jars or plastic bags in the
supermarket. Just make
sure the only ingredients
are cabbage and salt.
Inferior sauerkraut contains
preservatives, and that sold
in cans tastes tinny.*

ROASTED AND BRAISED DUCK
WITH SAUERKRAUT

MAKES 4 SERVINGS   TIME: 2 HOURS, LARGELY UNATTENDED

HERE'S A SIMPLE procedure for duck in which you first roast the bird and then braise it briefly. It keeps even the breast meat moist while making the legs ultratender. There are many options for the braising medium, but none provides more complementary flavor with less work than sauerkraut. The result is a moist bird with a sauce that doubles as a side vegetable. Although the cooking takes some time, you can practically ignore the duck as it roasts; if the oven temperature is moderate, it will brown more or less automatically and render its fat at the same time.

1 duck (about 4 pounds)

Salt and freshly ground black
    pepper

4 cups sauerkraut, rinsed (see Note)

2 teaspoons paprika

$1/2$ cup dry white wine or water

2 bay leaves

1. Preheat the oven to 375°F. Prick the duck all over with a fork, then sprinkle it with salt and pepper and put it in a large, deep ovenproof skillet or Dutch oven that can later be covered. Roast the duck, checking occasionally to make sure it is browning steadily, for about 1 $1/2$ hours. (If the duck is barely browning, increase the heat by 50 degrees; if it seems to be browning too quickly, reduce the heat slightly.) At that point it will be nicely browned and will have rendered a great deal of fat; pour off all but a few tablespoons of the fat and transfer the pan to the top of the stove. Don't worry if the duck does not appear to be fully cooked.

2. Scatter the sauerkraut around the duck, then sprinkle it with paprika, moisten it with the wine, and tuck the bay leaves in there. Turn the heat to low and cover. Simmer for about 15 minutes, then stir and put some of the sauerkraut on top of the duck.

3. Cook for another 15 minutes or so, until the duck is quite tender. Carve and serve.

BEEF AND VEAL

THE MINIMALIST'S MARINATED STEAK

MAKES 4 SERVINGS   TIME: 30 MINUTES

THERE ARE JUST two reasons for marinating before grilling: to add flavor and promote browning and crispness. Neither of these requires much time, although dunking the meat or fish for a few minutes in what is best labeled a grilling sauce may contribute to a slightly greater penetration of flavor. (On the other hand, if you really have no time at all, simply smear the food with the sauce as it's going on the grill.)

Promoting browning is easy: anything with sugar browns quickly—often too quickly, as you know if you've ever slathered a piece of chicken with barbecue sauce before grilling it.

Which flavor to add is a matter of taste. My favorite is soy sauce; I love its taste, and it always seems to contribute exactly the right amount of saltiness. Any marinade that is made with a sweetener will need some acid to balance it; lime goes best with soy, but almost any acidic liquid will do, from lemon to white vinegar.

One last note about marinades: Marinade that is applied to raw food should not be brushed on during the last few minutes of cooking, nor should it be used as a sauce unless it is boiled for a few minutes. And, as always, marinade brushes and other utensils that are used with raw food should not be used near the end of cooking.

$^{1}/_{4}$ cup soy sauce

1 teaspoon minced peeled fresh ginger

$^{1}/_{2}$ teaspoon minced garlic

1 tablespoon honey, molasses, or hoisin sauce

Freshly ground black pepper

Juice of $^{1}/_{2}$ lime

1 to $1^{1}/_{2}$ pounds boneless steak (like rib-eye, skirt, or strip) or $1^{1}/_{2}$ to 2 pounds bone-in steak (like rib-eye or T-bone)

1. Preheat a grill until hot and put the rack no more than 4 inches from the heat source. Mix together the first 6 ingredients; taste and add more of anything you like. Turn the steak in the sauce once or twice, then let it sit in the sauce until the grill is hot.

VARIATIONS

Many other ingredients can make this basic sauce somewhat more complex in flavor (as long as you don't add too many at once and end up muddying the flavor):

• 1 teaspoon to 1 tablespoon mustard

• About 1 teaspoon sesame or other roasted-nut oil

• About 1 tablespoon peanut butter or tahini (sesame paste); some sesame seeds or finely chopped peanuts are good, too

• Some onion, scallion, or shallot, minced or pureed

• 1 tablespoon or more horseradish or 1 teaspoon wasabi powder

• Some minced lemon, lime, or orange zest

• About 1 tablespoon minced fresh cilantro, plus more for garnish

• Up to 1 tablespoon ground cumin, up to 1 teaspoon coriander, or a combination

• Some minced jalapeño, hot red pepper flakes, or Tabasco or other hot sauce to taste

• About 1 tablespoon Worcestershire or fish sauce (nuoc mam or nam pla, sold at most Asian markets)

2. Turn the steak one more time, then put on the grill; spoon any remaining sauce over it. For rare, grill for about 3 minutes per side for steak under an inch thick. For larger or more well-done steak, increase the time slightly.

OVEN-"GRILLED" STEAK

MAKES 4 SERVINGS   TIME: 30 MINUTES

MAYBE YOU DON'T have a grill, maybe it's freezing outside, maybe you don't want to eat dinner in the choking cloud of smoke that stovetop steak cookery unfailingly produces. Fear not: a minimalist preparation if ever there was one, this technique will put a great crust on your steaks and keep your kitchen (largely) smoke free.

$1^1/2$ to 2 pounds strip or rib-eye
   steaks (2 large steaks should
   do it)

Salt and freshly ground black
   pepper

1. Preheat the oven to its maximum, 500°F or more, for at least 20 minutes; if it is equipped with a pizza stone, so much the better. About 10 minutes before you're ready to eat, put a cast-iron or other ovenproof heavy skillet large enough to hold the steaks (or use 2) over high heat. Wait 2 or 3 minutes, until the pan is beginning to smoke.

2. Add the steaks and let them sit on top of the stove as long as you can before the smoke becomes intolerable—probably no more than a minute. Immediately transfer the pan to the oven. Roast the steaks for about 4 minutes, or until nicely browned on the bottom, then turn and cook on the other side for another 3 or 4 minutes, until done. Sprinkle with salt and pepper and serve immediately.

SKIRT STEAK WITH COMPOUND BUTTER

MAKES 4 SERVINGS   TIME: 30 MINUTES

THE EASIEST WAY to make compound butter is to mince all the flavorings and then cream them and the butter together with a fork, just as you would butter and sugar in making a cake. But if your butter is ice-cold (or frozen), use a small food processor to combine all the ingredients quickly; there will be some waste here, as you'll never get all the butter out of the container and blade, but the process will take just seconds.

Skirt steak, the long, thin band of wonderfully marbled muscle (actually the cow's diaphragm), was not easy to get even a couple of years ago but is now almost ubiquitous. It ranges as high as ten dollars a pound, but can often be found for well under half that, especially at supermarkets. It's a moist, juicy steak, but not exactly tender—a little chewier than good strip steak—and does not respond well to overcooking. If someone insists on having it cooked beyond medium-rare, take no responsibility.

About 1 $^1/_2$ pounds skirt steak, cut into 4 portions
Salt and freshly ground black pepper

$^1/_2$ recipe of one of the compound butters on pages 307–308

1. Preheat a grill until very hot—so hot you can hold your hand over it for only a couple of seconds. (Or preheat the broiler or pan-grill the steak if you prefer.)

2. When the fire is ready, grill the steak for 2 minutes per side for rare, about a minute or two longer for medium-rare to medium. Season the steak with salt and pepper as it cooks. Let it rest for a few minutes after it comes off the grill before dressing it with the compound butter.

3. Spread each steak with about a tablespoon of the flavored butter and serve. Wrap and refrigerate or freeze the remaining butter for future use.

Aug 29 2007

STEAK WITH BUTTER AND GINGER SAUCE

MAKES 4 SERVINGS   TIME: 20 MINUTES

LIKE OVEN-"GRILLED" STEAKS, this is a great way of cooking steaks indoors without sacrificing a good crust or setting off the smoke detector: sear the steak quickly, then remove it from the pan before building a quick sauce in which you can finish cooking the meat. This is such a good technique, with so many options, that you're sometimes likely to eschew the grill just to do it this way. Use fairly thin steaks for this recipe. Judging the doneness of thicker ones can be tricky, and inevitably the sauce evaporates before the meat is cooked through. The ideal setup for four people is four small, boneless steaks, cut from the top blade, sirloin, or rib. But two larger steaks will work nearly as well, as long as they're thin. And though it isn't necessary to use butter in this preparation, a small amount—there is little more than a teaspoon per person in the recipe—adds not only creaminess but also flavor.

1 to 1^1/$_2$ pounds boneless top blade, skirt, sirloin, or rib-eye steak, ^{3}/$_4$ inch thick or less

1^1/$_2$ tablespoons butter

1 tablespoon minced peeled fresh ginger

2 tablespoons soy sauce

1. Preheat a large, heavy skillet over medium-high heat until it begins to smoke. Add the steaks and cook until nicely browned, 1 to 2 minutes. Turn and brown the other side, another minute or two. Remove the skillet from the heat and transfer the steaks to a plate.

2. When the skillet has cooled slightly, return it to the stove over medium heat. Add the butter and, when it melts, the ginger. About 30 seconds later, add the soy sauce and stir to blend. Return the steaks to the skillet, along with any of their accumulated juices. Cook the steaks for a total of about 4 minutes, turning three or four times. (If at any time the pan threatens to dry out entirely, add a couple of tablespoons of water.) At this point, the steaks will be medium-rare; cook for a little longer if you like and serve with the pan juices spooned over.

VARIATIONS

- Use garlic or shallots and a few leaves of tarragon instead of the ginger, and vinegar in place of the soy sauce for a French flair. Season the steak well with salt before you add it to the pan.
- Go Mediterranean: Substitute extra virgin olive oil for the butter, garlic for the ginger, and fresh lemon juice for the soy sauce. Be sure not to forget to salt the steaks.
- Give it a Thai accent: Substitute minced lemongrass for the ginger and nam pla for the soy sauce. You can substitute peanut oil for the butter or not.
- Add any minced herbs you like to the sauce, at about the same time you return the meat to the skillet.

GRILLED FLANK STEAK WITH PROVENÇAL SPICES

MAKES 4 SERVINGS   TIME: 30 MINUTES

FLANK STEAK, MORE than most others, is tolerant of medium doneness, but in any case it must be thinly sliced. Slicing meat against the grain is especially important for tougher cuts like flank and skirt: it cuts the long, tough muscles into shorter, easier-to-chew pieces, giving the impression of tenderness.

If you have a garden or a windowsill, both rosemary and lavender are easy to grow and maintain (and the small investment you will make in those plants will save you from paying the king's ransom supermarkets charge for fresh herbs). If you can't find any lavender, up the rosemary to 2 tablespoons. In any case, do not substitute dried herbs for fresh in this recipe: they will rob it of its charm.

3 tablespoons extra virgin olive oil

3/4 teaspoon salt

2 garlic cloves, peeled

1 1/2 teaspoons fresh rosemary
   leaves

1 1/2 teaspoons fresh lavender
   leaves

1 1/2 teaspoons fennel seeds

1 1/2 teaspoons fresh thyme leaves

1 teaspoon cracked black pepper

1 1/2 to 2 pounds flank steak

1. Start a grill or preheat the broiler. Combine all ingredients except the steak in a small food processor and blend until minced (you can, of course, mince by hand) but not pureed. Rub all over the steak.
2. When the fire is hot, grill for about 4 minutes per side, or until nicely browned, for medium-rare, turning only once. Remove from the fire and let rest for about 5 minutes before slicing thinly and serving.

GRILLED STEAK WITH ROQUEFORT SAUCE

MAKES 4 SERVINGS   TIME: 20 MINUTES

THIS DISH, WHICH often appears on bistro menus in France, fits the need for a good steak served with something powerfully salty and rich (anchovy butter or a combination of butter, soy sauce, and ginger will also do the trick). Some might consider the sauce overkill, but not those of us who crave it.

My favorite cheese for this sauce is Roquefort, which is made from sheep's milk. But it's entirely a matter of taste—Stilton, Gorgonzola, Maytag blue, or any high-quality, fairly soft blue cheese will work equally well. Don't bother, however, trying to make this sauce with commercially produced domestic blue cheese, such as that sold precrumbled for salads. Not only will its taste be inferior, but it will not give the sauce the same creaminess.

This is a case where the usually too-lean and mildly flavored tenderloin (filet mignon) will do just fine. Its tenderness is welcome and its blandness more than compensated for by the sauce. I'd still prefer a good strip steak or rib-eye, which are chewier and more flavorful, but you will notice their higher fat content when they're combined with the rich sauce.

1 tablespoon butter or grapeseed, corn, or other neutral oil

1/4 cup minced shallot

2 tablespoons white wine or cider vinegar

6 ounces Roquefort or other blue cheese, crumbled

Good pinch of cayenne

Salt and freshly ground black pepper

1 1/2 to 2 pounds strip steaks, filet mignon, or rib-eye steaks

Minced fresh parsley or chives for garnish (optional)

1. Preheat a grill or broiler until quite hot and put the rack no more than 4 inches from the heat source.

2. Put the butter in a small saucepan and turn the heat to medium; when the butter melts and its foam begins to subside, add the shallot and cook until soft, stirring occasionally, about 5 minutes. Add the

vinegar, stir, and cook until it is just about evaporated, 1 or 2 minutes. Turn the heat to low and stir in the cheese and the cayenne. Stir occasionally until the cheese melts, then taste and adjust the seasoning as necessary (the sauce probably won't need any salt). Keep warm while you grill the steaks.

3. Season the steaks well with salt and pepper, then grill or broil them for 3 to 4 minutes per side for medium-rare, longer or shorter according to your taste. Serve the steaks with a spoonful or two of sauce over each, garnished with the parsley or chives if you like.

SIRLOIN STEAK WITH CHIMICHURRI SAUCE

MAKES 4 SERVINGS   TIME: ABOUT 30 MINUTES

CHIMICHURRI IS A simple Argentinean steak sauce made almost entirely from parsley, with huge amounts of chopped garlic and red pepper. In spirit, it's not unlike pesto, but because everything is hand-chopped rather than ground or mashed, it has a bit more chew to it. And its powerful ingredients set it apart, making it the perfect complement for mild-tasting but meaty tenderloin.

$3/4$ cup chopped fresh parsley
 (about 1 large bunch)
$1/2$ cup extra virgin olive oil
$1/4$ cup fresh lemon juice
2 tablespoons finely chopped garlic

2 teaspoons hot red pepper flakes
Salt and freshly ground black
 pepper
$1^1/2$ pounds beef tenderloin steaks,
 each about 1 inch thick

1. Put the parsley in a bowl and whisk in the olive oil, lemon juice, garlic, hot pepper, and salt to taste. Taste and adjust the seasoning if necessary; let the sauce rest at room temperature for an hour or two if you have time.

2. Put a large skillet over high heat; season the steaks with salt and pepper. When the skillet is hot, a minute or two later, add the steaks and cook for about 3 minutes per side for medium-rare, a little longer for more well done. Serve the steaks whole or slice them; serve with the chimichurri spooned over them, passing more sauce at the table.

RIB-EYE STEAK WITH ANCHOVY–RED WINE SAUCE

MAKES 4 SERVINGS   TIME: 15 MINUTES

ANOTHER GREAT, SIMPLE sauce based on anchovies (there are two in the pasta chapter; see pages 263 and 271). You get acidity, astringency, and fruitiness from the wine, piquancy from the garlic and anchovy, complexity from the thyme, and a smooth finish from the butter—all in about the time it takes to preheat a grill for the steaks. You don't need great red wine for this sauce, but it should be one with a fair amount of fruit and at least a little structure.

2 cups fruity but sturdy red wine, like Côtes-du-Rhône, Zinfandel, or California Cabernet

$1/2$ teaspoon minced garlic

6 anchovy fillets with some of their oil

1 teaspoon fresh thyme leaves

4 rib-eye steaks (about 6 ounces each) or 2 larger steaks

2 tablespoons butter

Salt and freshly ground black pepper

1. Put the wine in a small saucepan and turn the heat to high. Reduce, stirring occasionally, to about $1/2$ cup. Meanwhile, start a grill.
2. When the wine is reduced, turn the heat down so the reduction simmers and stir in the garlic, anchovies, and thyme. Cook, stirring occasionally, until the anchovies dissolve. When the grill is ready, cook the steaks for about 3 minutes per side for medium-rare or a little longer or shorter according to your preference.
3. Beat the butter into the sauce until it is smooth, then season to taste. Slice the steaks, drizzle with the sauce, and serve.

BEEF WRAPPED IN LETTUCE LEAVES, KOREAN STYLE

MAKES 4 SERVINGS

TIME: 45 MINUTES, OR LONGER IF YOU HAVE THE TIME

FOR YEARS, I thought the in-table-grill was such an important part of cooking bul kalbi that I never even tried to make it at home. I realized, however, that the time the meat spends over the coals—certainly less than five minutes—might be long enough to add the mental image of wood flavor, but certainly not the reality. So, with what might be described as typical American arrogance, I set about reinventing this traditional Korean dish, and I'm happy with the results.

Grilling remains the best cooking technique—a couple of minutes over a very hot fire is ideal—but a stovetop grill or a very hot skillet works nearly as well, as long as you have a powerful exhaust fan to suck out the smoke. Alternatively, a good broiler will do the trick; just turn the slices once. Finally, if you set an iron skillet or a heavy roasting pan in an oven heated to its maximum, then throw the meat onto that, it will sear the meat and cook it through in a couple of minutes. No matter how you cook the meat, do not sacrifice internal juices for external browning; that is, it's better to serve lightly browned but moist meat than tough, overcooked meat with a lovely crust.

3 to 4 pounds beef short ribs

$1/2$ cup roughly chopped scallion, shallot, or onion

1 tablespoon roughly chopped peeled fresh ginger

6 garlic cloves, roughly chopped

1 tablespoon sugar

$1/2$ teaspoon ground black pepper

$1/2$ cup soy sauce

16 to 24 leaves of romaine or other lettuce, washed and dried

Soy sauce or ground bean paste for garnish (available at Asian markets; optional)

1. If time allows, freeze the meat for 30 minutes or so to facilitate slicing. Use a sharp knife to strip the meat from the ribs—it will come off easily and in one piece (reserve the bones and any meat that adheres to them for stock).

2. Combine the scallion, ginger, garlic, sugar, pepper, soy sauce, and $1/2$ cup of water in a blender and puree until very smooth. Slice the meat into pieces between $1/8$ and $1/4$ inch thick. Toss with the marinade and let sit for 15 minutes to 2 hours. Preheat a grill, broiler, or stovetop grill or preheat the oven to its maximum heat and put a heavy roasting pan in it.

3. Remove the meat from the marinade and grill, pan-grill, broil, or roast it just until done, no more than a couple of minutes per side; it's nice if the meat is browned on the outside and rare on the inside, but it's imperative that it not be overcooked. Serve with the lettuce leaves: to eat, wrap a piece or two of meat in a torn piece of lettuce; garnish with a drop or two of soy sauce or bean paste if you like.

NEGIMA (JAPANESE BEEF-SCALLION ROLLS)

MAKES 4 SERVINGS   TIME: 30 MINUTES

WRAPPING ONE FOOD with another is familiar, especially if meat, cheese, or vegetables make up the filling—think of ravioli, stuffed cabbage, or egg rolls. Making meat the wrapping is a nice role reversal, a neat twist that is extraordinary enough to allow a simple preparation to wow a crowd. Such is the case with the Japanese negima, in which beef is wrapped around chives or scallions, then brushed with soy sauce and grilled.

NOTE

The cuts of beef that supermarkets most frequently slice thin are from the round, which is not only tough but relatively tasteless, making chicken, veal, and pork (which are routinely sold as thin cutlets that can be made even thinner with a little gentle pounding) viable substitutes.

8 thin slices beef, chicken, veal, or pork, each about 3 inches wide and 5 to 6 inches long (about $1^1/4$ pounds; see Note)

$1/4$ cup soy sauce
Green parts from about 2 dozen scallions

1. Preheat a grill or broiler until quite hot.
2. Put the meat between two layers of wax paper or plastic wrap and pound it gently until about $1/8$ inch thick. Brush one side of each piece of meat with a little soy sauce.

3. Cut the scallions into lengths about the same width as the meat and put a small bundle of them at one of the narrow ends of each slice. Roll the long way, securing the roll with a toothpick or two. (You can prepare the rolls in advance up to this point; cover and refrigerate for up to 2 hours before proceeding.) Brush the exterior of the roll with a little more soy sauce.

4. Grill until brown on all sides, a total of about 6 minutes for chicken, 4 to 5 minutes for veal or pork, 4 minutes or less for beef.

ROAST SIRLOIN OF BEEF

MAKES 4 TO 6 SERVINGS   TIME: 45 MINUTES

FEW MEATS ARE as tender, juicy, and flavorful as roast beef, yet none is easier to prepare, given the appropriate cut and proper technique. But finding the right cut can be a challenge. Two of the best cuts for roasting, filet (or tenderloin) and standing rib, are not always ideal. The first is supremely tender but expensive and nearly tasteless; the second tends to be sold in large cuts that are too unwieldy for most weeknights. But the sirloin strip, also called *New York strip* (the same cut that makes for some of the best steaks), cut in a single large piece, is a perfect roast. The only drawback is that it is not routinely offered for sale. But if you tell the butcher you want a two- or three-pound piece of sirloin strip—essentially a steak cut as a roast—you should have it a few minutes later.

A meat thermometer can help you judge doneness, and it pays to undercook the meat slightly and let it sit for a few minutes before carving; this not only makes carving easier but prevents overcooking. It's worth noting that this technique will work for larger roasts of sirloin as well and, because the meat is of more or less uniform thickness, cooking time will not be appreciably longer for a roast of four or five pounds than it is for one of two or three.

Roast Sirloin with Pan Gravy

Discard all but a tablespoon or two of the cooking fat remaining in the pan. Put the pan over high heat and add 1 cup red wine, chicken or beef stock, or water and cook, stirring frequently, until the mixture is reduced to about $1/2$ cup. Stir in a tablespoon or more of butter, a few drops of fresh lemon juice, and salt and pepper to taste.

Roast Sirloin with Red Wine Sauce

Combine 2 cups red wine and $1/4$ cup minced shallots or 1 tablespoon slivered garlic and reduce over high heat until only about $1/2$ cup of syrupy liquid remains; stir in a tablespoon of butter and some salt and pepper.

One $2^1/2$- to 3-pound piece beef sirloin strip

Salt and freshly ground black pepper

1. Preheat the oven to 500°F; put an ovenproof skillet large enough to hold the roast into the oven so it preheats as well. Sprinkle the meat liberally with salt and pepper.

2. When the oven and pan are hot, add the roast to the pan, top (fatty) side down. Ten minutes later, turn and roast fatty side up. After 10 more minutes, roast for 5 minutes on each side so total cooking time is 30 minutes.

3. At this point the roast will be nicely browned all over. When a meat thermometer inserted into the center of the meat, about 1 inch from one of the ends, registers 120°F, the meat will be rare to medium-rare. Cook it longer if you like, but beware that from this point on it will increase a stage of doneness every 3 to 5 minutes.

4. Let the roast rest for 5 to 10 minutes, then carve and serve with its juices. Serve either thick, steaklike slices, or carve the meat more thinly, as you would a traditional roast beef.

POACHED BEEF TENDERLOIN WITH GARNISHES

MAKES 4 SERVINGS   TIME: 30 MINUTES

SERVE THE MEAT with a variety of garnishes, which you and your guests can combine any way you like.

One 2-pound piece beef tenderloin from the thick end, preferably at room temperature
6 cups boiling stock or water
Salt

Minced shallots, good mustard, chopped cornichons, coarse salt, soy sauce, and ketchup for garnish

1. Put the meat in a deep pan just large enough to hold it—a Dutch oven is usually ideal, but you can curve the meat into a wide saucepan too—and cover it with boiling stock or water. Add a large pinch of salt if you're using water or if the stock is unsalted. Adjust the heat so that the mixture bubbles gently—on my stove that's medium.

2. Cook until the meat reaches 120°F on an instant-read thermometer; 125°F if you prefer medium-rare. Remove the meat and let it sit for about 5 minutes, then cut into $1/2$- to 1-inch-thick slices. Serve immediately, with the garnishes.

ASIAN POT ROAST WITH TURNIPS

MAKES 4 SERVINGS
TIME: 3 TO 4 HOURS, LARGELY UNATTENDED

WHEN YOU'RE MAKING a pot roast, the vegetables you add at the beginning contribute to the development of the sauce, but those at the end draw on the sauce for flavor (like the turnip or rutabaga in this dish), often making them the best part.

You can skip browning the meat to save time (and mess) if necessary. Yes, browning creates complexity, but there is so much flavor in this particular pot roast that subtle complexity is overwhelmed.

1 tablespoon peanut or vegetable oil

One 3- to 4-pound beef brisket or boneless chuck

$1/3$ cup dark soy sauce or $1/2$ cup light soy sauce

5 nickel-sized slices fresh ginger (don't bother to peel)

4 whole star anise

2 to 3 cups cubed peeled rutabaga or white turnip

$1/2$ cup minced scallion

VARIATION

European Pot Roast with Carrots
Use olive oil for searing. Replace the soy-water mixture, ginger, and star anise with a mixture of 2 cups red wine, 20 peeled pearl onions (the frozen ones aren't bad), 5 peeled and lightly smashed garlic cloves, and 1 cup trimmed, chopped mushrooms. Add more wine (or water) if necessary to the simmering meat as it cooks. Substitute carrots for the rutabaga in step 2 and garnish with chopped fresh parsley in place of scallion.

1. Heat the oil in a large skillet over high heat, add the roast (you can cover the pot loosely to reduce spattering), and sear for about 5 minutes on each side, or until nicely browned. While the meat is browning, combine the soy sauce, ginger, star anise, and 2 cups of water in a casserole big enough to hold the meat snugly. Bring this mixture to a boil, then adjust the heat so it simmers.

2. When the meat is browned, add it to the simmering liquid and cover the pot. Cook, turning the meat once or twice an hour and adding more water if necessary, for about 3 hours, or until the meat is just about tender (poke it with a thin-bladed knife; when the meat is done, it will meet little resistance). Fish out the star anise and add the rutabaga, stirring to make sure it is coated with liquid (again, add more water if necessary). Re-cover and cook until the rutabaga is very tender, about 30 minutes.

3. Remove the meat and carve it, then return it to the pot (or put it on a platter with the sauce and the rutabaga). Garnish with the scallion and serve.

POT ROAST WITH CRANBERRIES

MAKES 4 TO 6 SERVINGS

TIME: ABOUT 1$\frac{1}{4}$ HOURS

UNLIKE THEIR COUSIN, the blueberry—which is sometimes used in savory cooking, although almost never successfully—cranberries are not at all sweet and so make a much more natural companion for meat.

One trick I've learned over the years is that dusting the meat with a sprinkling of sugar makes the browning process go much more rapidly and leaves behind a caramelized residue that lends a great complexity to the final dish. It's not an appropriate trick for every occasion, but it's perfect for this gutsy, appealing, and unusual pot roast.

Most pot roasts depend mightily for their flavor on the juices exuded

POT ROAST AND its ilk are true no-brainers: since they are always cooked well done, timing is pretty flexible, and since they are cooked in a covered pot with liquid, neither source nor level of heat matters much.

You can cook a pot roast on top of the stove or in the oven, at a very low heat, something more moderate, or even quite high. You can even cook it in advance and reheat it, or cut the meat up before cooking and call it beef stew.

Tender cuts of beef, like sirloin and even tenderloin, will markedly reduce the cooking time but will not produce the same rich, silky sauce created by the tougher cuts. Thus inexpensive cuts like

chuck and brisket are best—and you can use either one. Chuck becomes tender a little faster, but it is fattier; brisket becomes a little drier, but the sauce takes care of that, and it slices beautifully.

Remember that when you are browning the meat, a step called for in each of the following recipes, you should keep the heat high and not move the meat around. Only when it appears good and browned—really browned, not just colored—should you proceed to the next step.

The best part is that flavoring pot roast is no more than a matter of taste; you can hardly go wrong as long as the ingredients that go in the pot all appeal to you.

by the meat itself, but since the meat's contribution here is minimized by the powerful cranberry-based combination, a faster-cooking cut like tenderloin works perfectly, reducing the cooking time to just over an hour.

1 tablespoon butter or extra virgin olive oil

$^1/_2$ cup sugar

One 2- to 3-pound piece beef tenderloin (filet mignon)

Salt and freshly ground black pepper

$^1/_2$ cup sherry vinegar or good-quality wine vinegar

$^3/_4$ pound cranberries

1 orange

Cayenne

1. Put the butter or oil in a casserole or skillet that can later be covered and turn the heat to medium-high. Put the sugar on a plate and dredge all surfaces of the meat in it; reserve the remaining sugar. When the butter foam subsides or the oil is hot, brown the meat on all sides, seasoning it with salt and pepper as it browns.

2. When the meat is nicely browned, add the vinegar and cook for a minute, stirring, then add the cranberries and remaining sugar and stir. Strip the zest from the orange (you can do it in broad strips, with a small knife or vegetable peeler) and add it to the pot; juice the orange and add the juice also, along with a pinch of cayenne. Turn the heat to low and cover; the mixture should bubble but not furiously.

3. Cook, turning the meat and stirring for about 1 hour, or until the internal temperature is 125°F to 130°F (medium-rare); you can cook it longer if you like.

4. When the meat is done, taste and adjust the seasoning if necessary. Turn off the heat and let the roast rest for a few minutes, then carve and serve, with the sauce.

BEEF WITH CARAMELIZED SUGAR

MAKES 4 SERVINGS   TIME: 2 HOURS OR LESS

CARAMEL IS THE KEY to what makes this dish distinctive; though it is made from sugar, it gains a certain bitterness if you cook it long enough. Chances are no one will be able to figure out how you made this.

One 2-pound piece boneless beef
    chuck roast
1 large onion
Salt and freshly ground black
    pepper

1 cup stock or water
1 cup sugar
Juice of 1 lemon
1 tablespoon soy sauce

1. Heat a large, deep skillet over medium-high heat for a couple of minutes, then add the beef. Sear on one side until nicely browned, about 5 minutes, then sear on the other side. Transfer to a plate, turn the heat to medium, and add the onion. Season it with salt and pepper and cook, stirring occasionally, until tender, 5 to 10 minutes.

2. Return the meat to the pan and season it with salt and pepper; add the stock, bring to a boil, turn the heat to low, and cover the pan. It should bubble steadily but not vigorously. Cook until the meat is tender, at least an hour.

3. When the meat is done, put the sugar in a small, heavy saucepan over medium-high heat; add a couple of tablespoons of water. Cook, shaking the pan occasionally, until the sugar melts and turns dark golden brown. Carefully add about half the caramel to the beef mixture, then add the lemon and soy sauce. If the mixture is appealingly salty and bitter, it is done; if it is tame, add more salt, lemon juice, pepper, and/or some of the caramel. Carve the meat and serve it with the sauce.

JAPANESE-STYLE BEEF STEW WITH WINTER SQUASH
MAKES 4 SERVINGS
TIME: AT LEAST 1 HOUR, LARGELY UNATTENDED

BEEF STEWED IN dashi and mirin seems lighter and more delicate than beef stewed in stock or wine. It's a dish that's filling enough to satisfy on a fall or winter day but doesn't have the heaviness sometimes associated with pot roasts and stews. Serve it with prepared Japanese mustard or wasabi on the side.

2 pounds boneless beef chuck, cut into 1- to 1 1/2-inch chunks

2 cups dashi (see Note)

1/4 cup soy sauce

1/4 cup mirin, honey, or sugar

10 nickel-sized slices peeled fresh ginger

Salt and freshly ground black pepper

1 lemon

1 1/2 pounds peeled butternut, pumpkin, or other winter squash or sweet potatoes, cut into 1-inch chunks

TO MAKE DASHI

Combine 1 piece dried kelp (kombu), about 3 inches long, with 2 cups of water in a small pan over medium heat. Don't allow the mixture to come to a boil; as soon as it is about to, turn off the heat and remove the kelp. Stir in 1/2 to 1 cup dried bonito flakes, let sit for a couple of minutes, then strain. Use the dashi immediately, or refrigerate for up to 2 days.

1. In a large skillet, preferably nonstick, over medium-high heat, sear the meat until nicely browned; do it in 2 or 3 batches to avoid crowding. It will take only 5 minutes per batch, since it's sufficient to brown the meat well on one side. As you finish, transfer the chunks to a medium casserole.

2. When the meat is all browned, add the dashi to the skillet and cook over high heat, stirring and scraping occasionally, until all the solids are integrated into the liquid. Pour into the casserole with the soy sauce, mirin, ginger, and a couple of grinds of pepper. Peel the lemon and add the peel to the mixture; juice the lemon.

3. Cover and cook on top of the stove (or in a preheated 350°F oven), maintaining a steady simmer. Stir after 30 minutes and begin to check the meat at 15-minute intervals.

4. When the meat is tender, or nearly so, stir in the squash and continue to cook as before, checking every 15 minutes, until the squash is tender but not mushy. Add salt if necessary, then stir in the reserved lemon juice and serve.

SAUTÉED CHICKPEAS WITH MEAT

MAKES 4 SERVINGS   TIME: 30 MINUTES

THIS RECIPE, which is vaguely related to the classic chili, combines chickpeas, meat, and spices and takes advantage of all of those assets. The cooked chickpeas are sautéed over high heat until browned and slightly crisp, and the pan is ultimately deglazed with the reserved chickpea-cooking liquid.

$1/2$ pound ground beef or other
meat
4 cups cooked or canned
chickpeas (2 cups of the
cooking or canning liquid
reserved)
$1^1/2$ teaspoons ground cumin
$1/2$ ancho or chipotle chile, soaked,
stemmed, seeded, and minced,
or 1 teaspoon good-quality chili
powder, or to taste

$1^1/2$ teaspoons minced garlic
Salt and freshly ground black
pepper
1 tablespoon extra virgin olive oil
Minced fresh cilantro or parsley for
garnish (optional)

1. Turn the heat to high under a large, deep skillet and add the meat a little at a time, breaking it into small pieces as you do so. Stir and break up the meat a bit more, then add the chickpeas. Keep the heat high and continue to cook, stirring only occasionally, until the chickpeas begin to brown and pop, 5 to 10 minutes. Don't worry if the mixture sticks a bit, but if it begins to scorch, lower the heat slightly.

2. Add the cumin, chile, and garlic and cook, stirring, for about a minute. Add the reserved cooking liquid and stir, scraping the bottom of the pan if necessary to loosen any browned bits that have stuck. Season with salt and pepper, then turn the heat to medium-low; continue to cook until the mixture is no longer soupy but not completely dry.

3. Stir in the olive oil, then taste and adjust the seasoning if necessary. Garnish if you like and serve immediately, with rice or pita bread.

OSSO BUCO

MAKES 4 SERVINGS

TIME: AT LEAST 2 HOURS, LARGELY UNATTENDED

THERE IS NO promise of speed here: osso buco takes time. But this classic Italian dish of glorious, marrow-filled veal shanks (the name means "bone with hole"), braised until they are fork-tender, is dead easy to make and requires a total of no more than fifteen or twenty minutes of attention during its two hours or so of cooking. And it holds well enough overnight so that 90 percent of the process can be accomplished while you're watching television the night before you serve the dish.

Though I'll concede that starting with good-quality stock will yield the richest sauce, I'll volunteer that two hours of cooking veal shanks—which are, after all, veal bones—creates a very nice stock with no work, so I never hesitate to make osso buco with white wine or even water.

Try to buy slices of shank taken from the center, about one and a half inches thick. The slices from the narrow end have very little meat on them; those from the thick end contain little or no marrow. Center cuts give you the best of both worlds, though you shouldn't let it stop you if they are unavailable.

1 tablespoon olive oil

4 center-cut slices veal shank
   (2 pounds or more)

Salt and freshly ground black pepper

3 to 4 garlic cloves, lightly smashed
   and peeled

4 anchovy fillets

1 cup dry white wine, chicken or
   beef stock, or water

2 teaspoons butter (optional)

1. Heat a large, deep skillet over medium-high heat for a couple of minutes. Add the oil, swirl it around, and pour out any excess. Add the veal and cook until nicely browned on the first side (for even browning, you can rotate the shanks, but try not to disturb them too much), about 5 minutes. Turn and brown the other side.

2. When the second side is just about completely browned, sprinkle the shanks with a little salt and pepper and add the garlic and an-

TRADITIONALLY, OSSO BUCO is served with a condiment known as *gremolata*. To make it, mix together 1 tablespoon minced lemon zest, 2 tablespoons minced fresh parsley, and $1/4$ to 1 teaspoon minced garlic (remember that this will not be cooked, so go easy on the garlic).

chovies to the pan. Cook, stirring a little, until the anchovies dissolve and the garlic browns, about 2 minutes. Add the liquid and let it bubble away for about a minute.

3. Turn the heat to low and cover the skillet. Five minutes later, check to see that the mixture is simmering—just a few bubbles appearing at once—and adjust the heat accordingly. Cook until the meat is very tender and pulling away from the bone, at least $1^1/2$ hours and probably somewhat more; turn the veal every half hour or so. (When the meat is tender, you may turn off the heat and refrigerate the dish for up to 24 hours; reheat gently before proceeding.)

4. Transfer the meat to a warm platter and turn the heat to high. Boil the sauce until it becomes thick and glossy, about 5 minutes. Stir in the butter if you like and serve the meat with the sauce spooned over it.

BRAISED VEAL BREAST WITH MUSHROOMS

MAKES 4 OR MORE SERVINGS
TIME: AT LEAST $1^1/2$ HOURS, LARGELY UNATTENDED

FEW SLOW-COOKED foods are as rewarding as beef brisket, which at its best is tender, juicy, and flavorful. Doing it right takes so long—my favorite recipe is a twelve-hour job—that, at least in my house, a brisket is made only annually, or even less often than that. That's why I regret that

Braised Veal Breast with Fresh Mushrooms

Though I find that cooking the veal breast with dried porcini or shiitake mushrooms yields the best results and deepest flavor, you can prepare the dish with fresh mushrooms: Start with at least $1/2$ pound fresh mushrooms, button or other. Slice them, then cook them over medium-high heat in 2 tablespoons olive oil or butter, preferably with a couple of crushed peeled garlic cloves and a few fresh thyme sprigs, until tender, about 15 minutes. Proceed as directed, adding $1/2$ cup water, wine, or stock in place of the mushroom-cooking liquid.

Veal Brisket with Bacon and Onion

One of my favorite variations takes its cue from a classic coq au vin. Start by rendering about $1/4$ pound cubed bacon, preferably cut from a slab, over medium heat, stirring, until crisp. Then remove the bacon pieces with a slotted spoon. Brown the veal in the fat as directed. Remove the veal and cook $1 1/2$ cups chopped onion (or about 15 pearl onions) in the fat over medium heat until

I didn't make my "discovery" of veal brisket sooner. It had just never occurred to me until recently that you could get a delicious, tender, relatively quick-cooking form of brisket by removing the bones from a breast of veal.

Unfortunately, boneless breast of veal—which can also be called *veal brisket* and, like brisket of beef, is the flap that covers the front part of a cow's chest—is rarely sold that way. But any butcher (and, yes, this includes virtually every supermarket butcher) can quickly remove the bones from a veal breast and present you with a flat, boneless, relatively compact cut that contains little fat and becomes tender in less than two hours of unattended cooking.

Ask the butcher to start with a piece of breast that weighs four to six pounds. The yield is about half that, a piece of boneless meat of two or three pounds that will easily fit in a large skillet. (Consider asking the butcher for the bones, too—you're paying for them, and they are among the best for stock making.)

1 ounce dried mushrooms, preferably porcini

One 2- to 3-pound boneless veal breast

$1/2$ cup white wine or $1/2$ cup good-quality chicken or beef stock

Salt and freshly ground black pepper

1 tablespoon butter (optional)

1. Reconstitute the mushrooms by covering them with very hot water. Turn the heat under a 12-inch skillet to medium-high and let the pan sit for a minute. Add the veal and brown it on both sides, turning once, for a total of about 6 minutes.

2. Transfer the meat to a plate and turn the heat to medium. Add the mushrooms and about $1/2$ cup of their liquid (strained, if necessary, to remove sediment) along with the wine. Bring to a boil and cook for about 30 seconds, then return the veal to the skillet. Season with salt and pepper, turn the heat to low, and cover.

3. Cook for 1 to $1 1/2$ hours, turning once or twice during that period and checking now and then to make sure the liquid is bubbling slowly; adjust the heat accordingly.

4. When the meat is tender, transfer it to a cutting board. Turn the heat under the liquid in the skillet to high and reduce it to a thick, saucy consistency. Stir in the butter if you like and keep it warm. Carve the meat against the grain into $1/4$-inch-thick slices and serve with the sauce.

VEAL STEW OF SPRING

MAKES 4 SERVINGS   TIME: 1 HOUR

THE CHARM OF most braised dishes is that they result in succulent, tender meat and require little attention after an initial browning. The sad truth, however, is that most meats need hours—sometimes many hours—before they become truly tender. Not so with veal chunks taken from the shoulder or leg, which become tender in less than an hour and produce a superb stew.

And the smaller the chunks of meat, the shorter the cooking time. (This is a very basic and oft-ignored general principle of cooking: spend a little more time with the knife and you sometimes spend a lot less time at the stove.) Smaller chunks have another advantage as well: in just a few minutes, enough of their surface area browns that you can move to the next step of the recipe. This guarantees a full-flavored stew—the browning step is not essential but very desirable—and reduces stovetop mess.

1 tablespoon extra virgin olive oil

1 tablespoon butter (or more oil)

$1^1/2$ to 2 pounds boneless veal shoulder or leg, cut into pieces no larger than $1\,^1/2$ inches on any side.

1 fresh tarragon sprig or $^1/2$ teaspoon dried

1 pound spring onions, shallots, or scallions, cut in half if large

Salt and freshly ground black pepper

$^1/2$ cup white wine or water

1 cup shelled fresh peas, snow peas, or frozen peas

nicely browned. Proceed as directed, beginning by adding the mushrooms and their liquid and using red wine in place of the white wine.

• For any of these renditions, consider stirring in up to 4 tablespoons ($^1/2$ stick) of butter, a bit at a time, at the end of cooking to give the sauce a richness and suavity like you'd encounter in the best restaurants. (Trust me: that's how they make everything taste so good.)

VARIATIONS

Veal Stew, Provençal Style

In step 1, use all olive oil. In step 2, omit the tarragon and onions, adding instead 2 garlic cloves, peeled and crushed; 20 fresh basil leaves, roughly chopped; 2 cups seeded and chopped tomato (canned is fine, lightly drained); and 1 cup good-quality black olives; omit the wine or water. Add the salt and pepper and cook as directed. In step 3, omit the peas; uncover and reduce the liquid if necessary until the stew is thick. Garnish with more chopped basil.

Veal Stew with Paprika

In step 1, use all butter (or grapeseed, corn, or other light oil). In step 2, omit the tarragon; add 2 garlic cloves, peeled and crushed, and 2 teaspoons good-quality paprika. Add salt, pepper, and liquid and cook as directed. In step 3, omit the peas and stir in 1 cup sour cream and more paprika if necessary.

1. Put a 12-inch skillet over high heat and, a minute later, add the oil and butter. Add the meat in one layer (if you use the larger amount of meat, you may have to cook in batches to cook only in one layer; it's worth the effort). Cook, undisturbed, until the meat is nicely browned on the bottom, about 5 minutes.

2. Add the tarragon, onions, and some salt and pepper. Cook, stirring occasionally, until the onions soften and any bits of meat stuck to the bottom of the pan are released, about 5 minutes. Add the liquid (but don't add too much liquid; the meat and onions generate plenty of their own as the covered meat simmers gently), stir, reduce the heat to low, and cover. Cook for 30 to 40 minutes, or until the veal is tender.

3. Uncover, add the peas, and raise the heat to medium. Cook for about 5 minutes more, until the peas are done. Taste and adjust the seasoning if necessary and serve.

VEAL STEW WITH DILL

MAKES 4 SERVINGS

TIME: 1 TO 1 $^1/_2$ HOURS, LARGELY UNATTENDED

THE SMALLER THE pieces you cut, the shorter the cooking time, but I wouldn't make them too small or you'll rob yourself of some of the satisfaction of eating them. This stew is also excellent made with lamb shoulder.

1 $^1/_2$ pounds boneless veal shoulder, cut into roughly 1 $^1/_2$-inch chunks

4 shallots, peeled

8 to 12 very small new potatoes

Salt and freshly ground black pepper

2 carrots, cut into roughly pea-sized bits (optional)

1 cup shelled fresh or frozen peas

8 scallions, roughly chopped (optional)

$^1/_2$ cup snipped fresh dill for garnish, or more to taste

Lemon wedges for serving

1. Put the veal in a broad skillet over high heat; sear, undisturbed, for about 4 minutes, or until the underside is nicely browned (don't worry if not all of the pieces brown). Stir, then add the shallots and potatoes. Cook for another couple of minutes, then add salt, pepper, and 1 $^1/_2$ cups of water. Stir, scraping the bottom if necessary to loosen any bits of meat that may have stuck. Turn the heat to low, cover, and simmer for about 45 minutes, stirring once or twice during that period.

2. Uncover and add the carrots if you're using them; stir once, re-cover, and simmer for about 15 minutes more, or until the veal and potatoes are tender.

3. Uncover and add the peas and scallions if you like. Raise the heat if necessary to boil away excess liquid. Taste and adjust the seasoning, then serve, garnished with the dill and accompanied by a lemon wedge.

LAMB

CRISP ROASTED RACK OF LAMB

MAKES 4 SERVINGS TIME: 30 MINUTES

RACK OF LAMB—a row of unseparated rib chops—has been a restaurant feature for so long that many people assume there is some trick to cooking it. But there is not. You trim the rack of excess fat and roast it at high heat. Salt and pepper are good seasonings, there are a number of quick tricks for adding flavor to the exterior, and you can of course make a quick reduction sauce before serving. But these are options and by my standards unnecessary: the distinctive flavor of true lamb is an uncommonly fine treat.

Getting true lamb is part of the problem; the mild flavor of baby lamb has a more universal appeal than the gamier flavor of older meat. Be sure to tell the butcher you want a rack that weighs less than two pounds.

Because many restaurants offer a whole rack as a serving (six to eight ribs!), many people believe that to be a standard serving size. But there are almost no circumstances where even a small rack will not serve two people; a larger rack can accommodate three and sometimes four. To serve more, just cook two racks at a time; they will fit comfortably side by side in most roasting pans. I like to cut each rack in half before roasting. This makes for slightly more uniform cooking and also relieves you from separating each rack into individual ribs before serving.

The roasting itself is child's play. Your oven should be hot (it should also be well insulated, because high heat produces smoke). Cut the rack most of the way down between the ribs so that more meat is exposed to intense heat and therefore becomes crisp. ("Frenching" the ribs—scraping the meat off the bones to leave them naked and neater in appearance—is counterproductive; the crisp meat on the bones is one of the joys of rack of lamb.) Unless you're highly experienced, the most reliable method of judging doneness is with an instant-read thermometer; 125°F in the center will give you medium-rare meat.

2 racks of lamb (each about 1$\frac{1}{2}$ pounds)

Salt and freshly ground black pepper

VARIATIONS

Rack of Lamb Persillade: Combine 2 tablespoons olive oil, 1 cup plain bread crumbs, 1 small peeled garlic clove, and about $\frac{1}{2}$ cup fresh parsley leaves in a small food processor (or chop by hand). Process until minced, then rub into the meaty side of the racks before roasting.

• If you happen to have some port open and you're inclined to serve your rack of lamb with a sauce, you can make a port reduction while the rack rests: Pour off all but a tablespoon of the fat from the pan and put the roasting pan on a burner (or two burners if it is big) over high heat. Add 1 cup good-quality red wine or port and cook, stirring and scraping, until the liquid is reduced to about $\frac{1}{3}$ cup. Add any of the liquid that has accumulated around the lamb and stir. Season to taste, then spoon a little of this over each serving of rib.

1. Preheat the oven to 500°F. Strip most of the surface fat from the lamb (your butcher may already have done this). Cut between the ribs, almost down to the meaty eye. Divide each rack in half down the middle, sprinkle with salt and pepper to taste, and put in a roasting pan.

2. Roast for 15 minutes, then insert a meat thermometer straight in from one end into the meatiest part. If it reads 125°F or more, remove the lamb immediately. If it reads 120°F or less, put the lamb back for about 5 minutes. Remove and let sit for 5 minutes; this will give you medium- to medium-rare lamb on the outer ribs, medium-rare to rare in the center. Cook a little longer for more doneness. Serve, separating the ribs by cutting down straight through them.

BRAISED AND GRILLED LAMB SHANKS

MAKES 4 SERVINGS

TIME: AT LEAST 2^1/$_2$ HOURS, LARGELY UNATTENDED

WHY DO SO many recipes have you brown lamb shanks and other tough meats when the long braising needed to make them tender ends up breaking down the lovely, crisp crust? The simple answer is that browning creates complex flavors, but it also creates a spattery mess. So here's a solution: grill or broil the shanks after braising. This will give them the ultimate crust, and the braising liquid will serve as a succulent sauce.

4 lamb shanks (each about 1 pound)

1 cup port or red wine

8 garlic cloves (don't bother to peel them)

Salt and freshly ground black pepper

1 teaspoon red wine vinegar or fresh lemon juice, or to taste

VARIATION

Anise-Flavored Lamb Shanks (or Short Ribs)
For an Asian-flavored main course, braise the meat in a mixture of ^{1}/$_4$ cup soy sauce, 1 cup water, 5 thin slices peeled fresh ginger, 5 whole star anise, 4 garlic cloves, and 1 tablespoon sugar. Proceed as directed, finishing the sauce with rice or white wine vinegar.

1. Combine the lamb shanks, port, and garlic in a skillet just large enough to hold the shanks. Turn the heat to high and bring to a boil; cover and turn down the heat so that the mixture simmers gently. Cook, turning about every 30 minutes, until the shanks are tender and a lovely mahogany color, at least 2 hours and more likely longer.

2. Remove the shanks and strain the sauce. If time allows, refrigerate both separately; skim the fat from the top of the sauce. Preheat a grill or broiler until quite hot; the rack should be 4 to 6 inches from the heat source.

3. Grill or broil the shanks until nicely browned all over, sprinkling them with salt and pepper to taste and turning as necessary; total cooking time will be about 15 minutes. Meanwhile, reheat the sauce gently; season it with salt and pepper, then add the vinegar or lemon juice. Taste and add more seasoning if needed. Serve the shanks with the sauce.

BRAISED AND BROWNED LAMB WITH PEACHES

MAKES 4 SERVINGS

TIME: ABOUT 1 $^{1}/_{2}$ HOURS, LARGELY UNATTENDED

A LOGICAL COMBINATION, and glorious once you taste it, with the sweet juice of the peaches deftly cutting through the richness of the lamb without being piercing. A hint of cinnamon (or an even smaller one of allspice—maybe an eighth of a teaspoon) gives the dish a great aroma as it cooks and a slightly mysterious flavor at the table. A pinch of cayenne or other red pepper makes a nice addition.

Whereas most braises begin with browning, this one ends with it, like the Braised and Grilled Lamb Shanks on page 188. This method reduces both spattering and time—since the lamb's liquid is mostly gone by the end of cooking, it doesn't go flying from the hot fat, and the meat browns faster. And the peaches, browning lightly in the same cooking liquid, contribute some of their juices to the pan while becoming meltingly tender.

2 pounds boneless lamb shoulder, trimmed of fat and gristle and cut into 1- to $1^{1}/_{2}$-inch pieces

Salt

1 cinnamon stick or $^{1}/_{2}$ teaspoon ground cinnamon

$^{1}/_{4}$ teaspoon cayenne or other red pepper, or to taste

1 medium to large onion, cut in half

$^{1}/_{2}$ cup port, red wine, or water

4 medium to large ripe peaches

Juice of 1 lemon

1 cup roughly chopped fresh parsley

1. Put the lamb in a 12-inch skillet and turn the heat to medium-high. Season with salt and add the cinnamon, cayenne, onion, and wine. Bring to a boil, cover, and adjust the heat so that the mixture simmers steadily but not violently. Cook, checking and stirring every 15 minutes or so, adding a little more liquid in the unlikely event that the mixture cooks dry. (This probably means that the heat is too high; turn it down a bit.)

2. After 1 to $1^{1}/_{2}$ hours, the meat should be tender when poked with a small, sharp knife; remove the onion and cinnamon stick, then turn the heat to medium-high and cook off any remaining liquid, allowing the lamb to brown a little. Cut the peaches in half and remove their pits, then cut each of them into 12 or 16 wedges. Stir in the peaches and continue to cook, gently tossing or stirring the mixture, until the peaches are glazed and quite soft but still intact, about 5 minutes.

3. Stir in the lemon juice and most of the parsley; taste and adjust the seasoning. Garnish with the remaining bit of herb and serve.

LAMB WITH PEPPERS AND YOGURT SAUCE

MAKES 4 SERVINGS   TIME: 40 MINUTES

YOU MIGHT THINK of this Turkish dish as a kind of lamb shish kebab with a couple of twists. First of all, it can be executed indoors (though in good weather the initial browning could certainly be done on a grill). Second, it contains its own built-in sauce, a combination of yogurt and the juices exuded by lamb and roasted vegetables.

2 pounds boneless lamb, cut into
    2-inch chunks (see Note)

3 red or yellow bell peppers

2 or 3 mildly hot fresh chiles, such
    as Anaheim (optional)

1 onion, peeled and cut in half

Salt and freshly ground black
    pepper

2 cups plain yogurt

1 to 2 teaspoons fresh thyme leaves
    (optional)

NOTE
You can use either leg or shoulder. Leg is leaner and best kept on the rare side; shoulder, which has more fat, can be cooked a little longer without drying out, which means it can be left under the broiler for a few extra minutes to give it an extra-crisp crust.

1. Turn the heat to high under a cast-iron or other large, heavy skillet; a couple of minutes later, add the lamb and quickly sear on all sides. Don't worry about cooking it through, but brown the exterior well.

2. Remove the lamb and put the peppers and chiles if you're using them in the same skillet, still over high heat. Add the onion, cut sides down. Cook until the peppers blacken on all sides, turning as necessary (the onion will blacken quickly; remove it and set aside). When the peppers are beginning to collapse, after 10 to 15 minutes, remove the skillet from the heat and cover with foil or a lid. Preheat the broiler and put the rack 2 to 4 inches from the heat source.

3. When the peppers cool slightly, peel and seed them, then cut or tear into strips; separate the onion into rings. Combine the peppers and onions with the lamb, salt, pepper, and yogurt (and thyme leaves if you like) in a roasting pan just large enough to hold the lamb in one layer. Broil until charred on top, just a few minutes, then serve.

BONELESS LAMB SHOULDER ROAST

MAKES 6 TO 8 SERVINGS   TIME: ABOUT 2 HOURS

LAMB SHOULDER IS a bony cut of meat that easily can be turned into a boneless roast by any butcher, including those who work in supermarkets. The result is a round, tied piece of meat with lovely crevices into which you can stick a simple seasoning mixture like garlic and parsley. This is a traditional combination for lamb, and rightly so, because the flavors marry so well.

If you have them on hand, add two tablespoons of crushed coriander seeds (put them in a plastic bag and pound gently with a rolling pin, rubber mallet, or like object) to the parsley: they add a distinctive and alluring floral note to the dish.

1 cup fresh parsley leaves

4 medium or 2 large garlic cloves

Salt and freshly ground black pepper

2 tablespoons extra virgin olive oil, more or less

One 3- to 4-pound boneless lamb shoulder

1. Preheat the oven to 300°F. Mince together the parsley and garlic until quite fine (a small food processor will work for this). Add a big pinch of salt and some pepper and enough olive oil to make a slurry. Smear this on and into the lamb, being sure to get it into every nook and cranny you can reach. Put the lamb in a roasting pan (you can line the pan with foil to facilitate cleanup if you like).

2. Roast for about $1^{1}/2$ hours, basting with the pan juices every 30 minutes or so. When the internal temperature reaches 140°F, turn the heat to 400°F and roast for about 10 minutes more, or until the internal temperature is 150°F and the exterior has browned nicely.

3. Let the roast sit for about 10 minutes before carving, then carve and serve, with some of the juices that come out during carving.

GRILLED BONELESS LEG OF LAMB

MAKES AT LEAST 6 SERVINGS   TIME: ABOUT 40 MINUTES

THERE MAY BE no meat better for grilling than boneless leg of lamb. It cooks reasonably quickly, usually in less than half an hour, but still develops an irresistibly crunchy crust. Even better, that crust can be flavored in minutes before it is cooked with any of a dozen combinations of seasonings. Marinating is unnecessary, as the meat itself has exquisite flavor and really needs no more than salt.

The leg's irregular shape virtually guarantees that every eater will be happy—lamb is the only meat good at every stage of doneness. When the thickest parts have cooked to rare, the ends will be well done, the parts in between medium. Boneless legs sold at supermarkets are sometimes wrapped in an elastic net to form them into a round roast. For grilling, remove this so the meat lies flat. If the larger end of the meat is three or more inches thick, you might cut a flap to make that lobe thinner and flatter so that it cooks more evenly. Using a sharp, thin-bladed knife and working from the side of the lobe that faces the rest of the meat, make a horizontal cut about halfway down from top to bottom, most of the way through, and fold the meat out; in essence, you are butterflying the butterfly.

One 3- to 4-pound butterflied leg of lamb
1 tablespoon olive oil
1 teaspoon minced garlic
1 tablespoon minced fresh rosemary or 2 teaspoons dried
1 tablespoon chopped or crushed fennel seeds
Salt and freshly ground black pepper

1. Preheat a grill or broiler until quite hot; put the rack 4 inches from the heat source.
2. Trim the lamb of excess fat. Mix together the olive oil, garlic, rosemary, fennel seeds, salt, and pepper; rub this mixture well into the lamb, being sure to get some into all the crevices. (If time allows, it

VARIATIONS

If grilling isn't an option, you can cook this dish in the oven: Put the broiler rack 4 to 6 inches from the heat source. Keep an eye on the lamb to prevent burning; the cooking time will be a little shorter. Or roast it in the middle of the oven, at 450°F, turning occasionally; the cooking time will be about the same.

Grilled Boneless Leg of Lamb with Coriander and Ginger
Use a combination of 1 tablespoon coriander seeds, 1 teaspoon black peppercorns, 1 tablespoon garlic, and 1 tablespoon peeled fresh ginger, all minced or coarsely ground together; moisten with a little soy sauce.

Curried Boneless Leg of Lamb
Rub the lamb all over with 2 tablespoons curry powder mixed with $1/2$ cup yogurt.

Grilled Soy-and-Ginger Boneless Lamb Leg
Rub the lamb all over with 1 tablespoon olive oil, 2 teaspoons salt, 1 teaspoon cracked black pepper, 1 tablespoon minced garlic, $1/4$ cup soy sauce, 1 tablespoon peeled minced or grated fresh ginger. Serve with lemon wedges.

does no harm to let the prepared lamb sit in the refrigerator for up to 24 hours; just return the meat to room temperature before grilling.)

3. Sear the meat over the hottest part of the grill until nicely browned on both sides, 10 to 15 minutes. Continue to cook with the grill covered or uncovered for 5 to 15 minutes longer, until the internal temperature at the thickest part is about 125°F. Let rest for 5 minutes before slicing and serving.

BREADED LAMB CUTLETS

MAKES 4 SERVINGS   TIME: 20 MINUTES

THOUGH THIS IS an unusual preparation, in many ways lamb is the meat most suited to this simple treatment. Like all cutlet preparations, it's lightning-quick.

Eight 1-inch-thick medallions of lamb, cut from 2 racks or from the loin or leg

2 tablespoons extra virgin olive oil

2 eggs

Panko (Japanese bread crumbs) or other bread crumbs for dredging

Salt and freshly ground black pepper

1 teaspoon ground cumin or minced fresh rosemary (optional)

Chopped fresh parsley for garnish (optional)

1 lemon, cut into wedges

1. Preheat the oven to 200°F. If you're using rib or loin slices, pound them lightly with the heel of your hand until they are about $1/2$ inch thick. If you're using leg, put them between 2 sheets of wax paper or plastic wrap and pound with a mallet or rolling pin until they are about $1/2$ inch thick. Put a nonstick or well-seasoned skillet over medium-high heat and add the oil.

2. When the oil shimmers, dip a piece of lamb in the egg and press both sides into the bread crumbs. Add to the skillet; do not crowd—you will have to cook in batches. When the meat is in the skillet, season it with salt and pepper and sprinkle it with a pinch of cumin if you like.

3. As the meat browns, flip it and brown the other side; adjust the heat so that each side browns in about 2 minutes; the meat should remain rare. As the pieces finish, put them on an ovenproof platter and keep them warm in the oven. When they are all done, garnish with parsley if you like and serve with lemon wedges.

CUMIN-RUBBED LAMB CHOPS
WITH CUCUMBER SALAD

MAKES 4 SERVINGS   TIME: 1 HOUR, LARGELY UNATTENDED

LAMB CHOPS ARE among the best meats to grill; although they tend to catch fire, they cook so quickly—three minutes per side is usually more than enough—that there is no time for them to char, and the fire makes the exterior even crisper than it might be otherwise. The cucumbers are best if they're salted, which removes some of their bitterness and makes them extra-crisp. Start with one or two Kirby (small) cucumbers per person—or half of a medium cucumber or about a third of a long ("English") cucumber.

About $1^1/2$ pounds cucumbers, peeled and thinly sliced

Salt and freshly ground black pepper

$1/2$ cup coarsely chopped fresh mint

2 lemons

4 shoulder or leg lamb chops or 12 rib or loin chops (about 1 pound)

1 tablespoon cumin, preferably freshly ground

1. Put the cucumber slices in a colander and sprinkle with salt, just a little more than if you were planning to eat them right away. After 15 to 30 minutes, preheat a grill or broiler; put the rack about 4 inches from the heat source.

2. When the fire is hot, press the cucumbers to extract as much liquid as possible and toss them with the mint and the juice of one of the lemons. Rub the lamb chops with salt, pepper, and cumin and grill for about 3 minutes per side for rare, turning once.

3. Serve each of the lamb chops on a bed of the cucumber salad. Quarter the remaining lemon and serve it to squeeze over the lamb.

_____

BROILED LAMB CHOPS WITH MINT CHUTNEY

MAKES 4 SERVINGS   TIME: 30 MINUTES

ASPARAGUS MAY INTRODUCE spring, but mint screams it. The perennial herb is among the first edible greens out of the ground, and it's rampant enough to be considered a weed for those who aren't fond of it. Team it with lamb and you have a model spring dish.

Juice of 1 lime

1 garlic clove, peeled

One $1/2$-inch-long piece fresh ginger, peeled and roughly chopped

Fresh or dried chile to taste

$1/2$ cup whole-milk yogurt

$1^1/2$ teaspoons sugar

1 cup fresh mint leaves

Salt and freshly ground black pepper

4 shoulder or leg lamb chops or 12 rib or loin chops (about 1 pound)

1. Preheat a grill or broiler to moderately hot; put the rack 4 to 6 inches from the heat source.

2. Meanwhile, make the chutney: Combine the lime juice, garlic, ginger, chile, yogurt, and sugar in a food processor or blender and puree. Stir in the mint by hand, then add salt and pepper to taste.

3. When the chutney is ready, grill the chops for 3 to 4 minutes per side, by which time they will be medium-rare, or until they reach the desired degree of doneness. Serve the lamb chops with the chutney.

GRILLED LAMB RIBS

MAKES 4 SERVINGS   TIME: 30 MINUTES

IF YOU DON'T see lamb ribs in your supermarket, the chances are that they're being tossed. Both demand and profit are evidently so slim that they are not worth processing and putting out in the case. Which is a shame, because next to pork (spare) ribs, lamb ribs are the best down-and-dirty grill item I know. They're also the cheapest. Where I live, it's hard to pay more than a dollar a pound for them.

Like spareribs, lamb ribs are the bones of the breast, separated into individual pieces. The supermarket meat department or butcher may give you the entire breast, or he may separate the ribs for you. If he does not, be sure to ask him to at least remove or cut through the breastbone, which will make cutting in between the ribs fast and easy.

Lamb ribs require special treatment while grilling, because they are loaded with fat (this is one of the reasons they taste so good, of course). You can grill them very slowly or (my preference) parboil the ribs just for ten minutes or so, long enough to render enough of the fat so that it doesn't catch fire the instant you put the ribs on the grill. You'll still need to be careful during grilling; don't leave the fire for more than a minute or two. Broiling them makes this somewhat easier, but you still have to keep an eye out; left unattended, they will burn.

Any brushing sauce or spice rub you like is suitable here. My choice is a sweet but pungent amalgam of raw onion, strong mustard, and honey, marmalade, or maple syrup.

Salt and freshly ground black
    pepper
4 to 5 pounds lamb breast, cut into
    ribs

$^1/_4$ cup honey, orange marmalade,
    or maple syrup
$^1/_4$ cup Dijon mustard
1 small onion, peeled

1. Preheat a grill or broiler to moderately hot; put the rack at least 4 inches from the heat source. Bring a large pot of water to a boil; salt it. Put in the lamb and simmer for 10 minutes.
2. Drain the ribs. Grill or broil them for about 10 minutes, turning once

VARIATIONS

Once you've tracked down a source for lamb ribs, the options for what to do with them are almost endless:

• Rub the parboiled ribs with any spice rub, such as chili or curry powder, before grilling.

• Cook the ribs unadorned, then serve with a light drizzle of $^1/_2$ cup fresh lemon juice and hot sauce and salt to taste.

• You can make a fast, more typical barbecue sauce like this: Combine 1 cup ketchup with 1 tablespoon each Worcestershire sauce and chili powder; $^1/_4$ cup each red wine vinegar and minced onion; 1 garlic clove, minced; and salt and pepper. Combine this mixture in a saucepan and cook over medium-low heat, stirring occasionally, until warm, about 10 minutes. Taste and adjust the seasoning, then use as directed.

• Serve them with pesto: Make a light pesto of fresh basil, cilantro, or parsley, blending together about 2 tablespoons of oil to 1 cup of leaves, along with salt, a garlic clove, and enough water to make the mixture creamy. Don't brush the ribs with this mixture, but pass it at the table.

(continued)

(Variations, continued)

• Serve them with salsa: See page 295 or, for example, combine about $^1/_2$ cup chopped onion or scallion with 2 large tomatoes, chopped, and a little minced garlic, some cayenne or paprika, 1 tablespoon vinegar, and salt, pepper, and fresh lemon or lime juice to taste. Pass at the table.

• Lamb and cucumber make a natural combination: Make a cucumber salsa by peeling, seeding, and chopping 2 cucumbers, then coarsely chopping them in a blender or food processor with fresh mint and salt to taste. Pass at the table.

• Lamb takes to fruit surprisingly well: Try making a fast mango relish by combining the chopped flesh of 2 mangoes (or peaches) with $^1/_2$ cup minced onion, the juice of 2 limes, and salt, pepper, and chopped fresh cilantro to taste and passing at the table to accompany the lamb.

or twice and sprinkling them with a little salt and pepper. Meanwhile, combine the honey, mustard, and onion in a blender and whiz until smooth.

3. When the ribs begin to brown, brush them with the sauce and continue to cook, watching carefully so they do not catch fire. When they are brown and crisp all over—a matter of no more than 10 or, at the most, 15 minutes—remove from the grill and serve.

PORK

PORK CHOPS WITH MISO–RED WINE SAUCE

MAKES 4 SERVINGS   TIME: 20 MINUTES

MISO IS A superb thickener, adding a rich, creamy consistency when whisked into a small amount of liquid. With that in mind, it's the work of a moment to turn the pan juices remaining after searing a piece of meat into a great sauce. My choice here is pork for meat and red wine for liquid; the combination resulting from these three ingredients completely belies the amount of energy put into the dish.

Red miso (which is in fact brown) adds terrific color to the sauce and has the strongest flavor of all the misos; it's also the easiest to find. Miso must be handled gently, because high heat practically destroys its flavor; so be sure to keep the heat low when you stir it in.

For the pork, I prefer a bone-in chop, preferably from the rib end of the loin; it's a little bit fattier than other chops, and these days pork is so lean that the extra fat is a benefit rather than a detriment.

Four 1-inch-thick bone-in pork
    chops (each about 6 ounces)
Salt and freshly cracked black
    pepper
1 cup sturdy red wine, like Zinfandel
    or Cabernet Sauvignon

2 tablespoons red miso
$^1/_4$ cup roughly chopped fresh shiso
    (if available), basil, or parsley
    (optional)

1. Heat a heavy skillet over medium-high heat for 2 or 3 minutes, then add the chops. Sprinkle them with a little bit of salt and a lot of pepper, then brown them on one side for 4 to 5 minutes. Turn and brown the other side until firm and nearly cooked through, another 3 or 4 minutes. Transfer to a warm plate and turn the heat to medium.

2. Add the wine and cook, stirring occasionally with a wooden spoon to loosen any bits of meat that have stuck to the pan, until the wine reduces by about half. Turn the heat to low and add the miso; stir briskly to make a smooth mixture (a wire whisk will help here).

3. Taste the sauce and add more salt (unlikely) and pepper if necessary. Spoon it over the pork, garnish if you like, and serve.

VIETNAMESE-STYLE PORK CHOPS

MAKES 4 SERVINGS   TIME: 30 MINUTES

THIS DISH HAS the beguiling, distinctively Southeast Asian aroma of garlic, lots of it, nuoc mam (the Vietnamese fish sauce known more commonly by its Thai name, nam pla), and lime. But there are a couple of "secret" ingredients as well, including the mild acidity of lemongrass and the spiciness of black pepper in large quantities. Traditionally, this dish also contains the burnt sweetness that comes from caramelized sugar, but the intense heat of the grill makes honey a good substitute and a much easier one. So the marinade can be assembled in ten minutes, the grill preheated in another ten, and the pork grilled in ten: a great, intensely flavored, thirty-minute dish.

You can use pork chops for this dish, but so-called country-style ribs (actually the shoulder end of the pork loin) remain moister during grilling. And if you can find these "ribs" with the bone out, so much the better—you've essentially got a one-inch-thick pork loin steak that grills beautifully.

2 tablespoons minced lemongrass (see Note)

1 tablespoon minced garlic

3 tablespoons honey

1 tablespoon nam pla or soy sauce, or to taste

2 limes

Freshly ground black pepper

1 1/2 pounds country-style pork chops, preferably boneless

Chopped fresh Thai basil, mint, cilantro, or a combination for garnish (optional)

1. Combine the first 4 ingredients in a bowl; whisk to blend. Add the juice of one of the limes and lots of pepper—about a teaspoon. Marinate the pork in this mixture while you preheat a grill or broiler to moderately hot; put the grill rack about 4 inches from the heat source.

2. Grill or broil the pork, spooning the marinade over it as it cooks, until done, about 10 minutes. Turn only once, so that each side browns nicely. Serve with the remaining lime, garnished with the optional herb.

NOTE

To prepare lemongrass, first peel it like a scallion. Virtually the entire inner core is tender enough to mince (in the winter, when the stalks have been in storage, you may have to peel off layer after layer to find the edible center). Figure a yield of about a tablespoon of minced lemongrass per stalk.

VARIATION

Turn this dish into a full meal by pairing it with a simple, Vietnamese-inspired cabbage salad. Finely slice some cabbage, toss it with a few pinches of salt, and let it sit in a colander while the pork steaks marinate and grill. While the grilled meat is resting, toss the cabbage with lime juice (start with 1 lime and work up from there), a goodly amount of whatever herb you're serving the pork with, finely chopped, and a healthy, heady dose of freshly ground black pepper. Top the cabbage salad with the pork and serve.

ROAST PORK CHOPS
WITH FENNEL-ORANGE COMPOTE

MAKES 4 SERVINGS   TIME: 45 MINUTES

IT ISN'T OFTEN you can combine a few winter staples and create a novel, fresh-tasting dish that is easily varied, stands on its own, or forms the base for a variety of other foods. Yet a simple mélange of fennel and orange does all of these things and without a lot of effort. Take some slices of boneless pork, for example, marinate them briefly in olive oil, lemon juice, garlic, salt, and pepper, pan-roast them, then serve them on a bed of the compote: the mingled juices are sheer delight. (I've presented the recipe that way here, but it is easy to cook the fennel orange combination on its own.) Similarly, the compote works nicely as a bed for simple roasted cod, sautéed duck breast, and grilled chicken. There isn't much technique to speak of here; you'll know the dish is done when the orange juice bubbles become scarce. Just be sure not to cook the compote entirely dry; the orange juice sauce is a nice touch.

4 boneless pork chops (1 to 1 1/2 pounds)

Salt and freshly ground black pepper

1/4 cup extra virgin olive oil

Juice of 1 lemon

1 fennel bulb (1 pound or more)

2 navel oranges, peeled

1 medium onion, peeled

1 tablespoon fresh rosemary or 1 teaspoon dried

1 1/2 cups fresh orange juice

1. Sprinkle the pork chops with salt and pepper to taste and marinate them on a plate with 2 tablespoons of the olive oil and the lemon juice. Preheat the oven to 500°F.

2. Trim the fennel, reserving some of the dill-like fronds. Cut the fennel, oranges, and onion into 1/8- to 1/4-inch-thick slices.

3. Put the remaining olive oil in an 8-inch skillet or a saucepan that is at least 4 inches deep. Put half the fennel in the skillet, then top with half the orange, the onion, and the rosemary. Sprinkle with salt and pepper, then top with the remaining fennel and orange. Pour in the orange juice and add more salt and pepper.

VARIATIONS

• Substitute grapefruit for the oranges or add the juice of a lemon or a lime to the mix.

• Vary the herb. Classic Western European herbs like rosemary, thyme, tarragon, and parsley are all naturals, but cilantro or finely minced lemongrass also add nice touches.

• Add finely minced peeled fresh ginger along with some garlic and soy sauce. A teaspoon or so of sesame oil finishes the compote nicely. Substitute peanut oil for the olive oil if you have it, or use a neutral oil like canola.

• Any meat, like steak, can be cooked like the pork. Grilled chicken, on or off the bone, works well, as does sautéed duck breast. You can also make the dish with fish: Try roasted delicate fillets, like cod or red snapper; or grilled shrimp; or swordfish, tuna, or salmon steaks.

4. Bring to a boil on top of the stove and cook over fairly lively heat, pressing the solids down into the liquid from time to time. When the mixture is no longer swimming in juice but not yet dry—about 20 minutes—it is done. Hold it at minimum heat while you finish the pork chops.

5. Just before you judge the compote to be done, heat an ovenproof skillet over high heat for 3 or 4 minutes. Add the pork chops with their marinade and immediately transfer the skillet to the oven (if you have a powerful vent, you can pan-grill the chops on top of the stove). Roast for 2 minutes, then turn and roast for another 2 to 3 minutes, or until the chops are done.

6. Serve the chops on a bed of the compote. Mince the reserved fennel fronds and use as a garnish.

SAUSAGE WITH GRAPES

MAKES 4 SERVINGS   TIME: 30 MINUTES

ALTHOUGH I WAS told this dish—beautifully browned sausages nestled on a bed of grapes in varying stages of doneness, some lightly browned, some collapsed, some whole and nearly raw—is Umbrian in origin, it seems as if many workers of the land who produced sausages and picked grapes would have created this, even if by accident, no matter where they lived. It is an often overlooked recipe in cookbooks, perhaps because there's almost nothing to it. In any case, the wonderful marriage is incredibly easy to produce and easily worked into anyone's repertoire. With good bread and a salad, you've got a great weeknight meal in about half an hour.

1 to 1^1/2 pounds fresh Italian
    sausage
4 cups seedless grapes

2 teaspoons balsamic vinegar or
    fresh lemon juice, or to taste

1. Put the sausages in a 10- or 12-inch skillet over medium heat. Cook the sausages, turning from time to time, until nicely browned, about 15 minutes. Prick each sausage in a few places with a thin-bladed knife and cook for 5 minutes more.

2. Transfer the sausages to a warm platter. If more than a tablespoon or two of fat remains in the pan, remove the excess. Add the grapes and turn the heat to medium-high. Cook, stirring occasionally, until some of the grapes collapse. Add the vinegar or lemon juice, stir, and turn off the heat. Serve the sausages nestled in the grapes and their juices.

KALE, SAUSAGE, AND MUSHROOM STEW

MAKES 4 SERVINGS TIME: 30 TO 40 MINUTES

BY BUILDING THIS stew one ingredient at a time—in a manner not unlike that of making soup—the process is streamlined and nearly everything is browned. This makes the flavors so much more complex that the stew needs no stock to finish it off. (Should you have some stock on hand, however, by all means use it.) To make this stew even tastier, use a mixture of mushrooms or add a few reconstituted dried porcini and use their soaking liquid to replace some of the water.

1 tablespoon extra virgin olive oil

1 pound Italian sausage, sweet or hot, cut into 1-inch or smaller pieces

1 pound kale, leaves stripped from stems

1/2 pound mushrooms, trimmed and sliced

1 tablespoon roughly chopped garlic

1 teaspoon hot red pepper flakes, or to taste

Salt and freshly ground black pepper

2 cups stock or water

VARIATION

Bangers and Mash, Italian Style
Boil 1^1/2 to 2 pounds peeled potatoes in water to cover until soft; drain, reserving some of the cooking liquid. While the potatoes are hot, mash them with 1/2 teaspoon minced garlic, 2 tablespoons extra virgin olive oil, and enough of the reserved cooking liquid to make them smooth. Season to taste with salt and pepper. Meanwhile, cook the sausages. In step 2, just before adding the grapes, add 1 cup white wine or chicken stock to the skillet. Raise the heat to high and cook, stirring, until the liquid is reduced by about half. Stir in the grapes and proceed as directed. Serve with the mashed potatoes.

1. Put the olive oil in a large, deep skillet or casserole over medium-high heat; a minute later, add the sausage and cook without stirring until the sausage browns well on one side, about 5 minutes. Meanwhile, chop the stems of the kale into about $1/2$-inch lengths and shred the leaves.

2. Stir the sausage and let it brown a bit more. Remove it with a slotted spoon (don't worry if it isn't cooked through). Cook the mushrooms in the remaining fat with the heat still on medium-high, stirring occasionally, until lightly browned, about 10 minutes. Remove with a slotted spoon and keep warm.

3. Add the kale stems and cook, stirring frequently, until they begin to brown, 3 or 4 minutes. Turn the heat to medium and add the garlic, hot pepper, kale leaves, salt, and pepper; stir and cook for about 1 minute. Return the sausage to the pan and add the stock or water. Raise the heat to high and cook for about 5 minutes, stirring occasionally and scraping the bottom of the pan with a wooden spoon. Add salt and pepper to taste and ladle into bowls, topping with the reserved mushrooms.

FORTY-MINUTE CASSOULET

MAKES 4 TO 6 SERVINGS   TIME: 40 MINUTES

CASSOULET IN FORTY minutes or less is heresy, of course, but even "real" cassoulet was designed as a bean stew containing whatever meat, preferably fatty and flavorful, was available to throw in. That's the spirit here, too.

Although the pork tenderloin need not be browned before further cooking, the sausage benefits from a quick browning, definitely worth the five-minute effort. If you can get duck confit, just brown it lightly on both sides, adding both it and its fat to the stew in place of the duck breast.

4 cups chopped tomato with the
    juice (canned is fine)

1 tablespoon chopped garlic

4 cups white beans, nearly fully
    cooked, drained if canned or
    frozen

1 cup stock, dry red wine, bean-
    cooking liquid, or water

Salt

$1/8$ teaspoon cayenne, or to taste

1 pound Italian sausage, preferably
    in 1 piece

1 pound pork tenderloin, cut into
    1-inch cubes

1 boned duck breast

1. Combine the tomato and garlic in a large saucepan over medium heat. Bring to a boil and add the beans; bring to a boil again, stirring occasionally, then reduce the heat so the mixture bubbles regularly but not furiously. Cook for about 20 minutes, adding the liquid when the mixture becomes thick. Add the salt and cayenne when the beans are tender and flavorful.

2. Meanwhile, put the sausage in a skillet and turn the heat to medium-high; brown on both sides, turning only once or twice. Add the sausage to the tomato-bean mixture, along with the pork. Raise the heat a bit if necessary to keep a simmer going. Stir the beans occasionally so the pork chunks cook evenly.

3. Cut a $1/2$-inch cross-hatch pattern in the skin side of the duck breast, right down to the fat layer. Put the breast in the same skillet as the sausage, skin side down, and turn the heat to medium-high. Cook until nicely browned, pouring any rendered duck fat and juices into the bean mixture. Turn the duck and brown the meat side, then crisp up the skin side again for a minute or so, once more pouring any juice into the beans. Total cooking time for the breast will be 6 to 8 minutes.

4. To serve, carve the sausage and duck breast into serving pieces and put on each of 4 or 6 plates. Top with beans and pork.

VARIATION

An optional additional step (which is not particularly time consuming and certainly not at all difficult) that will give the dish the look of a traditional cassoulet: In step 4, combine the cut-up duck (or the browned duck confit if you were able to substitute it) with the beans and pork in a shallow baking dish. Finish the dish by toasting some bread crumbs, seasoned with salt and pepper, in the fat remaining from browning the duck. Sprinkle these on top of the stew, then run under the broiler to brown just before serving.

SPARERIBS, KOREAN STYLE

MAKES 4 SERVINGS   TIME: 45 MINUTES

THIS PREPARATION RESULTS in ribs that are dark, glossy, and so tender that just a tug of the teeth will pull the meat off the bone.

3 to 4 pounds spareribs, cut into
    2-inch sections
$1/4$ cup sesame seeds
2 tablespoons chopped garlic
$1/4$ cup sugar
5 nickel-sized slices peeled fresh
    ginger

$1/2$ cup soy sauce
2 tablespoons sesame oil
Salt and freshly ground black
    pepper
$1/2$ cup chopped scallion

1. Put a large skillet that can hold the ribs in one layer over high heat and add the ribs and $1/2$ cup of water. Boil, turning the ribs occasionally, until the liquid has evaporated, then reduce the heat to medium and brown the ribs in their own fat, turning occasionally, for about 5 minutes. Meanwhile, toast the sesame seeds by putting them in a small skillet over medium heat, shaking the pan occasionally until they brown slightly and begin to pop.

2. Add the garlic and half the sesame seeds and stir; cook for 30 seconds. Add the sugar, ginger, soy sauce, half the sesame oil, and another $1/4$ cup of water; turn the heat to medium-high, and cook, turning occasionally, until the liquid is thick and dark. If the ribs are tender at this point, they're ready. If not, add another $1/4$ cup of water and repeat the process.

3. Add salt and pepper to taste and the remaining sesame seeds and sesame oil. Stir once, sprinkle with the scallion, and serve.

BRAISED PORK WITH TURNIPS

MAKES 4 SERVINGS   TIME: 1 HOUR

THIS IS A classic spring or fall dish, times when you can get good, fresh turnips but don't mind long, slow cooking. Here turnips and pork are both browned for perfect color and then simmered in a little liquid until tender.

Don't ignore the instruction to preheat the skillet for at least a minute, then allow the butter and/or oil to become hot, and don't crowd the meat, or it won't brown properly. Make sure the first side of the pork cubes browns well and that the second is on its way to being browned before adding the turnips. The turnips themselves are so high in natural sugars that they brown almost instantly and continue to gain color as they braise.

1 tablespoon neutral oil, like
    grapeseed or corn
1 tablespoon butter (or more oil)
$1^1/_2$ pounds boneless pork shoulder
    or loin, trimmed of excess fat
    and cut into 1- to $1^1/_2$-inch
    chunks
$1^1/_2$ pounds purple-topped turnips
    or rutabaga, peeled and cut into
    1-inch chunks

$^3/_4$ cup white wine, chicken stock,
    or water
Salt and freshly ground black
    pepper
2 tablespoons minced fresh lovage,
    celery leaves, or parsley
    (optional)

1. Put a 12-inch skillet, preferably nonstick, over medium-high heat and let sit for at least a minute. Add the oil and butter. When the butter foam subsides or the oil is hot, add the pork, a few chunks at a time. When it is all in the skillet, turn the heat to high. Cook for about 5 minutes, undisturbed, until the pork is nicely browned on one side. Turn each piece, return the heat to medium-high, and cook for about 3 minutes more.

2. Add the turnip chunks and shake the skillet so that the pork and turnips are all sitting in one layer or nearly so. Cook for another 3 or

VARIATIONS

Creamy Pork with Turnips
In the final step, transfer the pork and turnips to a warm platter. Do not quite reduce the liquid to a glaze; when there is about $^1/_2$ cup left, reduce the heat to low, stir in 1 cup sour or sweet cream, and slowly bring back to a boil over medium heat. Stir the pork and turnips back into the sauce, garnish, and serve, preferably over rice.

Pork and Turnips with Mustard
You can do this in combination with the preceding variation if you like. Stir 1 tablespoon Dijon mustard, or more to taste, into the finished sauce. Heat through and serve.

4 minutes, or until the turnips begin to brown. Add the liquid and stir once or twice. Add salt and pepper to taste and half the lovage if you're using it, turn the heat to medium-low, and cover the skillet.

3. Cook, stirring every 10 minutes, until both pork and turnips are quite tender, about 30 minutes. Remove the cover and raise the heat to medium-high; boil the liquid until it is reduced to a syrupy glaze. Taste and add more salt and pepper if necessary, then garnish with the remaining herb if you like and serve.

─────────

ROAST PORK WITH APPLESAUCE

MAKES 4 SERVINGS   TIME: 1 HOUR

SPREADING A ROAST with a sweet coating—apricot jam comes to mind—adds an interesting contrast of flavor, and the sugar encourages browning. But the results are often too sweet. So I decided to experiment with alternative coatings for a small roast of pork—one that would cook quickly enough to be considered for weeknight dinners—and settled on applesauce, which has a not-too-obvious benefit. Because applesauce doesn't contain nearly the same percentage of sugar as jam, more of it can be used without overwhelming the meat with sweetness, and the thicker coating protects the meat and keeps it moist. This is important, because the superlean pork sold in supermarkets almost inexorably dries out as it cooks.

VARIATION

Roast Pork with Jam or Marmalade
This is the original version, which some will prefer: Substitute 1 cup apricot jam or orange marmalade for the applesauce; warm it over low heat, stirring in 1 tablespoon fresh lemon juice to thin it slightly. Proceed as directed.

2 cups applesauce, preferably unsweetened
One 1^1/$_2$- to 2-pound boneless pork loin
Oil for the pan
Salt and freshly ground black pepper

1. Preheat the oven to 500°F; set the oven rack as close to the top of the oven as is practical (take the thickness of the roast into account). Meanwhile, put the applesauce in a fine strainer over a bowl or in the sink to allow excess liquid to drain. Line a roasting pan with a double thickness of aluminum foil (to avoid tough cleanup) and brush the foil with a little oil.

2. When the oven is hot, sprinkle the roast with salt and pepper, then spread an even layer of the applesauce all over it, using up all the applesauce. Sprinkle with a little more salt and pepper and roast, checking every 15 minutes or so to make sure the applesauce doesn't burn. It's fine if it darkens and browns, or even turns dark brown, as long as the top doesn't blacken.

3. Begin checking the pork with an instant-read thermometer after 45 minutes. When the internal temperature reaches 155°F, remove the meat from the oven. Let it rest for 5 minutes before carving. Serve the sliced meat with any accumulated juices.

CRISPY PORK BITS WITH JERK SEASONINGS

MAKES 4 SERVINGS   TIME: 2 HOURS, LARGELY UNATTENDED

YOU'LL FIND STRONGLY seasoned, crunchy pork everywhere in Latin America, and it's always irresistible.

$1^1/2$ pounds boneless pork shoulder, trimmed of excess fat and cut into large chunks

5 garlic cloves, peeled and crushed

1 tablespoon coriander seeds

1 dried chipotle or other chile

1 cinnamon stick

Several gratings of nutmeg

Salt

$1/2$ cup chopped fresh cilantro

2 limes, cut into wedges

1. Put the pork in a deep skillet or wide saucepan; wrap the garlic, coriander, chile, and cinnamon in a piece of cheesecloth and add to the pan, along with the nutmeg and salt to taste. Add water to cover and bring to a boil over high heat. Turn the heat to low and simmer until the pork is very tender, about $1^1/4$ hours, adding water as necessary.

2. When the pork is soft, remove the cheesecloth sack and discard. Raise the heat to medium-high and boil off all the liquid.

3. If you choose not to grill, you can now brown the pork in its own remaining fat. Garnish with cilantro and serve with lime wedges. Or thread the pork onto 8 skewers and, when you're ready to eat, grill them lightly on all sides to brown before garnishing and serving.

THE MINIMALIST'S CHOUCROUTE

MAKES 6 SERVINGS

TIME: ABOUT 2 HOURS, LARGELY UNATTENDED

IN ITS HOMELAND of Alsace, choucroute garnie is no more special than a frank and sauerkraut, with which it has much in common. But while the French treat this archetypally hearty combination of sauerkraut, spices, wine, and smoked meats as common fare, here it has become the province of restaurants. In any case, choucroute is a flexible combination of wintertime staples, the perfect cold-weather dish, featuring sauerkraut cooked in a little goose fat (or duck fat or lard) and wine, then "garnished"—this is some garnish—with a variety of candidly heavy meats, some smoked, some fresh or salted. Note that good sauerkraut does not come in cans but is sold fresh from barrels or in plastic. It should contain no more than cabbage and salt—beyond that, the less the better.

VARIATIONS

• Add several tablespoons of duck fat or lard to the simmering sauerkraut (a traditional addition).
• Use any sausages you like, including those made from chicken, veal, turkey, or seafood.
• Add 12 small potatoes to the pot when about 45 minutes of cooking time remain.
• Add 2 to 3 peeled, cored, and grated apples to the sauerkraut when about 15 minutes of cooking remain.
• Stir 2 tablespoons kirsch into the sauerkraut about 5 minutes before serving.

3 pounds sauerkraut

1 large onion, chopped

10 juniper berries

2 cups dry white wine, preferably Alsatian Riesling

1 pound slab bacon in 1 piece

1 pound kielbasa or similar dark sausage

3 bratwursts or similar "white" sausage

3 smoked pork loin chops

Salt and freshly ground black pepper

Hot mustard for serving

1. Rinse the sauerkraut and drain it well. Combine it with the onion, juniper berries, and wine in a large skillet or broad pot and add enough water to come about two-thirds of the way up the side of the sauerkraut (in some pots, the wine may provide enough liquid). Turn the heat to high and bring to a boil.

2. Turn down the heat and nestle the bacon in the sauerkraut. Cover and cook for 1 hour, then add the sausages and pork chops. Re-cover and cook for another 30 minutes. The sauerkraut should be tender but retain some crunch; cook for another 15 minutes if necessary, then taste and season with salt and pepper to taste.

3. To serve, cut the meat into pieces and serve it on a platter with the sauerkraut along with hot mustard.

SLOW-GRILLED RIBS

MAKES 4 TO 8 SERVINGS   TIME: AT LEAST 2 HOURS

THIS IS THE way to get tender, moist ribs without burning them. They take some time, but not much attention.

2 to 4 racks spareribs   Salt and freshly ground black
                                      pepper

1. Start a not-too-fierce fire on a covered grill big enough to bank the coals to one side once they get hot (on a gas grill, turn the heat to medium on one side and keep it off on the other; if there are three burners, you can light the 2 side ones and cook in the middle). When the grill is hot, put the spareribs on the less hot part of the grill, and cover the grill. Walk away for about 30 minutes.

2. Turn the ribs and continue to cook them, adding to the fire if necessary. They should be browning very slowly, firming up, and drying out. When the meat begins to pull away from the bone and the meat between the bones is easily pierced with a thin-bladed knife, the meat is nearly done. At this point you can cool the ribs slightly, then wrap well in foil and put in the refrigerator or continue to cook.

3. When you're ready to serve the ribs, brown them on both sides over direct heat, being careful not to burn them. When they're done, season them with salt and pepper and serve.

CHINESE-STYLE SLOW-COOKED RIBS

MAKES 4 SERVINGS   TOTAL TIME: 3 HOURS

THIS IS A really easy dish that takes some time. But once you get it started (which will take just five minutes or so), you can all but ignore it during the cooking, just checking every now and then to turn the ribs and make sure the liquid doesn't dry out.

To make this into a whole-meal stew, use two cups of water and add some peeled and chunked carrots or turnips, whole pearl onions or shallots, or all of these. Some shredded cabbage added during the last half hour or so of cooking is also good.

2 pounds pork spareribs, cut into pieces, or beef short ribs

$1/4$ cup plus 2 tablespoons soy sauce

1 whole star anise

1 small dried chile

5 slices fresh ginger (don't bother to peel)

2 garlic cloves, lightly crushed

2 teaspoons sugar

1. Combine the meat, $1/4$ cup soy sauce, the anise, chile, ginger, garlic, and sugar with $1/2$ cup of water in a skillet just broad enough to hold the meat.

2. Bring to a boil, then turn the heat to low, cover, and simmer for 2 hours or so, turning the meat occasionally and adding water $1/2$ cup at a time if and when the pan dries out. The meat is done when it is tender and nearly falling from the bone.

VEGETABLES

ROASTED ASPARAGUS WITH PARMESAN

MAKES 4 SERVINGS   TIME: 25 MINUTES

THERE ARE TWO things I love about pencil-thin asparagus: one is that it requires no peeling, because its outer sheath is far more tender than that of its thick cousin; the other is that it cooks much faster.

This is especially important when you turn to methods other than boiling or steaming—most notably roasting. What I like to do is roast thin spears until they're just about tender, then top them with a fool-proof two-ingredient topping: coarse bread crumbs and Parmigiano-Reggiano cheese. Run that under the broiler, and you get roasted asparagus with a crunchy, high-impact crust. Keep your eye on the dish while it's under the broiler—the time needed there is only a minute or two.

1 thick slice good-quality bread
(about 1 ounce)

1 small chunk Parmigiano-Reggiano cheese (about 1 ounce)

1¹/₂ pounds thin asparagus, more or less

3 tablespoons butter, extra virgin olive oil, or a combination

Salt and freshly ground black pepper

VARIATION

Roast Asparagus with Soy and Sesame
Omit the bread and cheese. Use 1 tablespoon peanut oil in place of the olive oil or butter. Halfway through the roasting, add 1 tablespoon soy sauce to the asparagus. Top with about 2 tablespoons sesame seeds; run under the broiler until they begin to pop, about 1 minute. Finish with a sprinkling of soy sauce, just a teaspoon or two.

1. Preheat the oven to 500°F; while it's preheating, put the bread in there and check it frequently until it is lightly toasted and dry. Coarsely grind or grate the bread and cheese together (a small food processor is perfect for this)—if possible, keep the crumbs from becoming as fine as commercial bread crumbs.

2. Rinse the asparagus and break off the woody ends. Lay them in a baking dish that will accommodate them in two or three layers. Toss with bits of the butter and/or oil, sprinkle lightly with salt and pepper, and put in the oven.

3. Roast for 5 minutes, then shake the pan to redistribute the butter or oil. Roast for another 5 minutes, then test the asparagus for doneness by piercing a spear with the point of a sharp knife; it is done when the knife enters the asparagus but still meets a little resistance.

You can prepare the recipe in advance up to this point up to a couple of hours before serving; allow the asparagus to sit at room temperature during that time.

4. Turn on the broiler and put the rack as close as possible to the heating element. Sprinkle the asparagus with the crumbs and carefully brown the top—it will take only a minute or two. Serve the asparagus hot or at room temperature.

GRILLED ASPARAGUS
WITH LEMON DRESSING
MAKES 4 SERVINGS   TIME: 20 MINUTES

VARIATION
You could serve these grilled asparagus with any of the vinaigrettes on page 304 in lieu of the lemon-shallot-parsley mixture here. If you were serving them as part of an Asian-themed meal, you might swap out the dressing in this recipe for Soy-Ginger Dressing: Combine $1/4$ cup soy sauce with $1/2$ teaspoon minced garlic, 1 teaspoon minced peeled fresh ginger, $1/2$ teaspoon sugar, 2 teaspoons rice or other mild vinegar, and a few drops of sesame oil. Serve over the asparagus.

THIS PREPARATION FAVORS thick spears of asparagus, which become tender and remain moist inside while their exteriors char. Those that weigh an ounce or two each—that is, eight to sixteen per pound—are the best. The only difference between thick and pencil asparagus is that thick asparagus must be peeled before cooking to remove the relatively tough skin; use a vegetable peeler or paring knife.

$1^1/2$ to 2 pounds thick asparagus
About 2 tablespoons olive oil
Salt and freshly ground black
   pepper

Juice of 3 lemons
2 tablespoons minced shallot or
   scallion
$1/4$ cup minced fresh parsley

1. Snap off the woody ends of the asparagus; most spears will break naturally an inch or two above the bottom. Peel the stalks up to the flower bud. Meanwhile, start a grill or preheat a cast-iron or other heavy skillet over medium-high heat until it smokes.

2. To grill the asparagus, toss them with about 1 tablespoon of the oil, mixing with your hands until they're coated. Season well with salt and pepper to taste. Grill until tender and browned in spots, turning once or twice, a total of 5 to 10 minutes.

3. To pan-grill the asparagus, do not oil or season them. Just toss them in the hot skillet and cook, turning the individual spears as they brown, until tender, 5 to 10 minutes. Remove as they finish and season with salt and pepper.

4. Mix together the lemon juice and shallot, then stir in enough olive oil to add a little body and take the edge off the sharpness of the lemon; the mixture should still be quite strong. Season it with salt and plenty of black pepper and stir in the parsley. Serve the asparagus hot or at room temperature with grilled or broiled swordfish, monkfish, or other sturdy fish. Spoon the sauce over all.

ROSEMARY-LEMON WHITE BEAN DIP

MAKES 4 SERVINGS

TIME: 10 MINUTES (WITH PRECOOKED OR CANNED BEANS)

LIKE MOST BEAN DISHES, this puree is best if you use freshly cooked dried beans, but it is still good with canned beans. One-quarter pound of dried beans will yield about one cup, the amount needed for this recipe, although you can double the quantities if you like. If you use dried beans, cook them in unsalted water to cover (presoaking is unnecessary), with a couple of bay leaves, until very tender. If you use canned beans, you'll need almost a full fifteen-ounce can to get one cup (there's a lot of water in those cans).

2 cups cooked cannellini or other white beans, drained but quite moist

2 garlic cloves, peeled

Salt and freshly ground black pepper

$^1/_4$ cup extra virgin olive oil

1 tablespoon minced fresh rosemary

Grated zest of 1 lemon

1. Put the beans in a food processor with the garlic and a healthy pinch of salt. Turn the machine on and add half the olive oil in a steady stream through the feed tube; process until the mixture is smooth.

2. Put the mixture in a bowl and use a wooden spoon to beat in the rosemary, lemon zest, and remaining olive oil. Taste and add salt and pepper as needed. Use immediately or refrigerate for up to 3 days.

GREEN BEANS AND TOMATOES

MAKES 4 SERVINGS

TIME: AT LEAST 1 HOUR, LARGELY UNATTENDED

THIS DISH OF slow-cooked green beans yields soft and sweet beans. It is a perfect side dish for a midwinter meal because it does not depend on sun-ripened tomatoes or crisp just-picked beans for its appeal.

2 tablespoons extra virgin olive oil

1 pound green beans, trimmed

1 pint cherry or grape tomatoes, washed

Salt and freshly ground black pepper

1. Put 1 tablespoon of the olive oil in a large skillet and turn the heat to high. Add the beans and cook, undisturbed, until they begin to brown a little on the bottom. Add the tomatoes, turn the heat to low, and cover. Cook for about an hour, stirring occasionally, until the beans are very tender. (You can cook even more slowly if you like, or cook until done, turn off the heat, and reheat gently just before serving.)

2. Season with salt and pepper and stir in the remaining olive oil. Serve hot or at room temperature.

BEET ROESTI WITH ROSEMARY

MAKES 4 TO 6 SERVINGS   TIME: 30 MINUTES

THIS THICK BEET PANCAKE, cooked slowly on both sides until the beet sugars caramelize, sports a crunchy, sweet crust that, I swear, is reminiscent of crème brûlée. It must be cooked in a nonstick skillet, preferably a twelve-inch one (if you have only a ten-inch skillet, use only one and a half pounds of beets and the same quantity of the other ingredients), over moderate heat: too-high heat and too-quick cooking will burn the sugary exterior of the pancake while leaving the inside raw.

Remember that beets bleed, so it is wise to peel them over the sink and wash the grater or food processor as soon as you're done with it.

2 pounds beets (about 3 very large or 4 to 6 medium)

2 teaspoons coarsely chopped fresh rosemary

Salt and freshly ground black pepper

1/2 cup flour

2 tablespoons butter or olive oil

Minced fresh parsley or a few rosemary leaves for garnish

1. Trim the beets and peel them as you would potatoes; grate them in a food processor or by hand. Begin preheating a 12-inch nonstick skillet over medium heat.

2. Toss the grated beets in a bowl with the chopped rosemary, salt, and pepper. Add about half the flour; toss well, add the rest of the flour, then toss again.

3. Put the butter in the skillet and heat until it begins to turn nut-brown. Scrape the beet mixture into the skillet and press it down with a spatula to form a round. With the heat at medium to medium-high—the pancake should be sizzling gently—cook, shaking the pan occasionally, until the bottom of the beet cake is nicely crisp, 8 to 10 minutes. Slide the cake out onto a plate, top with another plate, invert the two plates, and return the cake to the pan. Continue to cook, adjusting the heat if necessary, until the second side is browned, another 10 minutes or so. Garnish, cut into wedges, and serve hot or at room temperature.

STEAMED BROCCOLI
WITH BEURRE NOISETTE

MAKES 4 SERVINGS   TIME: 30 MINUTES

BEURRE NOISETTE IS BROWNED, or nut-colored, butter, a French classic that fully qualifies as a sauce yet contains only one ingredient. If you've never had it, beurre noisette's complex flavor and beguiling aroma, redolent of hazelnuts, will amaze you. And if you like it over broccoli, you'll probably find that you like it over almost any other sturdy, full-flavored vegetable.

1 pound broccoli

3 tablespoons butter

Salt and freshly ground black
   pepper

$1/2$ to 1 tablespoon fresh lemon
   juice

1. Trim the broccoli as necessary (the thick stems should be peeled with a vegetable peeler or paring knife to make them less tough). Cut into equal-size pieces.

2. Put the butter in a small saucepan over medium heat. Cook, swirling the pan occasionally, until the butter stops foaming and begins to brown. Remove from the heat immediately and season lightly with salt and pepper; keep warm if necessary.

3. Steam the broccoli over boiling water (or boil in salted water to cover) until tender and bright green, usually less than 10 minutes. Drain if necessary and sprinkle with salt. (Or run under cold water and refrigerate. To reheat, put a little olive oil or butter in a pan over medium heat and turn the broccoli in it until hot.) Swirl the lemon juice into the beurre noisette and drizzle it over the broccoli; serve immediately.

GLAZED CARROTS

MAKES 4 SERVINGS   TIME: ABOUT 30 MINUTES

THIS IS MY favorite way of making a side of carrots to go with a meal. Part of its appeal is its ease and quickness; the other is how easy it is to vary. You can add almost any flavoring you like to these carrots during their final minutes in the pan, like a healthy grating of lemon or orange zest or a tablespoon of grated ginger or a clove of minced garlic, to flavor them to your taste.

1 pound carrots, cut into chunks
Salt
2 tablespoons butter

Chopped parsley, chervil, or mint
for garnish (optional)

1. Put the carrots in a saucepan with a pinch of salt and water to come about halfway up their height. Add the butter, cover the pan, and turn the heat to medium-high. Simmer until the carrots are nearly tender, about 20 minutes.

2. Uncover; much of the water will have evaporated. Continue to cook until the carrots are shiny, about 5 minutes longer; if they threaten to burn, add a tablespoon or two of water. When the carrots are done, taste and adjust the seasoning if necessary, garnish if you like, and serve.

CAULIFLOWER WITH GARLIC AND ANCHOVY

MAKES 4 SERVINGS   TIME: ABOUT 30 MINUTES

BUY SNOW-WHITE cauliflower with no brown spots; use broccoli or one of the hybrids (broccoflower, romanesco broccoli, and so on) if the cauliflower does not look good. And though it is a full-flavored dish, remember that cooking will mellow the assertive flavors of the anchovies and garlic, so don't skimp on either. This dish is just as good warm as it is hot.

1 large head of cauliflower (at least 2 pounds), trimmed and cut or broken into florets

Salt

1/4 cup plus 2 tablespoons extra virgin olive oil

5 to 10 anchovy fillets, to taste, chopped

1 tablespoon minced garlic

1 teaspoon hot red pepper flakes, or to taste (optional)

Minced fresh parsley for garnish

1. Put the cauliflower in a steamer above an inch or two of salted water. Cover and cook until it is just tender, about 10 minutes, then plunge into a bowl of ice water to stop the cooking.

2. Combine the oil, anchovies, garlic, and hot pepper if you're using it in a large, deep skillet and turn the heat to medium-low. Cook, stirring occasionally, until the anchovies begin to break up and the garlic begins to color, about 5 minutes.

3. Add the cauliflower and raise the heat to medium-high. Continue to cook, stirring, for about 5 minutes more, until the cauliflower is coated with oil and heated through. Garnish and serve hot or at room temperature.

ANCHOVIES

ANCHOVIES COME IN three forms: canned, paste, and salted. Canned are most familiar and a nearly ideal convenience food. It's worth pointing out that you want to buy those packed in olive oil, never soy or cottonseed; the ingredients should read "anchovies, olive oil, salt"—no more.

Anchovy paste is marginally more convenient.

But it's more than twice as expensive by weight as canned anchovies, and it often contains cream, butter, preservatives, and other unnecessary ingredients. Salted anchovies, which are sold in bulk in Italian markets from a large can or bucket, are delicious, but a hassle: before using them, you must rinse them and peel each fillet off the skeleton.

GRILLED CORN

MAKES 4 SERVINGS   TIME: 20 MINUTES

DURING THE SUMMER, rushing home with a bag of farmstand corn—which you can get in almost any part of the country—and cooking it out on the grill is a real treat. But if you can't find locally grown, just-picked corn, you shouldn't count yourself out of the fun—new breeds of corn retain their sweetness very well. Even if you are buying your corn from the supermarket, just remember that it declines in sweetness as it ages, so it will be best to cook it as soon as possible after you bring it home.

If your fire is raging hot, remove the inner silks from the corn and grill them in their husks. But if it's in the normal range, grill the shucked corn directly over the fire. Ideally, some of the kernels will brown and even char.

4 ears fresh corn
Melted butter (optional)

Salt and freshly ground black pepper

1. Start a grill. Shuck the corn.
2. Grill or roast the corn, turning occasionally. When some of the kernels char a bit and others are lightly browned—5 to 15 minutes, depending on the heat of the grill—the corn is done. Brush with melted butter if you like and serve with salt and pepper.

———————————————

GRILLED EGGPLANT DIP

MAKES 4 SERVINGS   TIME: ABOUT 1 HOUR

GRILLING IS AN important part of this dish, as it gives the eggplant a smoky flavor that's hard to come by otherwise. Serve this dip with grilled flatbreads or slices of baguette, or pitas.

1 medium or 2 small eggplants (about 1 pound)

2 tablespoons fresh lemon juice

2 tablespoons extra virgin olive oil

Pinch of minced garlic, or more to taste

Salt and freshly ground black pepper

Minced fresh parsley for garnish

1. Start a grill; pierce the eggplant in several places with a thin-bladed knife or skewer. Grill, turning occasionally, until the eggplant collapses and the skin blackens, 15 to 30 minutes, depending on size. Remove and cool.

2. When the eggplant is cool enough to handle, part the skin (if it hasn't split on its own), scoop out the flesh, and finely mince it. Mix it with the lemon juice, oil, garlic, salt, and pepper. Taste and adjust the seasonings, then garnish and serve.

======

ENDIVES BRAISED IN BROTH WITH PARMESAN

MAKES 4 SERVINGS   TIME: 40 MINUTES

GROWN INDOORS IN the dark, endives are among the perfect winter vegetables, usually used in salads but also lovely when cooked. This simple gratin benefits from good, dark stock, but the addition of Parmigiano-Reggiano will cover you if you resort to canned stock.

4 whole Belgian endives

1 cup good-quality stock

Salt and freshly ground black pepper

$^1/_4$ cup freshly grated Parmigiano-Reggiano cheese

1. Remove just a couple of the outer leaves from each of the endives; rinse them and put them in a skillet in one layer. Add the stock and sprinkle with salt and pepper. Cover and cook over medium heat until tender, 20 to 30 minutes. Preheat the broiler.

2. Cover the endives with the cheese and run under the broiler, just long enough to slightly brown the cheese. Serve with a slotted spoon.

FENNEL WITH OLIVE OIL DIPPING SAUCE

MAKES 4 SERVINGS   TIME: 15 MINUTES

FENNEL REMAINS EXOTIC enough to be a treat for many people, and this simple preparation simply elevates its stature a bit. Trim and discard the hard, hollow stalks that jut out from the top of the bulb; if you get your hands on a bulb with its fronds still attached, roughly chop them and add them to the hot oil with the garlic.

$1/4$ cup olive oil

1 garlic clove, peeled and lightly crushed

Salt and freshly ground black pepper

Zest of $1/2$ lemon, minced

$1/2$ fennel bulb, trimmed and cut into strips

1. Combine half the olive oil with the garlic in a small saucepan and turn the heat to medium-low. Cook, shaking the pan occasionally, until the garlic begins to sizzle. Remove the garlic from the oil and the pan from the heat.

2. Add the cold oil to the hot, along with salt, pepper, and lemon zest. Serve the fennel with the dipping sauce.

FENNEL GRATIN

MAKES 4 SERVINGS   TIME: 20 MINUTES

THIS IS AN almost universal technique for vegetables, an honest, simple gratin with a topping of just a couple of ingredients. Since one of them is rich, flavorful blue cheese, butter isn't even included. My vegetable of choice here is fennel—an underappreciated and almost always available bulb—but you could put this topping on almost any vegetable. For the cheese, you can use Gorgonzola, the soft Italian cheese; bleu d'Auvergne, a mild cheese from France; Maytag blue, the premier domestic variety; Stilton, the classic English blue; or Roquefort, which is made from sheep's milk. All are good, but my preferences are for the stronger cheeses, such as Roquefort and Maytag.

1 fennel bulb (about 1 pound) $1/4$ cup crumbled blue cheese
$1/2$ cup coarse bread crumbs   Freshly ground black pepper

1. Preheat the oven to 400°F. Bring a pot of water to a boil.
2. Trim the fennel, then cut it into about $1/4$-inch-thick slices and cook in the boiling water until just tender, less than 5 minutes. Drain and layer in the shallow baking dish. (You can also drain the vegetables, then stop their cooking by plunging them into ice water, then drain again. In this manner you can finish the cooking up to a day or two later; increase the baking time to 20 minutes.)
3. Top the fennel with the bread crumbs, then with the cheese; season all with pepper to taste (hold off on salt, because the cheese is salty). Put in the oven until the cheese melts, about 10 minutes.
4. Run the baking dish under the broiler until the top browns, checking every 30 seconds. Serve hot or at room temperature.

FIGS STUFFED WITH GOAT CHEESE

MAKES 4 SERVINGS   TIME: 15 MINUTES

FALL IS THE time for fresh figs, which people who live in Mediterranean climates (including many Californians) take for granted but which are a real treat for the rest of us. Fresh figs may be green or dark purple; color does not affect flavor (ripeness and variety do), but most people perceive purple figs as more attractive. This is obviously a fruit dish, but the fruit functions like a vegetable in this preparation.

3 to 4 ounces soft fresh goat cheese

1 tablespoon good-quality balsamic vinegar

12 fresh figs

1. Use your fingers to roll the goat cheese into 24 small balls, each $1/2$ inch or less in diameter. Put them on a plate and drizzle with the vinegar. Shake the plate gently to coat the cheese balls evenly.
2. Cut the figs in half and press a cheese ball into the center of each. As the figs are stuffed, return them, stuffed side up, to the plate where the cheese was marinating. Serve within an hour.

COOL COOKED GREENS WITH LEMON

MAKES 4 SERVINGS   TIME: 20 MINUTES

A CLASSIC PREPARATION, useful year-round, and especially convenient when you want to cook the greens in advance.

Salt and freshly ground black pepper

2 pounds dark leafy greens, like collards, kale, or spinach

Several tablespoons extra virgin olive oil

2 lemons, cut in half

1. Bring a large pot of water to a boil and salt it. Trim the greens of any stems thicker than $^1/_4$ inch; discard them. Wash the greens well.

2. Simmer the greens until tender, just a minute or two for spinach, up to 10 minutes or even longer for older, tougher greens. Drain them well and cool them quickly by running them under cold water.

3. Squeeze the greens dry and chop them. (You may prepare the salad in advance up to this point; cover and refrigerate for up to a day, then bring to room temperature before proceeding.) Sprinkle with olive oil, salt, and pepper, and serve with lemon halves.

STIR-FRIED LEEKS WITH GINGER

MAKES 4 SERVINGS   TIME: 30 MINUTES

A BIG DEAL is often made of washing leeks—they can be very sandy— but since you're going to be chopping these, it's easy.

2 large leeks (about 1 $^1/_2$ pounds)

2 tablespoons peanut or olive oil

2 tablespoons minced peeled fresh ginger

Salt and freshly ground black pepper

1 $^1/_2$ teaspoons soy sauce

1. Cut off the last couple of inches of dark green leaves, those without any pale green core, from the leeks. Then stand each leek up on its tail and use a sharp knife to "shave" the remaining bits of tough, dark green leaves off the stalk. When only white and pale green leaves remain, cut off the root, slice the leeks in half (or, if they're large, into quarters), and chop them roughly. Then wash in a salad spinner (or a colander inserted into a large bowl) until no traces of sand remain.

2. Put the oil in a large skillet, preferably nonstick, and turn the heat to high. When a bit of smoke appears, add the leeks, all at once. Let sit for a couple of minutes, then cook, stirring only occasionally, for about 10 minutes.

3. When the leeks dry out and begin to brown, sprinkle with the ginger. Cook, stirring for 2 or 3 minutes, then add some salt (just a little) and pepper, along with the soy sauce. Taste and adjust the seasoning, then serve.

―――――――――

PORCINI-SCENTED "WILD" MUSHROOM SAUTÉ

MAKES 4 SERVINGS   TIME: 30 MINUTES

HOW TO GET great flavor out of ordinary white mushrooms? Add a handful of dried porcini. You will not believe the difference.

$1/2$ cup dried porcini

$1/4$ cup extra virgin olive oil

1 pound button mushrooms, trimmed and sliced

Salt and freshly ground black pepper

1 teaspoon minced garlic

2 tablespoons minced fresh parsley

1. Pour boiling water over the porcini to reconstitute; let them sit for about 10 minutes, or until tender, then drain and trim off any hard spots.

2. Put the olive oil in a large skillet over high heat; a minute later, add the porcini and button mushrooms, along with a big pinch of salt and some pepper, and cook, stirring occasionally, until the mushrooms give off most of their liquid and begin to brown, about 10 minutes. Turn the heat to medium-low and add the garlic. Continue to cook for a few more minutes, until the mixture is tender and glossy. Taste and adjust the seasoning, stir in the parsley, and serve hot or warm.

DRIED MUSHROOMS

THE BEST-TASTING dried mushrooms are dried porcini (also called *cèpes*), which have come down about 50 percent in price over the last few years. Try to find dried porcini sold in bulk, not in tiny little packages of less than an ounce each (these are a complete rip-off). If you live in a big city, a major Italian or specialty food market will have them; otherwise, you can find good sources on the Internet. I usually buy about a pound at a time, which usually costs about fifty bucks and lasts me a couple of years.

SAUTÉED SHIITAKE MUSHROOMS

MAKES 4 SERVINGS   TIME: ABOUT 20 MINUTES

I KNOW PORTOBELLO mushrooms are all the rage, but shiitakes are the closest thing you can find to wild mushrooms without going to a specialist. To me, they are invaluable, and prepared this simple, traditional way, they are spectacular. If you do happen to have some chanterelle, morel, or other wild mushrooms on hand, this is an excellent way to cook them.

1/4 cup extra virgin olive oil

1 pound shiitake mushrooms, trimmed of their stems (which can be reserved for stock but are too tough to eat) and sliced

Salt and freshly ground black pepper

1 teaspoon minced garlic or 2 tablespoons chopped shallot

Chopped fresh parsley for garnish (optional)

1. Put the olive oil in a large skillet over medium heat. When it is hot, add the mushrooms, then some salt and pepper. Cook, stirring occasionally, until tender, 10 to 15 minutes.

2. Add the garlic or shallot and turn the heat to high. Cook, stirring occasionally, until the mushrooms begin to brown and become crisp at the edges. Taste and adjust the seasoning if necessary, garnish with the parsley if you like, and serve hot or at room temperature.

GARLIC-MUSHROOM FLAN

MAKES 4 SERVINGS   TIME: 40 MINUTES

WE USUALLY THINK of custards as desserts, but they may be savory as well, and in that form they make luxurious starters or light, flavorful main courses. Custards like garlic flan are often served in top restaurants, but the simplicity and ease of this preparation makes them good options for home cooks. Here's one with a surprise in it: cooked shiitakes. It will be a hit.

1 tablespoon butter
1 teaspoon minced garlic
1/2 cup thinly sliced shiitake
    mushroom caps

Salt and freshly ground black
    pepper
1 1/2 cups chicken or beef stock
4 eggs

1. Put the butter in a small saucepan over medium heat. Add the garlic and mushrooms and cook, stirring occasionally and sprinkling with salt and pepper, until the garlic is fragrant and the mushrooms begin to soften, just 5 minutes or so. Stir the mixture into the stock.

2. Beat the eggs lightly and combine with the stock mixture. Put about an inch of water in a baking pan or skillet just large enough to hold four 6-ounce ramekins and turn the heat to high. When the water boils, turn the heat to low, pour the egg mixture into the ramekins, and put the ramekins in the water. Cover tightly with foil and/or a lid.

3. Simmer for 15 to 20 minutes, then check; the moment the custards are set—they should still be quite jiggly—remove them from the water. Serve hot or at room temperature.

MARINATED OLIVES

MAKES 4 SERVINGS   TIME: 1 HOUR, LARGELY UNATTENDED

THE EASE WITH which this dish can be thrown together and the range of meals it happily accompanies (menus with European, Middle Eastern, or Northern African accents are game, as are good old American cookouts) guarantee that it makes regular and frequent appearances on my dinner table.

An assortment of olives is far preferable to just one kind. Try, for example, some oil cured, some big fat green Sicilians, and some Kalamatas—just that simple combination will look bright and pretty. If you can lay your hands on more varieties, so much the better.

2 cups assorted olives

4 garlic cloves, peeled and lightly
   crushed

2 tablespoons extra virgin olive oil

1 teaspoon fresh rosemary leaves

1 small lemon, cut in half and
   segmented like a grapefruit

1. Toss all the ingredients together in a bowl. Marinate for an hour or longer at room temperature.

2. After the first day, refrigerate, then remove from the refrigerator an hour or two before serving. These will keep for weeks.

ROASTED PEPPERS

MAKES 4 SERVINGS

TIME: ABOUT $1\frac{1}{2}$ HOURS, LARGELY UNATTENDED

ROASTING GIVES AMAZING depth to vegetables, especially peppers. The simplest way to serve these is to drizzle them with extra virgin olive oil, along with some salt and pepper, but you can also add a few drops of vinegar. The next step is to garnish with anchovies, capers, and/or herbs.

4 large red bell peppers (about 2
    pounds)
Salt and freshly ground black
    pepper

2 tablespoons extra virgin olive oil

1. Preheat the oven to 500°F. Line a roasting pan with enough foil to later fold over the top. Put the peppers in the pan and the pan in the oven. Roast, turning the peppers about every 10 minutes, until the peppers collapse, about 40 minutes.

2. Fold the foil over the peppers and allow them to cool. Work over a bowl and remove the core, skin, and seeds from each of the peppers. It's okay if the peppers naturally fall into strips during this process. Sprinkle with salt, pepper, and olive oil and serve at room temperature. (You can refrigerate these, tightly wrapped or covered, for a few days; bring to room temperature before serving.)

GRILLED RED PEPPERS WITH OLIVE OIL AND SHERRY VINEGAR

MAKES 4 SERVINGS   TIME: 30 MINUTES

THE STANDARD GRILLED pepper should be a part of every home cook's repertoire. They're a perfect accompaniment to nearly any simply grilled dish. Feel free to use a mix of yellow, orange, and red bell peppers if it appeals to you.

4 red bell peppers
2 tablespoons extra virgin olive oil
1 tablespoon sherry vinegar
1 tablespoon drained capers
    (optional)

Salt and freshly ground black
    pepper

1. Start a grill or preheat the broiler; put the rack about 4 inches from the heat source. When the fire is hot, put the peppers directly over the heat. Grill, turning as each side blackens, until they collapse, about 15 minutes. Wrap in foil and cool until you can handle them, then remove the skin, seeds, and stems. You will inevitably shred them in this process, and that's fine.

2. Drizzle the peppers with the olive oil and vinegar, then sprinkle with the capers if you like and some pepper. Taste and add salt if necessary, then serve.

CANAPÉS WITH PIQUILLO PEPPERS AND ANCHOVIES

MAKES 4 SERVINGS   TIME: 20 MINUTES

PIQUILLO PEPPERS ARE wood-roasted peppers from Spain, sold in cans or jars. If you cannot find them, substitute homemade roasted peppers or canned "pimientos."

Eight thick slices (roughly $^3/_4$ inch) French or Italian bread, cut in half

1 teaspoon minced garlic

8 piquillo peppers, cut in half, or 4 or 5 roasted peppers (page 234)

16 anchovies

Extra virgin olive oil

Lightly toast the bread. Top each piece with a tiny bit of garlic, then layer with a piece of piquillo and an anchovy. Drizzle with a little anchovy oil and/or olive oil. Serve within an hour.

ROAST NEW POTATOES WITH ROSEMARY

MAKES 4 TO 6 SERVINGS   TIME: 45 MINUTES

TREAT NEW POTATOES simply, using what little work you need to do to highlight their fresh and full potato flavor. I like to use heartier herbs, like rosemary, lavender, or thyme, to flavor roasted potatoes.

This preparation is classic and easy, as long as you remember it's better to overcook the potatoes than undercook them.

2 pounds new potatoes, the smaller the better, washed and dried

2 tablespoons extra virgin olive oil

1 scant tablespoon fresh rosemary leaves or 1 teaspoon dried

8 garlic cloves (optional)

Salt and freshly ground black pepper

1. Preheat the oven to 425°F. Put the potatoes in an ovenproof casserole or saucepan and toss with all the remaining ingredients. Cover and roast, shaking the pan occasionally, until the potatoes are tender, 30 to 45 minutes.

2. Uncover, stir once or twice, and serve.

NEW POTATOES WITH BUTTER AND MINT

MAKES 4 SERVINGS   TIME: 40 MINUTES

TO SEASON BOILED POTATOES, I like to use delicate herbs like mint, tarragon, or parsley. Mint makes a huge difference here, countering the potatoes' earthiness with its bright flavor.

About 2 pounds waxy new potatoes, the smaller the better

Salt

Several fresh mint sprigs

2 tablespoons butter, or more to taste

Minced fresh mint for garnish

1. Put the potatoes in a pot with salted water to cover; bring to a boil over high heat. Add the mint and turn the heat down to medium. Cook at a gentle boil until the potatoes are nice and tender, 20 to 40 minutes, depending on their size.

2. Drain the potatoes and return them to the pot over the lowest heat possible. Add the butter and cook, shaking the pan occasionally, until all traces of moisture have disappeared, about 5 minutes. Garnish and serve hot.

FAST POTATO GRATIN

MAKES 4 SERVINGS   TIME: 40 MINUTES

THIS IS A fast method for producing a delicious potato gratin. I discovered it accidentally, and it's since become a personal favorite.

2 pounds all-purpose potatoes,
    peeled and thinly sliced
Salt and freshly ground black pepper
1 teaspoon minced garlic or a
    grating of nutmeg (optional)

2 tablespoons butter
3 cups half-and-half or milk, or
    more

1. Layer the potatoes in a large nonstick ovenproof skillet or roasting pan, sprinkling salt and pepper and, if you like, garlic or nutmeg between the layers. Dot with the butter, then add enough half-and-half or milk to come about three-quarters of the way to the top. Preheat the oven to 400°F.

2. Turn the heat under the potatoes to high and bring to a boil. Turn the heat to medium-high and cook for about 10 minutes, or until the level of both liquid and potatoes has subsided somewhat. Put in the oven and cook, undisturbed, until the top is nicely browned, about 10 minutes. Turn the oven heat down to 300°F and continue cooking un-

til the potatoes are tender (a thin-bladed knife will pierce them with little or no resistance), about 10 minutes more. Serve immediately or keep warm in the oven or over very low heat for up to 30 minutes.

MASHED POTATOES

MAKES 4 SERVINGS   TIME: ABOUT 40 MINUTES

MASHED POTATOES ARE easy to make. If you like them lumpy, mash them with a fork or potato masher; if you like them creamy, use a food mill or ricer. If you like them lean, omit the butter and substitute some of the potato-cooking water for the milk.

2 pounds baking potatoes, like
    Idaho or russet, peeled and cut
    into quarters
Salt and freshly ground black
    pepper

3 tablespoons butter
$^3/_4$ cup milk, gently warmed

1. Boil the potatoes in salted water to cover until soft, about 30 minutes.
2. When the potatoes are done, drain them, then mash them well or put them through a food mill. Return them to the pot over very low heat and stir in the butter and—gradually—the milk, beating with a wooden spoon until smooth and creamy. Season with salt and pepper. Serve immediately, keep warm, or reheat in a microwave.

PAN-CRISPED POTATOES

MAKES 4 SERVINGS   TIME: 45 MINUTES

THE LATE, GREAT Pierre Franey—author of *The 60-Minute Gourmet*—showed me how to make these twenty years ago (of course he used butter), and I have been making them weekly ever since.

2 pounds waxy red or white potatoes, peeled and cut into $1/2$- to 1-inch cubes	Salt and freshly ground black pepper
	$1/4$ cup olive oil, more or less
	1 teaspoon minced garlic

1. Bring the potatoes to a boil in salted water to cover, then lower the heat to simmer until nearly tender, 10 to 15 minutes. Drain well.

2. Heat the oil over medium-high heat in a 12-inch nonstick skillet for 3 or 4 minutes. You can use more oil for crisper potatoes or less oil to cut the fat. (You can also use butter or a combination if you prefer.) Add the potatoes along with a healthy sprinkling of salt and pepper and cook, tossing and stirring from time to time (not constantly), until they are nicely browned all over, 10 to 20 minutes.

3. Add the garlic and continue to cook for 5 minutes more, stirring frequently. Taste and adjust the seasoning if necessary, then serve.

―――――――――――

QUICK SCALLION PANCAKES

MAKES 4 SERVINGS   TIME: ABOUT 30 MINUTES

THESE ARE SIMPLER than traditional scallion pancakes, which are made from a breadlike dough, and they taste more like scallions, because the "liquid" is scallion puree. The flavor is great, the preparation time is cut to about twenty minutes, and the texture is that of a vegetable fritter.

Salt and freshly ground black
    pepper
4 bunches of scallions (about
    1 pound)
1 egg

1 teaspoon soy sauce
1/2 cup flour
Peanut, corn, or olive oil as
    needed

VARIATIONS
The same method can be
used to make pancakes
with many members of the
onion family, especially
shallots and spring onions
(which look like scallions on
steroids). Or add:
• About 1 tablespoon
toasted sesame seeds
• About 2 tablespoons
roughly chopped peanuts
• About 1/4 cup minced
chives, added along with
the uncooked scallions
• A tablespoon or so
minced peeled fresh ginger

1. Bring a pot of salted water to a boil while you trim the scallions.
Roughly chop about three-quarters of them and mince the remainder.
2. Add the larger portion of scallions to the water and cook for about
5 minutes, or until tender. Drain, reserving about 1/2 cup of the cooking liquid. Puree the cooked scallions in a blender, adding just enough
of the cooking liquid to allow the machine to do its work.
3. Mix the puree with the egg and soy sauce, then gently stir in the
flour until blended; add pepper and the reserved minced scallions.
Film a nonstick or well-seasoned skillet with oil and turn the heat to
medium-high. Drop the batter by the tablespoon or 1/4 cup and cook
the pancakes for about 2 minutes per side, or until lightly browned. If
necessary, the pancakes can be kept warm in a 200°F oven for about
30 minutes.

TENDER SPINACH AND
CRISP SHALLOTS

MAKES 4 SERVINGS   TIME: 30 MINUTES

THERE ARE A number of ways to make simple dishes of greens more
appealing. Among my favorites is to prepare a topping of crisp-fried
shallots. By themselves, these are irresistible; when combined with tender greens they create an alluring contrast in flavor and texture. Furthermore, the oil in which the shallots have been fried is a great addition to
the greens and, in the days following, to many other dishes.

1/2 cup or more neutral oil, like grapeseed or corn

5 large shallots (1/2 pound or more), thinly sliced

Salt and freshly ground black pepper

1 pound spinach

1. Put the oil in a small to medium saucepan or narrow skillet at least an inch deep. Turn the heat to high and wait a few minutes; the oil should reach 350°F. (If you do not have a frying thermometer, just put a couple of slices of shallot in there; when the oil around them bubbles vigorously, it's ready.)

2. Add the shallots and cook, adjusting the heat so that the bubbling is vigorous but not explosive. Cook, stirring, until the shallots begin to darken, 8 to 12 minutes. As soon as they turn golden brown, remove them immediately with a slotted spoon—be careful, because overcooking at this point will burn the shallots. Drain the shallots on paper towels and sprinkle with salt and pepper; they'll keep for a couple of hours this way.

3. Meanwhile, bring a large pot of water to a boil and salt it. When it is ready, add the spinach and cook until it wilts, about 1 minute. Remove the spinach with a strainer or slotted spoon and plunge it into a large bowl filled with ice water to stop the cooking. When it's cool, drain and chop. (You can store the spinach, covered and refrigerated, for up to a couple of days if you like.)

4. Take 1 tablespoon of the shallot oil and place it in a skillet; turn the heat to medium-high. Turn the spinach into this skillet and cook, stirring frequently and breaking up any clumps, until the spinach is hot, about 5 minutes. Season with salt and pepper and serve, topped with the crisp shallots.

CURRIED TOFU WITH SOY SAUCE

MAKES 4 SERVINGS   TIME: 30 MINUTES

GIVEN THAT TOFU itself does not add much body to a dish, you need a substantial sauce, like one with canned coconut milk as its base, to make up for the tofu's blandness. Like heavy cream, coconut milk will thicken a sauce, making it luxurious in almost no time.

The onion must be browned carefully and thoroughly: keep the heat high enough so that this happens in a timely fashion—it should take about ten minutes and in no case more than fifteen—but not so high that the onion burns. I call this level of heat "medium-high," but all stoves are different; the oil should be bubbling but not smoking, and you must stir the onion every minute or so.

2 tablespoons peanut, corn, or grapeseed oil

1 large onion, minced

1 tablespoon curry powder, or to taste

1 cup roughly chopped walnuts or unsalted cashews

One 12- to 14-ounce can unsweetened coconut milk

1 block firm tofu (about 1 pound), cut into roughly $3/4$-inch cubes

2 tablespoons soy sauce, or to taste

Salt and cayenne

1. Put the oil in a 10- or 12-inch nonstick skillet over medium-high heat. A minute later, add the onion and cook, stirring occasionally, until the edges of the onion pieces are well browned, about 10 minutes (for best flavor, the onions must brown but not burn). Add the curry powder and cook, stirring, for 30 seconds or so; add the nuts and cook, stirring occasionally, for about a minute.

2. Add the coconut milk. Stir, bring to a boil, and reduce the heat to medium. Add the tofu, stir, and let the tofu heat through for about 3 minutes. Stir in the soy sauce, then taste and adjust the seasoning with soy sauce, salt, and/or cayenne as necessary. Serve.

SIMMERED TOFU WITH GROUND PORK
(MA-PO TOFU)

MAKES 4 SERVINGS   TIME: 20 MINUTES

THIS IS NOT a stir-fry but a simmered dish, easy and fast. The cooking time totals about ten minutes, and the preparation time is about the same, so be sure to start the rice first.

1 tablespoon peanut or other oil

1 tablespoon minced garlic

1 tablespoon minced peeled fresh
    ginger

$^1/_8$ teaspoon hot red pepper flakes,
    or to taste

$^1/_4$ pound ground pork

$^1/_2$ cup chopped scallion, green
    part only

$^1/_2$ cup stock or water

1 pound soft or silken tofu, cut into
    $^1/_2$-inch cubes

2 tablespoons soy sauce

Salt

Minced fresh cilantro for garnish
    (optional)

1. Put the oil in a deep 12-inch skillet or wok, preferably nonstick, over medium-high heat. A minute later, add the garlic, ginger, and hot pepper and cook just until they begin to sizzle, less than a minute. Add the pork and stir to break it up; cook, stirring occasionally, until it loses most of its pink color.

2. Add the scallion and stir; add the stock. Cook for a minute or so, scraping the bottom of the pan with a wooden spoon if necessary to loosen any stuck bits of meat, then add the tofu. Cook, stirring once or twice, until the tofu is heated through, about 2 minutes.

3. Stir in the soy sauce, taste, and add salt and hot pepper as necessary. Garnish with the cilantro if you like and serve.

SPANISH TORTILLA

MAKES 3 TO 6 SERVINGS　　　TIME: ABOUT 40 MINUTES

THE SPANISH TORTILLA has nothing in common with the Mexican tortilla except its name, which comes from the Latin *torta*—a round cake. In its most basic form, the Spanish tortilla is a potato-and-egg frittata, or omelet, which derives most of its flavor from olive oil. Although the ingredients are simple and minimal, when made correctly—and there is a straightforward but very definite series of techniques involved—this tortilla is wonderfully juicy. And because it is better at room temperature than hot, it can and in fact should be made in advance. (How much in advance is up to you. It can be fifteen minutes or a few hours.)

$1^{1}/_{4}$ pounds potatoes (3 to 4 medium)

1 medium onion

1 cup olive oil

Salt and freshly ground black pepper

6 extra-large or jumbo eggs

1. Peel and thinly slice the potatoes and onion; it's easiest with a mandoline. Meanwhile, heat the oil in an 8- or 10-inch nonstick skillet (a nonstick skillet is a must for this dish) over medium heat. After the oil has been heating for 3 or 4 minutes, drop in a slice of potato. When tiny bubbles appear around the edges of the potato, the oil is ready; add all of the potatoes and onion along with a good pinch of salt and a liberal sprinkling of pepper. Gently turn the potato mixture in the oil with a wooden spoon and adjust the heat so that the oil bubbles lazily.

2. Cook, turning the potatoes gently every few minutes and adjusting the heat so they do not brown, until they are tender when pierced with the point of a small knife. If the potatoes begin to break, they are overdone—this is not a tragedy, but stop the cooking immediately. As the potatoes cook, beat the eggs with some salt and pepper in a large bowl.

3. Drain the potatoes in a colander, reserving the oil. Heat an 8- or 9-inch nonstick skillet (it can be the same one, but wipe it out first)

VARIATIONS

Although potatoes are the most widely enjoyed filling, the tortilla is often filled with a variety of ingredients. Just make sure that any additions are either cooked in olive oil or thoroughly drained of other liquids.

• Replace the potatoes with onion or scallion, in equal amounts.

• Replace the potatoes with greens cooked as on page 229 (start with about a pound). Squeeze the greens dry and chop them, then sauté in just a couple of tablespoons of olive oil before adding the eggs.

• Add about 1 cup red bell pepper strips to the potatoes as they cook.

• Add $^{1}/_{4}$ cup or more diced chorizo, cooked bacon or shrimp, or dry-cured ham like prosciutto to the eggs.

• Add $^{1}/_{2}$ cup or more canned or cooked fresh peas, lima beans, or chickpeas to the eggs.

over medium heat for a minute and add 2 tablespoons of the re-served oil. Gently mix the warm potatoes with the eggs and add them to the skillet. As soon as the edges firm up—this will take only a minute or so—reduce the heat to medium-low. Cook for 5 minutes.

4. Run a rubber spatula all around the edges of the cake to make sure it will slide from the pan. Carefully slide it out—the top will still be quite runny—onto a plate. Cover with another plate and, holding the plates tightly, invert them. Add another tablespoon of oil to the skil-let and use a rubber spatula to coax the cake back in. Cook another 5 minutes, then slide the cake from the skillet to a plate. (Alterna-tively, finish the cooking by putting the tortilla in a 350°F oven for about 10 minutes.) Serve warm (not hot) or at room temperature. Do not refrigerate.

BREAD, NOODLES, AND RICE

FASTEST FRENCH BREAD

MAKES 1 LOAF

TIME: $1^1/_4$ HOURS, MORE IF YOU HAVE TIME, LARGELY UNATTENDED

I WON'T CLAIM that this is the best bread you've ever eaten, but it's the fastest yeast bread imaginable, and it's better than anything you can buy at many supermarkets. It requires little effort, less attention, and rounds out most simple dishes into filling meals.

3 cups all-purpose flour, plus more
    as needed
2 teaspoons instant yeast (see
    Note)

2 teaspoons salt

NOTE
I specify instant yeast (such as SAF) in this recipe and all my baking recipes. This is yeast that can be mixed, dry, with the flour—it's fuss-free, keeps forever in the fridge, and is sold at every supermarket.

1. Combine the flour, yeast, and salt in a bowl or food processor. Add $1^1/_4$ cups of warm water all at once, stirring with a wooden spoon or with the machine on. Continue to mix, for a minute or two longer by hand, for about 30 seconds total with the food processor. Add water by the tablespoon if necessary, until a ball forms.

2. Shape the dough into a flat round or long loaf, adding only enough flour to allow you to handle the dough. Put the dough on a baking sheet or a well-floured pizza peel. Let it rise in the warmest place in your kitchen, covered, while you preheat the oven to 425°F. (If you have time, let the dough rise for an hour or so.)

3. Bake the bread on the sheet, or slide it onto a baking stone. Bake until done, 30 to 45 minutes; the crust will be golden brown, crisp, and firm.

CORN BREAD

MAKES ABOUT 6 SERVINGS   TIME: ABOUT 45 MINUTES

CORN BREAD IS a quick bread—that is, risen with baking powder, not yeast—and the most useful one of all. Everyone loves it, too.

2 tablespoons butter or olive oil

$1^1/2$ cups cornmeal

$1/2$ cup flour

$1^1/2$ teaspoons baking powder

1 teaspoon salt

2 tablespoons sugar

1 egg

$1^1/4$ cups buttermilk, milk, or yogurt

1. Preheat the oven to 375°F. Put the fat in a medium nonstick or well-seasoned ovenproof skillet or in an 8-inch square baking pan over medium heat; heat until good and hot, about 2 minutes, then turn off the heat.

2. Meanwhile, combine the dry ingredients in a bowl. Mix the egg into the buttermilk, then stir the liquid mixture into the dry ingredients, combining well; if it seems too dry, add another tablespoon or two of milk. Pour the batter into the preheated fat, shake the pan once or twice, and put in the oven.

3. Bake for about 30 minutes, until the top is lightly browned and the sides have pulled away from the pan; a toothpick inserted into the center will come out clean. Serve hot or warm.

OLIVE OIL CROUTONS

MAKES 4 SERVINGS   TIME: 10 TO 15 MINUTES

A CROUTON IS not only a little cube of bread you use in salads or for stuffing, but a perfectly toasted slice that makes a wonderful side dish and a sensational way to use stale bread.

$^1/_4$ cup extra virgin olive oil

1 garlic clove, smashed and peeled

4 thick slices good-quality bread

Salt

1. Put the olive oil in a large skillet and turn the heat to medium-low. Add the garlic and cook, turning occasionally, until it is lightly browned.

2. Add the bread slices and cook, turning occasionally and adjusting the heat so they brown nicely. Remove and sprinkle lightly with salt; serve hot or at room temperature.

BREAD PUDDING WITH SHIITAKE MUSHROOMS

MAKES 8 SERVINGS

TIME: ABOUT 1 HOUR, LARGELY UNATTENDED

THIS BREAD CASSEROLE is a major upgrade from stuffing. Like most puddings and custards, it should be removed from the oven when it still appears slightly underdone, because its retained heat will firm it up just fine. Use good-quality white bread—torn from a loaf, not presliced—and the pudding will be much better.

Butter or extra virgin olive oil for greasing the baking dish, plus 2 tablespoons

$1/2$ pound good-quality white bread, cut or torn into chunks no smaller than 1 inch in diameter

2 cups milk

4 eggs

Salt and freshly ground black pepper

2 ounces Parmigiano-Reggiano cheese, freshly grated

$1/4$ pound Emmenthal or other semisoft cheese, freshly grated

1 cup sliced shiitake mushroom caps

1 teaspoon fresh thyme leaves or $1/4$ teaspoon dried

1. Butter or oil an 8-inch soufflé or baking dish and put the bread in it. Combine the milk, eggs, salt, pepper, and cheeses and pour this mixture over the bread. Submerge the bread with a weighted plate and turn the oven to 350°F. Meanwhile, heat the butter or oil in a skillet over medium-high heat and sauté the mushrooms, stirring occasionally, until they begin to brown, about 10 minutes. Sprinkle them with salt and pepper and thyme and stir them into the bread mixture.

2. Bake until the pudding is just set but not dry, 35 to 45 minutes. The top will be crusty and brown. Serve hot, warm, or at room temperature.

PIZZA IS EASY, even when you make the dough yourself. And although we have practically been force-fed pizza with cooked tomato sauce, pizza is even easier when topped with raw ingredients.

What the following pizzas have in common is their uncooked toppings; once you get the hang of it, you'll find it easy enough to improvise with both raw and cooked ingredients.

PIZZA DOUGH

MAKES 2 12- TO 13-INCH PIES,

ENOUGH FOR 4 PEOPLE　　　　TIME: 1 HOUR OR MORE

PEOPLE CAN NEVER seem to get enough pizza, and how many a pizza will serve depends on the heartiness of the toppings, the thickness of the crust, and whether you're serving anything along with it. But I've found generally that this dough recipe will make two twelve- or thirteen-inch pizzas and that pizzas made with the following toppings will serve at least four people.

3 cups all-purpose or bread flour, plus more as needed

2 teaspoons instant yeast

2 teaspoons coarse kosher or sea salt, plus extra for sprinkling

2 tablespoons olive oil

1. Combine the flour, yeast, and salt in a food processor. Turn the machine on and add 1 cup of warm water and the oil through the feed tube.

2. Process for about 30 seconds, adding more water, a little at a time, until the mixture forms a ball and is slightly sticky to the touch. If it is dry, add another tablespoon or two of water and process for another 10 seconds. (In the unlikely event that the mixture is too sticky, add flour, a tablespoon at a time.)

3. Turn the dough onto a floured work surface and knead by hand for a few seconds to form a smooth, round dough ball. Put the dough in

a bowl and cover with plastic wrap; let rise until the dough doubles in size, 1 to 2 hours. (You can cut this rising time short if you are in a hurry, or you can let the dough rise more slowly, in the refrigerator, for up to 6 to 8 hours.) Proceed to step 4, or wrap the dough tightly in plastic wrap and freeze for up to a month. (Defrost in a covered bowl in the refrigerator or at room temperature.)

4. When the dough is ready, form it into a ball and divide it into 2 or more pieces if you like; roll each piece into a round ball. Put each ball on a lightly floured surface, sprinkle with a little flour, and cover with plastic wrap or a towel. Let rest until they puff slightly, about 20 minutes. Proceed with any of the recipes that follow.

PIZZA-MAKING TIPS

- Be sure to allow the dough to relax, stretching it a little bit at a time, when you're ready to roll it out; pressing the dough onto an oiled baking sheet is the easiest way to get this done. And bear in mind that it's easier to handle small pies than large ones.

- You can bake the pies or grill them. An oven lined with a baking stone (or several uncoated quarry tiles) is ideal, but it requires a peel (a flat sheet of wood or metal with a long handle) to move the pizza about. A baking sheet, with or without a lip, is much easier, because you can press the dough right onto its surface. Since you use olive oil to prevent sticking, the process is a snap.

- Generally, toppings should never be too wet, or the dough will become soggy. In practice, this means fresh tomatoes should have some of their juice squeezed out and be thinly sliced, and preferably salted for a little while, before using; the same holds true for other moist vegetables like zucchini.

- It may be that there are more possible combinations of pizza toppings than moves in chess or atoms in the universe; in any case, there are a lot. Simple combinations are best, however; too many ingredients merely serve to muddy the flavors.

PIZZA WITH TOMATOES, ONIONS, AND OLIVES

MAKES 2 TO 4 SERVINGS

TIME: 35 MINUTES WITH PREMADE DOUGH

1 recipe Pizza Dough (page 253)

4 or 5 ripe tomatoes

Coarse salt

1 medium red onion or 4 shallots, chopped

20 black olives, such as Kalamata or oil-cured, pitted and chopped

Olive oil as needed

1. For grilled pizza, start a medium-hot charcoal or wood fire or pre-heat a gas grill to the maximum. Roll or lightly press each dough ball into a flat round, lightly flouring the work surface and the dough as necessary (do not use more flour than you need to). Let the rounds sit for a few minutes, then roll or pat out the dough, as thinly as you like, turning occasionally and sprinkling the top with flour as necessary.

For baked pizza, preheat the oven to 500°F. Oil one or more baking sheets, then press each dough ball into a flat round directly on the oiled sheet(s). Then pat out the dough, as thinly as you like, oiling your hands if necessary. If your oven is equipped with a baking stone, roll or pat out the dough as for grilled pizza, putting it on a peel to transfer it to the oven.

2. Meanwhile, core the tomatoes, cut them in half horizontally, and gently squeeze out the liquid and most of the seeds. Slice as thinly as possible, lightly salt and let the slices sit for at least 10 minutes. Drain off any excess liquid.

3. To grill the pizza, slide it directly onto the grill. Cook until brown grill marks appear, 3 to 5 minutes, depending on your grill heat. Turn with a spatula or tongs, top with the tomatoes, onion, and olives, and drizzle with olive oil. Cover the grill and cook until the bottom is crisp and brown and the tomatoes hot, 7 to 10 minutes.

To bake the pizza, top with tomatoes, onions, olives, and a little olive oil, slide the baking sheet into the oven (or the pizza itself onto the stone), and bake for about 15 minutes, depending on the oven heat, or until nicely browned.

PIZZA WITH ZUCCHINI AND SAUSAGE

MAKES 2 TO 4 SERVINGS
TIME: 45 MINUTES WITH PREMADE DOUGH

1 recipe Pizza Dough (page 253)

4 small or 2 medium zucchini

Coarse salt

2 or 3 sweet Italian sausages, the meat removed from the casing and crumbled

2 teaspoons minced garlic

Olive oil as needed

1. For grilled pizza, start a medium-hot charcoal or wood fire or pre-heat a gas grill to the maximum. Roll or lightly press each dough ball into a flat round, lightly flouring the work surface and the dough as necessary (do not use more flour than you need to). Let the rounds sit for a few minutes, then roll or pat out the dough, as thinly as you like, turning occasionally and sprinkling the top with flour as necessary.

For baked pizza, preheat the oven to 500°F. Oil one or more baking sheets, then press each dough ball into a flat round directly on the oiled sheet(s). Then pat out the dough, as thinly as you like, oiling your hands if necessary. If your oven is equipped with a baking stone, roll or pat out the dough as for grilled pizza, putting it on a peel to transfer it to the oven.

2. Meanwhile, thinly slice the zucchini. Salt the slices lightly and let them sit for at least 20 minutes, then drain off any accumulated liquid.

3. To grill the pizza, slide it directly onto the grill. Cook until brown grill marks appear, 3 to 5 minutes, depending on your grill heat. Turn with a spatula or tongs, then top with the zucchini, sausage, and garlic. Cover the grill and cook until the bottom is crisp and brown and the sausage cooked through, 7 to 10 minutes.

To bake the pizza, top with the zucchini, sausage, and garlic, slide the baking sheet into the oven (or the pizza itself onto the stone), and bake for about 15 minutes, depending on the oven heat, or until nicely browned and the sausage is cooked through.

PIZZA WITH GREEN TOMATOES

MAKES 2 TO 4 SERVINGS

TIME: 40 MINUTES WITH PREMADE DOUGH

1 recipe Pizza Dough (page 253)

2 large or 4 small green tomatoes

Coarse salt

1 cup freshly grated Parmigiano-
Reggiano cheese

$^1/_2$ cup coarsely chopped or torn
fresh basil

Olive oil as needed

1. For grilled pizza, start a medium-hot charcoal or wood fire or preheat a gas grill to the maximum. Roll or lightly press each dough ball into a flat round, lightly flouring the work surface and the dough as necessary (do not use more flour than you need to). Let the rounds sit for a few minutes, then roll or pat out the dough, as thinly as you like, turning occasionally and sprinkling the top with flour as necessary.

For baked pizza, preheat the oven to 500°F. Oil one or more baking sheets, then press each dough ball into a flat round directly on the oiled sheet(s). Then pat out the dough, as thinly as you like, oiling your hands if necessary. If your oven is equipped with a baking stone, roll or pat out the dough as for grilled pizza, putting it on a peel to transfer it to the oven.

2. Meanwhile, thinly slice the tomatoes. Salt the slices lightly and let them sit for at least 20 minutes, then drain off any accumulated liquid.

3. To grill the pizza, slide it directly onto the grill. Cook until brown grill marks appear, 3 to 5 minutes, depending on your grill heat. Turn with a spatula or tongs, then top with the tomato, Parmigiano-Reggiano, and basil. Cover the grill and cook until the bottom is crisp and brown and the top hot.

To bake the pizza, top with the tomato and Parmigiano-Reggiano, slide the baking sheet into the oven (or the pizza itself onto the stone), and bake for about 10 minutes, depending on the oven heat, or until nearly done. Sprinkle with the basil and cook until the pizza is nicely browned.

VARIATIONS

Here is a list of ideas for basic and flavorful combinations for pizza, none of which requires precooking:

White Pizza

Drizzle with about 2 tablespoons olive oil, then sprinkle with coarse salt, about 1 tablespoon fresh rosemary leaves (or a teaspoon or two of dried), and, if you like, a bit of minced garlic, chopped onion, or chopped shallot.

Pizza Romano

Drizzle with about 2 tablespoons olive oil, then top with a lot of cracked black pepper and a good cup of freshly grated pecorino Romano.

Pizza with Parmigiano-Reggiano and Sage

Top with at least 1 cup freshly grated Parmigiano-Reggiano, then sprinkle with 20 or 30 fresh sage leaves, coarsely chopped.

Pizza with Shallots and Thyme

Drizzle with about 2 tablespoons olive oil, then sprinkle with coarse salt and freshly cracked black pepper, 1 cup slivered shallot, and about 1 teaspoon fresh thyme leaves (or a few pinches of dried).

(continued)

PIZZA WITH FOUR CHEESES AND BASIL

MAKES 2 TO 4 SERVINGS
TIME: 30 MINUTES WITH PREMADE DOUGH

1 recipe Pizza Dough (page 253)
$1/2$ cup shredded or cubed mozzarella cheese
$1/2$ cup shredded or cubed fontina or Taleggio cheese
$1/2$ cup freshly grated pecorino Romano cheese
$1/2$ cup freshly grated Parmigiano-Reggiano cheese
$1/2$ cup coarsely chopped or torn fresh basil
Olive oil as needed

1. For grilled pizza, start a medium-hot charcoal or wood fire or preheat a gas grill to the maximum. Roll or lightly press each dough ball into a flat round, lightly flouring the work surface and the dough as necessary (do not use more flour than you need to). Let the rounds sit for a few minutes, then roll or pat out the dough, as thinly as you like, turning occasionally and sprinkling the top with flour as necessary.

For baked pizza, preheat the oven to 500°F. Oil one or more baking sheets, then press each dough ball into a flat round directly on the oiled sheet(s). Then pat out the dough, as thinly as you like, oiling your hands if necessary. If your oven is equipped with a baking stone, roll or pat out the dough as for grilled pizza, putting it on a peel to transfer it to the oven.

2. To grill the pizza, slide it directly onto the grill. Cook until brown grill marks appear, 3 to 5 minutes, depending on your grill heat. Turn with a spatula or tongs, then top with the cheeses and basil. Cover the grill and cook until the bottom is crisp and nicely brown and the cheeses melted.

To bake the pizza, top with the cheeses, slide the baking sheet into the oven (or the pizza itself onto the stone), and bake for about 10 minutes, depending on the oven heat, or until nearly done. Sprinkle with the basil and finish cooking until nicely browned.

PIZZA WITH ARUGULA, CORN, AND BACON

MAKES 2 TO 4 SERVINGS

TIME: 40 MINUTES WITH PREMADE DOUGH

1 recipe Pizza Dough (page 253)

6 cups loosely packed shredded
   arugula

Kernels from 4 ears corn

$1/2$ cup minced bacon

Olive oil as needed

1. For grilled pizza, start a medium-hot charcoal or wood fire or pre-heat a gas grill to the maximum. Roll or lightly press each dough ball into a flat round, lightly flouring the work surface and the dough as necessary (do not use more flour than you need to). Let the rounds sit for a few minutes, then roll or pat out the dough, as thinly as you like, turning occasionally and sprinkling the top with flour as necessary.

For baked pizza, preheat the oven to 500°F. Oil one or more baking sheets, then press each dough ball into a flat round directly on the oiled sheet(s). Then pat out the dough, as thinly as you like, oiling your hands if necessary. If your oven is equipped with a baking stone, roll or pat out the dough as for grilled pizza, putting it on a peel to transfer it to the oven.

2. To grill the pizza, slide it directly onto the grill. Cook until brown grill marks appear, 3 to 5 minutes, depending on your grill heat. Turn with a spatula or tongs, then top with the arugula, corn, and bacon. Cover the grill and cook until the bottom is crisp and brown and the bacon cooked through.

To bake the pizza, top with the arugula, corn, and bacon, slide the baking sheet into the oven (or the pizza itself onto the stone), and bake for about 15 minutes, depending on the oven heat, or until nicely browned and the bacon cooked through.

(Variations, continued)

Pesto Pizza
Spread with about 1 cup pesto or simply a handful or two of fresh basil, along with some garlic and a couple of tablespoons of extra virgin olive oil.

Pizza with Mozzarella
Top with a couple of hand-fuls of grated mozzarella, some sliced tomatoes, and a lot of chopped fresh basil, along with a sprinkling of salt and pepper and a drizzle of olive oil.

If you have a moderately well-stocked pantry— for example, if you have some olives, capers, chickpeas, dried chiles, canned tomatoes, and so on—you can make any of these delicious variations in less than a half hour.
• Add a couple of dried chiles to the oil along with the garlic. Discard before tossing with the pasta. Alternatively, sprinkle the pasta with hot red pepper flakes or pass some at the table.
• Add 1 cup cooked, drained chickpeas to the garlic-oil mixture about a minute before tossing with the pasta.
• Add 1 to 2 tablespoons capers to the garlic-oil mixture about a minute before tossing with the pasta.
• Add $1/4$ to $1/2$ cup minced pitted black olives (preferably imported) to the garlic-oil mixture about a minute before tossing with the pasta.
• Add a mixture of about 1 cup fresh herbs to the pasta when tossing it with the garlic-oil mixture. You probably will need more olive oil or some of the pasta-cooking water.

LINGUINE WITH GARLIC AND OIL

MAKES 4 TO 6 SERVINGS   TIME: 30 MINUTES

SINCE OLIVE OIL is the backbone of this dish, use the best you can lay your hands on and be sure to keep the heat under the oil medium-low, because you want to avoid browning the garlic at all costs. (Well, not at all costs. If you brown the garlic, you'll have a different, more strongly flavored kind of dish, but one that is still worth eating.) Garnish with a good handful of chopped parsley. For thirty seconds' work, this makes an almost unbelievable difference.

Salt
2 tablespoons minced garlic
$1/2$ cup extra virgin olive oil
1 pound linguine, spaghetti, or other long, thin pasta

$1/2$ cup loosely packed chopped fresh parsley (optional)

1. Bring a large pot of water to a boil and salt it. Meanwhile, combine the garlic, oil, and a pinch of salt in a small skillet over medium-low heat. Allow the garlic to simmer, shaking the pan occasionally, until it turns golden; do not allow it to turn dark brown.
2. When the water boils, cook the pasta until it is tender but firm. When it is done, drain it, reserving a bit of the cooking water. Reheat the garlic and oil mixture briefly if necessary. Dress the pasta with the sauce and parsley, if using, adding a little more oil or some of the cooking water if it seems dry.

LINGUINE WITH SPINACH

MAKES 4 TO 6 SERVINGS   TIME: 30 MINUTES

IT IS PASTA'S nature to be simple. I've long made a vegetable sauce by poaching greens such as spinach in the pasta water, then removing them and adding the pasta, a neat trick. But my friend Jack Bishop, author of *Vegetarian Italian Cooking,* mentioned that he'd gone one step further, cooking the greens right in with the pasta and adding seasonings at the last minute. The method relies on the fact that there is a period of two or three minutes between the moment when the pasta's last traces of chalkiness disappear and the point where it begins to become mushy. If, just before the pasta is done, you add the greens, whose tough stems have been removed, greens and pasta will finish cooking at the same time.

When making this dish and others like it, you must adhere to the often ignored canon of allowing at least a gallon of water per pound of pasta, because you need a pot large enough to accommodate the greens and because they cannot be allowed to slow down the cooking too much.

Salt and freshly ground black pepper

1 garlic clove

1/2 teaspoon hot red pepper flakes, or to taste (optional)

1/4 cup plus 1 tablespoon extra virgin olive oil

1 pound linguine or other long pasta

1 pound spinach, tough stems removed, roughly chopped

1. Bring a large pot of water to a boil and salt it. Meanwhile, mince the garlic as finely as possible and combine it in the bottom of a warm bowl with the hot pepper if you're using it and olive oil.

2. Add the pasta to the pot and cook until it is nearly done (test it for doneness by tasting). Plunge the spinach into the water and cook until it wilts, less than a minute. Drain quickly, allowing some water to cling to the pasta, and toss in the bowl with the garlic and olive oil mixture. Season with salt and black pepper to taste and serve.

VARIATIONS

One-Pot Pasta and Greens, Asian Style

Use Asian wheat noodles and substitute 1/4 cup peanut oil plus 1 tablespoon sesame oil for the olive oil. Add 1 tablespoon soy sauce to the hot pepper and garlic; garnish with 2 tablespoons lightly toasted sesame seeds.

• Toss the pasta with freshly grated Parmigiano-Reggiano or pecorino cheese to taste.

• Add any of the following to the garlic-pepper-oil mixture, singly or in combination: about 15 Kalamata or other olives, pitted and roughly chopped; about 1/4 cup chopped sun-dried tomatoes packed in oil; about 2 tablespoons drained capers; about 1/2 cup toasted bread crumbs; about 1/4 cup minced prosciutto or other dry-cured ham.

PASTA WITH GORGONZOLA AND ARUGULA

MAKES 4 TO 6 SERVINGS   TIME: 30 MINUTES

THERE ARE PASTA sauces you can make in the time it takes the pasta-cooking water to come to a boil, and there are those that are really fast—those that can be made in the eight to ten minutes it takes to actually cook the pasta. This is one of the latter, one that boasts just a couple of main ingredients and a supporting cast of two staples.

2 tablespoons butter

$^1/_4$ pound ripe Gorgonzola

6 ounces arugula

1 pound cut pasta, like ziti or
    farfalle

Salt and freshly ground black
    pepper

1. Bring a large pot of water to a boil for the pasta and salt it. Meanwhile, melt the butter in a small saucepan over low heat; add the Gorgonzola and cook, stirring frequently, until the cheese melts. Keep warm while you cook the pasta.

2. Tear the arugula into bits, or cut it up with scissors—the pieces should not be too small. Cook the pasta until it is tender but not mushy. Remove and reserve a little of the cooking water, then drain the pasta and toss it with the arugula and the cheese mixture, adding a bit of the water if the mixture seems dry.

3. Taste and adjust the seasoning—the dish should take plenty of black pepper—and serve.

PASTA WITH ANCHOVIES AND ARUGULA

MAKES 4 TO 6 SERVINGS   TIME: 30 MINUTES

A QUICK WAY to add great flavor to many simple dinner dishes is already sitting in your pantry or cupboard: anchovies. Anchovies are among the original convenience foods and contribute an intense shot of complex brininess that is more like Parmigiano-Reggiano than like canned tuna. Use them, along with garlic, as the base for a bold tomato sauce or combine them, as I do here, with greens, garlic, oil, and chiles for a white sauce that packs a punch.

Salt and freshly ground black
   pepper

$1/4$ cup extra virgin olive oil

4 large garlic cloves, slivered

8 anchovy fillets, or more to taste,
   with some of their oil

1 pound linguine or other long pasta

2 cups arugula, chopped

$1/2$ teaspoon or more hot red
   pepper flakes

1. Bring a large pot of water to a boil and salt it. Put half of the olive oil in a deep skillet over medium heat. A minute later, add the garlic and the anchovies. When the garlic sizzles and the anchovies break up, turn the heat to the minimum.

2. Cook the pasta until it is tender but not mushy. Reserve 1 cup of the cooking liquid and drain. Add the pasta and the arugula to the skillet, along with enough of the reserved cooking water to make a sauce; turn the heat to medium and stir for a minute. Add salt and black pepper to taste, plus a pinch or more of the hot pepper..

3. Turn into a bowl, toss with the remaining olive oil, and serve.

SPAGHETTI WITH ZUCCHINI

MAKES 4 TO 6 SERVINGS   TIME: 30 MINUTES

THIS DISH—which has zucchini as its focus—is simply amazing when made in midsummer with tender, crisp squash, but it isn't half bad even when made in midwinter with a limp vegetable that's traveled halfway around the world to get to your table. Either way, it is an unusual use for zucchini, which here substitutes for meat in a kind of vegetarian spaghetti carbonara, the rich pasta dish featuring eggs, bacon, and Parmigiano-Reggiano. Made with zucchini instead of bacon, the dish becomes a little less fat-laden, obviously, but it is still rich and delicious.

Salt and freshly ground black pepper

3 tablespoons olive oil

3 or 4 small zucchini (about 1 pound), sliced $1/8$ to $1/4$ inch thick

2 eggs (see Note)

1 cup freshly grated Parmigiano-Reggiano cheese

1 pound spaghetti, linguine, or other long pasta

$1/2$ cup roughly chopped fresh mint, parsley, or basil

1. Bring a large pot of water to a boil and salt it. Put the olive oil in a 10- or 12-inch skillet over medium-high heat. A minute later, add the zucchini; cook, stirring only occasionally, until very tender and lightly browned, 10 to 15 minutes. Season with a little salt and a lot of pepper.

2. Meanwhile, beat the eggs and $1/2$ cup of the Parmigiano-Reggiano together. Add the pasta to the boiling water and cook until it is tender but firm. When it is done, drain it and combine it immediately with the egg-cheese mixture, tossing until the egg appears cooked. Stir in the zucchini, then taste and add more salt and pepper if necessary.

3. Toss in the herb and serve immediately, passing the remaining Parmigiano-Reggiano at the table.

VARIATION

Fettuccine Alfredo
Omit the zucchini. Just toss the pasta (preferably fettuccine) with eggs, cheese, and enough heavy cream to bind the sauce. Best served as a small first course for 6 to 8.

NOTE

The eggs will cook fully from the heat of the pasta. If this makes you at all nervous, however, do the final tossing of eggs, cheese, and pasta in the cooking pot, over the lowest heat possible.

PENNE WITH BUTTERNUT SQUASH

MAKES 4 TO 6 SERVINGS   TIME: 30 MINUTES

THIS DISH IS a minimalist's take on the northern Italian autumn staple of tortelli filled with zucca, a pumpkinlike vegetable whose flesh, like that of butternut or acorn squash, is dense, orange, and somewhat sweet. The flavor and essential nature of that dish can be captured in a thirty-minute preparation that turns the classic inside out, using the squash as a sauce and sparing you the hours it would take to stuff the tortelli.

1 pound peeled (see Notes) and seeded butternut squash (about $1^1/_2$ pounds whole squash)

Salt and freshly ground black pepper

2 tablespoons butter or olive oil

1 pound penne or other cut pasta

$1/_8$ teaspoon freshly grated nutmeg, or to taste

1 teaspoon sugar (optional; see Notes)

$1/_2$ cup freshly grated Parmigiano-Reggiano cheese

1. Cut the squash into chunks and put it in a food processor. Pulse the machine on and off until the squash appears grated. Alternatively, grate or chop the squash by hand. Bring a large pot of salted water to a boil for the pasta.

2. Put a large skillet over medium heat and add the butter or oil. A minute later, add the squash, salt and pepper to taste, and about $1/_2$ cup of water. Cook over medium heat, stirring occasionally. Add water, about $1/_4$ cup at a time, as the mixture dries out, but be careful not to make it soupy. When the squash begins to disintegrate, after 10 or 15 minutes, begin cooking the pasta. While it cooks, season the squash with the nutmeg, sugar if desired, and additional salt and pepper if needed.

3. When the pasta is tender, scoop out about $1/_2$ cup of the cooking liquid and reserve it, then drain the pasta. Toss the pasta in the skillet with the squash, adding the reserved pasta-cooking water if the mixture seems dry. Taste and add more of any seasonings you like, then toss with the Parmigiano-Reggiano and serve.

NOTES

Peel the squash with a knife, not a vegetable peeler, which is likely to break. And don't worry if you take a bunch of the flesh along with the peel; remember that squash is almost always inexpensive.

Some butternut squash is sweeter than others, and there's no way to predict this by appearance. Since this sauce relies on sweetness for its character, if the squash seems a little bland as it cooks, add about a teaspoon of sugar. It will brighten the flavor considerably.

PASTA WITH CAULIFLOWER

MAKES 4 TO 6 SERVINGS   TIME: ABOUT 40 MINUTES

THE FUNDAMENTAL PROCEDURES required to make this pasta dish are easy, but this is as instructional as any simple recipe I know, and one that builds a wonderfully flavorful dish with just a few ingredients.

Salt and freshly ground black pepper

1 head of cauliflower (about 1 pound)

1/4 cup olive oil

1 tablespoon minced garlic

1 pound penne, ziti, or other cut pasta

1 cup coarse bread crumbs (see Note)

NOTE

The bread crumbs are best when freshly made from good but slightly stale bread; coarse bread crumbs, such as those made in a food processor, are infinitely preferable to the finer store-bought variety.

VARIATION

Feel free to add 3 or 4 anchovy fillets, with their oil, to the skillet along with the garlic if you like; when I'm cooking for a group that enjoys bold flavors, I always do.

1. Bring a large pot of water to a boil. Trim the cauliflower and divide it into florets. Salt the water and cook the cauliflower in it until it is tender but not mushy. Remove the cauliflower and set it aside; when it is cool enough to handle, chop it roughly into small pieces. (If you have a little extra time, you can poach the cauliflower whole—even leaving the leaves on if you like; they'll add a little extra flavor to the water, and therefore to the pasta—which will save you the trouble of cutting it into florets).

2. Meanwhile, cook the oil and garlic together in a large, deep skillet over medium-low heat, stirring occasionally, until the garlic is golden; start the pasta in the same water as you used for the cauliflower.

3. When the garlic is ready, add the cauliflower and bread crumbs to the skillet and turn the heat to medium. Cook, stirring occasionally. When the pasta is just about done—it should be 2 or 3 minutes shy of being the way you like it—drain it, reserving about a cup of the cooking liquid.

4. Add the pasta to the skillet with the cauliflower and toss with a large spoon until well combined. Add salt and pepper to taste along with some of the pasta water to keep the mixture from drying out. When the mixture is hot and the pasta tender and nicely glazed, serve.

LINGUINE WITH FRESH HERBS

MAKES 4 TO 6 SERVINGS   TIME: ABOUT 30 MINUTES

ALL WINTER I dream of the time when there are so many fresh herbs that it seems imperative to use them at almost every meal. One of my favorite ways to take advantage of this abundance is to mix large quantities of herbs with pasta and a simple base of olive oil and garlic. In winter, a dish like this would not only seem exotic but would also cost a small fortune. In summer, however, it is an inexpensive no-brainer.

$^1/_4$ cup olive oil, or more to taste

1 teaspoon minced garlic

1 cup or more mixed fresh herbs, like parsley, dill, chervil, basil, tarragon, thyme, oregano, marjoram, or mint, woody or thick stems discarded

1 tablespoon butter (optional)

Salt and freshly ground black pepper

1 pound linguine or other long pasta

1. Bring a large pot of water to a boil. Combine the olive oil and garlic in a small saucepan over medium-low heat. Cook gently, just until the garlic begins to color, then remove from the heat. Meanwhile, wash and mince the herbs. Put them in a bowl large enough to hold the pasta. Cut the butter into bits if you're using it and add it to the bowl.

2. Salt the water and cook the pasta until tender but not mushy. Reserve $^1/_2$ cup of the pasta-cooking water, then drain the pasta and toss with the herbs and reserved olive oil–garlic mixture. Add a little more olive oil or some of the pasta water if you did not use butter and the mixture seems dry. Season with salt and pepper and serve.

PASTA WITH GREEN BEANS, POTATOES, AND PESTO

MAKES 4 TO 6 SERVINGS   TIME: 30 MINUTES

PESTO HAS BECOME a staple, especially in late summer when basil is best. But pasta with pesto does have its limits; it's simply not substantial enough to serve as a main course. The Genoese, originators of pesto, figured this out centuries ago, when they created this dish, which augments the pesto with chunks of potatoes and chopped green beans, making it a more complex, more filling, and more interesting dish. Recreating this classic dish is straightforward and easy.

Note that if you start the potatoes and pasta simultaneously, then add the green beans about halfway through cooking, they will all be finished at the same time and can be drained and tossed with the sauce in a snap. This technique may sound imprecise, but it works.

Salt

2 cups fresh basil leaves

2 garlic cloves, peeled

$^1/_2$ cup grated pecorino Romano or other hard sheep's milk cheese, or Parmigiano-Reggiano

$^1/_2$ cup extra virgin olive oil, or more

2 tablespoons pine nuts

2 medium potatoes (about $^1/_2$ pound), preferably waxy boiling potatoes, peeled and cut into $^1/_2$-inch cubes

1 pound trenette or linguine

$^1/_2$ pound green beans, trimmed and cut into 1-inch lengths

1. Bring a large pot of water to a boil and salt it. Combine the basil, garlic, salt to taste, and cheese in a blender or food processor; pulse until roughly chopped. Add the olive oil in a steady stream and continue to blend until the mixture is fairly creamy, adding a little more olive oil or some water if necessary. Add the pine nuts and pulse a few times to chop them into the sauce.

2. Add the potatoes to the boiling water and stir; then add the pasta and cook as usual, stirring frequently, about 10 minutes in all. When the pasta is about half done—the strands will bend but will not yet be tender—add the beans.

3. When the pasta is done, the potatoes and beans should be tender. Drain the pasta and vegetables, toss with the pesto and more salt or olive oil if you like, and serve.

PASTA WITH WALNUTS

MAKES 4 TO 6 SERVINGS   TIME: 20 MINUTES

YOU MIGHT THINK of this as winter pesto, with a higher percentage of walnuts and the always-available parsley filling in for summer's basil— though if you can find good basil, by all means use it.

Salt and freshly ground black
  pepper
1 cup walnut or pecan halves
$^{1}/_{2}$ cup loosely packed fresh parsley
  or basil leaves, washed

1 garlic clove, peeled
$^{1}/_{2}$ cup extra virgin olive oil
1 pound linguine, spaghetti, or other
  long pasta

1. Bring a large pot of water to a boil and salt it. Meanwhile, combine the nuts, parsley, and garlic in a small food processor (or use a mortar and pestle) and turn the machine on. With the machine running, add the oil gradually, using just enough so that the mixture forms a creamy paste. Season to taste with salt and pepper.

2. Cook the pasta, stirring occasionally, until it is tender but not mushy. When it is ready, drain it—reserve some of the cooking water—and toss with the sauce; if the mixture appears too thick, thin with a little of the pasta-cooking water or more olive oil. Serve.

SPAGHETTI WITH FRESH TOMATO SAUCE

MAKES 4 TO 6 SERVINGS   TIME: 20 MINUTES

THE DISH HAS a thick creaminess that you can never duplicate with canned tomatoes, no matter how good they are. So the season when you can make it—when there are good, ripe tomatoes in the market—is fairly short; where I live, just two or at the most three months a year.

There is an ideal instant for serving this sauce: When the tomatoes soften and all of their juices are in the skillet, the sauce suddenly begins to thicken. At that moment, it is at its peak; another minute or two later, many of the juices will have evaporated and, although the essence of the sauce is equally intense, it won't coat the pasta as well. If this happens, just add a little fresh olive oil or butter to the finished dish.

VARIATIONS

• Add about 1 teaspoon minced garlic to the butter or oil, just before the tomatoes. Garnish with minced fresh parsley instead of Parmigiano-Reggiano.
• Add about 1 tablespoon minced shallot to the butter or oil.
• Cook the tomatoes with a couple of branches of basil, remove them before serving, and stir about 1/2 cup or more roughly chopped basil leaves into the pasta.
• Toss the pasta with about 1 cup cubed (1/2 inch or less) mozzarella, preferably fresh.
• Add hot red pepper flakes to taste along with the tomatoes.

Salt and freshly ground black pepper
3 tablespoons butter or olive oil
1 1/2 to 2 pounds fresh tomatoes (preferably plum), cored and roughly chopped

1 pound spaghetti, linguine, or other long pasta
1/2 cup freshly grated Parmigiano-Reggiano cheese

1. Bring a large pot of water to a boil and salt it. Put the butter or oil in an 8- or 10-inch skillet over medium heat. When the butter melts or the oil is hot, add the tomatoes and turn the heat to high.
2. Cook, stirring occasionally, until the tomatoes begin to juice up, then turn the heat to low and cook, stirring occasionally, until the sauce thickens.
3. Cook the pasta until it is tender but firm. Drain and toss with the tomatoes and cheese. Season with salt and pepper to taste, toss again, and serve immediately.

FRESH TOMATOES SHOULD always be cored before being used (remove a cone-shaped wedge from the stem end). Peeling is optional—if you object to little bits of skin in your sauce, it's worth the effort. Just drop the tomatoes into boiling water for ten seconds, remove with a slotted spoon, and slip the peel right off. (Alternatively, you can also fish out the skin as the sauce simmers; it automatically separates from the flesh.)

LINGUINE WITH TOMATO-ANCHOVY SAUCE

MAKES 4 TO 6 SERVINGS   TIME: 30 MINUTES

FEW THINGS ARE simpler than a quick tomato sauce over pasta, but as an unending diet it can become somewhat tiresome. Here it's completely jazzed by the addition of a hefty amount of garlic and a few anchovies. The transformation is as easy as it is remarkable. Canned anchovies—packed in olive oil—are the easiest to use here. Salted anchovies, if you have them, are fine also, but you must mince them first (after cleaning them, of course, which you do under running water, stripping the meat from the skeleton).

Salt and freshly ground black
    pepper
2 tablespoons extra virgin olive oil
1 teaspoon minced garlic
4 to 6 anchovy fillets, with some of
    their oil

One 28-ounce can tomatoes,
    crushed or chopped and drained
1 pound linguine or other long pasta

1. Bring a large pot of water to a boil and salt it. Put the olive oil in a deep skillet and turn the heat to medium. A minute later, add the garlic and the anchovies. When the garlic sizzles and the anchovies break up, add the tomatoes.

2. Turn the heat to medium-high and bring to a boil. Cook, stirring occasionally, until the mixture becomes saucy, about 15 minutes.

3. Cook the pasta until it is tender but firm. Season the sauce to taste and serve over the linguine.

===

PASTA WITH CLAMS AND TOMATOES

MAKES 4 TO 6 SERVINGS   TIME: 30 MINUTES

THIS IS A technique popular in Liguria—the Italian Riviera—in which all of the clam liquid is used as part of the sauce, but without much effort. The result is delicious pasta in a little rich, thick sauce—along with a pile of clams.

Use the smallest clams you can find; cockles are fine, too. Figure eight to twelve littlenecks or twenty-four cockles per person. Wash and scrub the clamshells very well, as they will cook in the sauce and any unremoved sand will find its way into your mouth. Discard any open or cracked clams before cooking; those that remain shut after cooking may be opened with a knife.

VARIATION

White Pasta with Clams
Omit the tomatoes and substitute about $3/4$ cup dry white wine, adding it to the clams about a minute before the pasta.

Salt and freshly ground black
    pepper
$1/4$ cup extra virgin olive oil
36 to 48 littleneck clams
1 tablespoon minced garlic

1 pound linguine or other long pasta
2 or 3 plum tomatoes, cored and
    chopped
Chopped fresh parsley for garnish

1. Bring a large pot of water to a boil and salt it. Meanwhile, put 2 tablespoons of the olive oil in a large, deep skillet that can later be covered and turn the heat to high. A minute later, add the clams, reduce the heat to medium-high, give the pan a shake, and cover. Continue to cook the clams, shaking the pan occasionally, until they begin to open, as little as 5 minutes later. Add the garlic and cook until most of the clams are open.

2. Meanwhile, cook the pasta. When it is nearly tender, remove a cup of its cooking water and drain. When the clams are ready, add the pasta and the tomatoes to the skillet and cook, tossing frequently, until the pasta is tender and hot; add some of the pasta-cooking water if the mixture is too dry.

3. Add the remaining olive oil and taste and adjust the seasoning if necessary; garnish with the parsley and serve.

PASTA WITH SAUSAGE

MAKES 4 TO 6 SERVINGS   TIME: 30 MINUTES

MOST OF US associate pasta and sausage with a dense, heavy tomato sauce, the kind that is so Italian-American it is just about indigenous. Yet sausage can contribute to a relatively light, almost delicate pasta sauce, especially if it is used in small amounts. In fact, sausage is the ideal meat to use in a quick pasta sauce, because it is preseasoned and cooks almost instantly.

Salt and freshly ground black
    pepper
1 tablespoon butter
$1/2$ pound sweet or hot Italian
    sausage, removed from the
    casing

1 pound ziti or other cut pasta
$1/2$ cup or more freshly grated
    Parmigiano-Reggiano cheese

1. Bring a large pot of water to a boil and salt it. Put the butter in a medium skillet over medium-low heat. As it melts, crumble the sausage meat into it, making the bits quite small, $1/2$ inch or less in size. Add $1/2$ cup of water and adjust the heat so that the mixture simmers gently.

2. Cook the pasta until it is tender but not at all mushy. Reserve about $1/2$ cup of the pasta-cooking water.

VARIATIONS

White Pasta with Sausage and Onions
Before adding the sausage, gently cook about 1 cup minced onion in the butter until it is translucent. Proceed as directed.

Red Pasta with Sausage
Still far lighter than the pasta with sausage you're expecting. Core, cut up, seed, and drain 5 to 6 plum tomatoes; they may be fresh or canned. Add them to the sauce along with the sausage.

• Add about 1 teaspoon minced garlic or a couple of tablespoons minced shallot to the butter as it melts.
• Toss in a handful of chopped fresh parsley or basil at the last moment or add about 1 teaspoon fresh thyme leaves or minced fresh sage along with the sausage.
• Use red wine as the cooking liquid; its astringency offsets the sweet richness of butter and meat beautifully.

3. Drain the pasta and dress with the sauce, adding some of the reserved cooking liquid if necessary. Taste and add salt and pepper as necessary. Toss with the Parmigiano-Reggiano and serve.

PASTA WITH FAST SAUSAGE RAGU

MAKES 4 TO 6 SERVINGS   TIME: 30 MINUTES

TRUE RAGU IS **a magnificent pasta sauce, a slow-simmered blend of meat, tomatoes, and milk. The real thing takes hours, for the meat must become tender and contribute its silkiness to the sauce, the tomatoes must dissolve, and the milk must pull the whole thing together. But a reasonable approximation of ragu can be produced using ground beef or pork or, even better, prepared Italian sausage.**

Salt and freshly ground black pepper
1 tablespoon extra virgin olive oil
1/2 large or 1 medium onion, chopped
1/2 pound Italian sausage, removed from the casing
1 cup milk
1/4 cup tomato paste
1 pound long pasta
About 1 cup freshly grated Parmigiano-Reggiano cheese

1. Bring a large pot of water to a boil and salt it. Put the oil in a 10-inch skillet and turn the heat to medium; a minute later, add the onion. Cook, stirring occasionally, until it softens, about 5 minutes. Add the sausage in bits and turn the heat to medium-high; cook, stirring occasionally, until the sausage is nicely browned, 5 to 10 minutes.

2. Add the milk and tomato paste, along with some salt and pepper; stir to blend and simmer for about 5 minutes, or until thick but not dry. Keep it warm if necessary and, if it becomes too thick, add a little more milk, water, or chicken stock.

3. Meanwhile, cook the pasta until tender but not mushy. Drain it and toss with the sauce and about half the Parmigiano-Reggiano. Taste and adjust the seasoning, and serve, passing the remaining Parmigiano-Reggiano

ZITI WITH CHESTNUTS AND MUSHROOMS

MAKES 4 TO 6 SERVINGS TIME: 30 MINUTES

CHESTNUTS AND DRIED MUSHROOMS have a wonderful affinity for each other. Their unusual flavors and textures seem distantly related; they are both meaty and complex, chewy but neither tough nor crunchy. With shallots and plenty of black pepper for bite, the combination makes a great pasta sauce.

And though chestnuts are a pain in the neck (the fingers, actually) to peel, the good news is that their complex, fragrant flavor is so powerfully distinctive that just a few can have an enormous impact on a dish. So although it may take thirty seconds to a minute to process a single chestnut, if you need only a dozen or so for a dish, the work amounts to about ten minutes. And in a creation like this one, the time is well worth the effort.

15 chestnuts

1 ounce dried mushrooms—porcini, shiitake, black trumpets, morels, or an assortment

Salt and freshly ground black pepper

3 tablespoons butter or extra virgin olive oil

$^1/_2$ cup sliced shallot

1 pound ziti or other cut pasta

1. Cut a ring around each chestnut, then put them in boiling water to cover and cook for 3 minutes. Remove them from the water, a few at a time, and peel while still hot. Meanwhile, soak the mushrooms in about $1^1/_2$ cups of very hot water.

2. Bring a large pot of water to a boil and salt it. Put half the butter or oil in a skillet, turn the heat to medium-high, and, a minute later, add the shallot. Sprinkle lightly with salt and cook, stirring, until softened, 3 to 5 minutes. Chop the chestnuts into $1/2$- to $1/4$-inch chunks, then measure about 1 cup. Add them to the skillet along with a little more salt.

3. Cook, stirring occasionally, until the chestnuts deepen in color, about 5 minutes. Remove the mushrooms from their soaking liquid; reserve and strain the liquid. Chop the mushrooms and add them to the skillet; cook, stirring, for a minute or two, then add the strained mushroom-soaking liquid. Turn the heat to low and season to taste with salt and lots of black pepper.

4. Cook the pasta until tender but not mushy. If the sauce is too thick, add a little of the pasta-cooking water to it when the pasta is nearly done. Stir in the remaining butter or oil, then drain the pasta and dress with the sauce. Serve immediately.

PEELING CHESTNUTS

THERE ARE MANY WAYS to peel chestnuts, which like most nuts have a hard outer shell and a soft inner skin. Removing them both is a three-step process. First, use a paring knife—a curved one with a sharp point makes this quick and easy—to cut a ring around the equator of each nut or make an X on the flat side. Plunge the nuts into boiling water to cover for about three minutes, then turn off the heat, leaving the chestnuts in the water. Remove two or three at a time and, using the knife and your fingers, peel off both shell and skin; use a towel to protect your hands from the heat if necessary. If you're doing a large batch—say, twenty or more—you'll notice that as the water cools the skins become more difficult to remove. Bring the pot back to a boil and they'll begin to slip off again. And, although the exact count of chestnuts for this dish is not critical, I begin with fifteen, because there are usually a couple of rotten ones, or some whose inner skin refuses to come off. These must be discarded.

PASTA WITH MEATY BONES

MAKES 4 TO 6 SERVINGS   TIME: AT LEAST 1 HOUR

ONE OF MY favorite elaborations on a simple tomato sauce is the recipe for pasta with meaty bones. It requires considerably more time but almost no extra effort, and it boasts the wonderful depth of flavor, silken texture, and satisfying chewiness of slow-cooked meat. Southern Italian in origin, it begins with bony meat (or meaty bones) and requires lengthy simmering. Otherwise, it's little different from basic tomato sauce.

Whatever you use, the idea remains constant: meat is a supporting player, not the star, so an eight- to twelve-ounce piece of veal shank, for example, provides enough meat, marrow, and gelatin to create a luxuriously rich sauce. Just cook until the meat falls off the bone, then chop it and return it to the sauce along with any marrow.

This sauce is rich enough without grated cheese; a better garnish is a large handful of coarsely chopped parsley or basil. Either freshens the sauce while adding color and flavor.

2 tablespoons olive oil

2 small dried hot red chiles (optional)

1 meaty veal shank ($^1/_2$ to 1 pound)

3 garlic cloves, roughly chopped

Salt and freshly ground black pepper

One 28-ounce can whole plum tomatoes with juice

1 pound ziti, penne, or other cut pasta

$^1/_2$ cup or more roughly chopped fresh parsley or basil

1. Put the olive oil in a saucepan over medium heat. After a minute, add the chiles if you like and cook for about 30 seconds. Add the veal shank and raise the heat to medium-high; cook, turning as necessary, until the meat is nicely browned, 10 minutes or more. When the meat is just about done, add the garlic and salt and pepper to taste.

2. When the garlic has softened a bit, crush the tomatoes and add them along with their juice. Turn the heat to medium-low to maintain a steady simmer. If you are using a broad pot, cover it partially. Cook,

Pasta with Ribs

This is one of the best ways to use a small amount of meat in a highly satisfying way. Substitute 6 to 8 meaty spareribs for the veal shank (you can even use a couple more). The cooking time may be a little shorter. Serve the pasta topped with sauce along with a couple of ribs on the side.
• Carrots make a nice addition to this sauce; add about a cup, cut into chunks, along with the tomatoes. Some chopped onion won't do any harm either.

stirring occasionally, until the meat is tender and just about falling off the bone, at least 1 hour.

3. Bring a large pot of water to a boil and salt it. Cook the pasta until it is tender but firm. Remove the veal shank, scoop out any marrow, chop the meat coarsely, and return the meat to the sauce (discard the bone). Remove and discard the chiles.

4. Drain and sauce the pasta; sprinkle it with the herb, toss, and serve.

ZITI WITH BUTTER, SAGE, AND PARMIGIANO-REGGIANO

MAKES 4 TO 6 SERVINGS   TIME: 30 MINUTES

THE FLOUR-ENRICHED water in which pasta has cooked is never going to be an essential component of fine cooking, and it seldom appears in recipes. Yet from its origins as a cost-free, effortless substitute for stock, olive oil, butter, cream, or other occasionally scarce or even precious ingredients, pasta-cooking water has become a convenient and zero-calorie addition to simple sauces.

When you compare a lightly creamy sauce like the one in this recipe to the highly flavorful and ever-popular Alfredo sauce of butter, cream, eggs, and cheese, the latter seems relatively heavy. Substituting water for much of the butter and all of the cream and eggs produces a sauce with a perfect balance of weight and flavor. The water lends a moist quality, not unlike that produced by tomatoes, as opposed to the slickness contributed by straight fat.

This is best as a starter, not a main course, but it's still pretty rich. I would stick with a light fish preparation to follow, even a big salad.

Salt and freshly ground black pepper

1 pound ziti, penne, or other cut pasta

2 tablespoons butter

30 fresh sage leaves

About 1 cup freshly grated Parmigiano-Reggiano cheese

1. Bring a large pot of water to a boil and salt it. Cook the pasta until it is tender but a little short of the point at which you want to eat it.

2. Meanwhile, put the butter in a skillet or saucepan large enough to hold the cooked pasta; turn the heat to medium and add the sage. Cook until the butter turns nut-brown and the sage shrivels, then turn the heat down to a minimum.

3. When the pasta is just about done, scoop out a cupful of the cooking water. Drain the pasta, immediately add it to the butter-sage mixture, and raise the heat to medium. Add $\frac{1}{2}$ cup of the water and stir; the mixture will be loose and a little soupy. Cook for about 30 seconds, or until some of the water is absorbed and the pasta is perfectly done.

4. Stir in the cheese; the sauce will become creamy. Thin it with a little more water if necessary, season liberally with pepper and salt to taste, and serve immediately, passing more cheese at the table if you like.

VARIATIONS

• Try fresh parsley, thyme, chervil, or other green herbs in place of sage.

• Cook $\frac{1}{4}$ to $\frac{1}{2}$ cup minced shallot or onion in the butter, just until translucent.

• Toast $\frac{1}{2}$ cup bread crumbs or chopped nuts in the butter, just until lightly browned.

• Substitute extra virgin olive oil for some or all of the butter. The result will be good if not as creamy.

PASTA WITH POTATOES

MAKES AT LEAST 8 SERVINGS   TIME: 1 HOUR

THIS IS ABOUT as unlikely a dish as I've ever come across, a soupy combination containing little more than the two main ingredients and canned tomatoes. Not only does the thought of it tweak the mind—doesn't this sound something like a bread sandwich?—but it counters a number of the conventions that have been drummed into our collective consciousness.

Chief among these is that the dish is at its best when the pasta is cooked until it is fat, juice-laden, and quite soft. Here there is no need to seize the ideal moment at which the pasta is al dente; in fact you cook the pasta somewhat past that point, and it is even acceptable for it to sit for a while. Nor need you worry about the "correct" pasta shape; pasta with potatoes requires several different shapes, in varying quanti-

- After the potatoes begin to brown, add 1 to 2 cups chopped onion and cook, stirring, until it softens before proceeding.
- Add small bits of cooked or raw meat—up to 2 cups—along with the potatoes.
- Add chunks of carrot and/or celery—up to 2 cups—along with the potatoes.
- Cook a few stems of basil in the stew. Remove before serving, then garnish with plenty of chopped fresh basil.
- Serve with freshly grated pecorino or Parmigiano-Reggiano cheese.
- Or make Pasta and Potato Soup: Add 2 to 4 cups of water (or, much better, chicken stock) in step 5. Heat and serve with a spoon.

ties, preferably broken (it began as a way to use up the bits and pieces of dried pasta lying around in the cupboard).

Finally, not only may you serve pasta with potatoes as a leftover, but it's just as good after sitting for a day. So feel free to make a half batch of this pasta if you like, but since it's no more work to make this amount and it keeps for days, I advise making the full recipe.

2 tablespoons olive oil

About $1/2$ cup minced pancetta or bacon (optional)

3 to 4 potatoes (about $1^1/2$ pounds), peeled and cut into bite-sized chunks

1 tablespoon chopped garlic

3 to 4 small dried hot red chiles or about 1 teaspoon hot red pepper flakes, or to taste

One 28-ounce can whole plum tomatoes, with juice

About $1^1/2$ pounds assorted leftover dried pasta

Salt and freshly ground black pepper

Several cups of water, kept at a simmer in a pot or kettle

1. Put the olive oil in a large saucepan and turn the heat to medium. If you're using pancetta or bacon, add it to the oil and cook, stirring occasionally, until it becomes slightly crisp, about 10 minutes. (If you are omitting the meat, proceed to the next step.)

2. Add the potatoes, garlic, and chiles and raise the heat to medium-high. Cook, stirring occasionally, until the potatoes begin to brown all over, about 10 minutes.

3. Add the tomatoes and their juice, along with 2 cups of water, and bring to a boil. Turn the heat down to medium-low and cook, uncovered, stirring occasionally to break up the tomatoes and prevent sticking.

4. While the potatoes are cooking, break long pasta, like spaghetti, into several lengths; place cut pasta, such as ziti, in a bag and smack it into pieces with the back of a pot or a hammer. After the potatoes have simmered for about 10 minutes, add the pasta and plenty of salt and pepper to the pot. Simmer, stirring and adding water as necessary—the mixture should remain thick and stewy, never dry.

5. When the potatoes and pasta are both quite tender—this will take 20 minutes or more—the dish is done. Be careful not to cook the dish too dry. If, at the last minute, the pasta has absorbed nearly all the liquid, stir in another cup or so of water and cook for a minute or two longer. (It may be covered and refrigerated for a day or two or put in a closed container and frozen for several weeks; it's likely that you will need to add more liquid when you reheat it.) Check the seasoning and add some hot pepper, black pepper, and/or salt if needed. Serve hot, in bowls.

PASTA ALLA GRICIA

MAKES 4 TO 6 SERVINGS   TIME: 30 MINUTES

THERE IS AN important and splendid group of pasta recipes that is associated with Rome and the area around it; all the variations begin with bits of cured meat cooked until crisp. Around these delightfully crispy bits—and, of course, their rendered fat—are built a number of different sauces of increasing complexity. The first contains no more than meat and grated cheese and is called *pasta alla gricia;* the second, in which eggs are added, is the well-known pasta (usually spaghetti) carbonara, one of the first authentic nontomato sauces to become popular in the United States, about thirty years ago; and the third is pasta all'Amatriciana, which adds the sweetness of cooked onion and the acidity of tomato.

Salt and freshly ground black pepper

2 tablespoons extra virgin olive oil

1/2 cup (about 1/4 pound) minced guanciale, pancetta, or bacon (see Notes)

1 pound linguine or other long pasta

1/2 cup grated pecorino Romano cheese (see Notes), or more to taste

VARIATIONS

Spaghetti Carbonara
While the pasta is cooking, warm a large bowl and beat 3 eggs in it. Stir in about 1/2 cup freshly grated Parmigiano-Reggiano and the pancetta and its juices. When the pasta is done, drain it and toss with the egg mixture. If the mixture is dry (unlikely), add a little reserved cooking water. Add plenty of black pepper and some more Parmigiano-Reggiano to taste and serve.

NOTE
The eggs will cook fully from the heat of the pasta. If this makes you at all nervous, however, do the final tossing of eggs, cheese, and pasta in the cooking pot, over the lowest heat possible.

(continued)

Pasta all'Amatriciana
In step 1, remove the pancetta with a slotted spoon and, in the juices left behind, sauté a medium onion, sliced, over medium heat, stirring occasionally, until well softened, about 10 minutes. Turn off the heat and let the mixture cool a bit. Stir in 2 cups chopped tomato (canned is fine; drain it first) and turn the heat back to medium. Cook the sauce, stirring occasionally, while you cook the pasta. When the pasta is done, drain it and toss it with the tomato sauce, the reserved pancetta, and at least $1/2$ cup freshly grated pecorino Romano or Parmigiano-Reggiano cheese.

1. Bring a large pot of water to a boil and salt it. Combine the olive oil and meat in a small saucepan over medium heat. Cook, stirring occasionally, until the meat is nicely browned, about 10 minutes. Turn off the heat.
2. Cook the pasta until it is tender but not mushy. Before draining the pasta, remove about a cup of the cooking water and reserve it.
3. Toss the drained pasta with the meat and its juices; stir in the cheese. If the mixture is dry, add a little of the pasta-cooking water (or a little olive oil). Toss in lots of black pepper and serve.

NOTES

Cookbooks and articles about Italian cooking insist that the "genuine" meat for these recipes is pancetta—salted, cured, and rolled pork belly. Pancetta is available in almost any decent Italian deli and in many specialty stores, but for those of us who could not obtain pancetta, bacon—which is also pork belly, but cured and smoked—is an adequate substitute. (In fact, the first choice for these dishes is guanciale, salted and cured pig jowl; but that's hard to find.)

Similarly, pecorino Romano is "essential" to pasta alla gricia, Parmigiano-Reggiano is the most commonly used cheese in carbonara, and the Amatriciana-style sauce is at home with either. But, again, you can choose whatever you like—no one is looking.

SPAGHETTI WITH RED WINE SAUCE
MAKES 4 TO 6 SERVINGS   TIME: 30 MINUTES

IN THIS DISH, the pasta takes on a fruity acidity from the reduced wine—smoothed by the last-minute addition of butter—and a beautiful mahogany glaze that's like nothing you've ever seen.

The kind of wine you use is of some importance, although it need not be expensive. Try a decent Chianti Classico, a light wine from the Côtes-du-Rhône, or a good-quality (red) Zinfandel. This is a true starter, not a main course; follow it with something gutsy, like grilled meat or fish, or something grand like Crisp Roasted Rack of Lamb (page 187).

Salt and freshly ground black
   pepper
$1/2$ cup extra virgin olive oil
1 tablespoon minced garlic
1 teaspoon hot red pepper flakes, or
   to taste

1 pound spaghetti
1 bottle light red wine, like Chianti
1 tablespoon butter

1. Bring a large pot of water to a boil and salt it. Put the oil, garlic, and hot pepper in a large, deep skillet.

2. When the water boils, add the pasta; turn the heat under the skillet to high. Cook the pasta as usual, stirring. As soon as the garlic begins to brown, sprinkle it with salt and pepper to taste and add three-quarters of the bottle of wine (a little more than 2 cups); bring to a boil and keep it there.

3. When the pasta begins to bend—after less than 5 minutes of cooking—drain it and add it to the wine mixture. Cook, stirring occasionally, adding wine a little at a time if the mixture threatens to dry out completely.

4. Taste the pasta frequently. When it is done—tender but with a little bite—stir in the butter and turn off the heat. When the butter glazes the pasta, serve it immediately.

VARIATIONS

• You can easily add another dimension to this dish by tossing in about 1 cup chopped walnuts—pieces of about $1/4$ inch, no smaller—along with the butter.

• A garnish of chopped fresh parsley or basil will make the presentation more attractive and the flavor somewhat brighter.

PASTA, RISOTTO STYLE

MAKES 4 TO 6 SERVINGS   TIME: 30 MINUTES

WHY NOT COOK pasta as you do risotto? That is, add broth a bit at a time and stir frequently, with the goal being a creamy, quickly made pasta (no waiting for the requisite gallon of water to boil!) that requires only marginally more attention than the standard variety. The concept is simple, it makes sense—pasta, like Arborio and other rices used for risotto, is plenty starchy enough—and it takes just the use of good-quality stock and a vegetable to make the dish delicious.

• Substitute carrots, cut into small chunks, for the asparagus; they add vivid color and a marked sweetness. Or experiment with other vegetables.
• Any sharp grated cheese will fill in well for the Parmigiano-Reggiano, especially pecorino Romano.

If you're using canned stock and have a little time, heat it with an onion, a carrot, and a garlic clove before beginning to add it to the pasta. And don't salt the dish until you're finished cooking; canned stock can be overly salty.

1 pound asparagus

3 tablespoons butter or extra virgin olive oil

1 medium onion, chopped

1 pound penne, gemelli, or other cut pasta (long pasta will be far too unwieldy)

6 to 8 cups good-quality stock, heated

Salt and freshly ground black pepper

Freshly grated Parmigiano-Reggiano cheese (optional)

1. Break the woody ends from the asparagus and peel the stalks if necessary. (If you use thin asparagus, you won't have to peel them at all; thicker asparagus should be peeled from the bottom of the flower to the end of the stalk.) Break or cut off the flower ends and cut the stems into $1/2$-inch sections (it looks a little nicer if you cut the stems on a diagonal, but this is hardly essential).

2. Put half the butter or oil in a deep 10- or 12-inch skillet or a broad saucepan and turn the heat to medium-high; when it melts, add the onion and cook, stirring occasionally, until softened and beginning to brown, 3 to 5 minutes. Add the pasta and cook, stirring occasionally, until it begins to brown, about 5 minutes more.

3. Add a ladleful of stock. As the stock is absorbed and the pasta swells, add more stock and continue to stir once in a while, until the pasta is beginning to get tender, about 5 minutes. Add the asparagus stalks and continue to add stock as needed until the pasta is just about done, another 5 minutes or so.

4. Add the asparagus tips and a little more stock, stirring until the tips are crisp-tender, the pasta is cooked to your liking, and the mixture is moist but not soupy (add a little more stock if necessary). Stir in the remaining butter or oil and the Parmigiano-Reggiano to taste if you like and serve.

A FEW TIPS FOR MAKING PARMESAN CUPS

BE CAREFUL not to grate the cheese too finely; you don't want the same powdery consistency you might prefer on pasta. One of the larger holes of a box grater works well, and so does the steel blade of the food processor, which produces small, even pellets of cheese.

Baking the cheese disks doesn't present much of a problem, and it's easy enough to tell when they're done because the edges begin to brown. But removing them from the baking sheet can be tricky: be sure to allow the rounds to cool slightly so that they can firm up a bit—thirty to sixty seconds is right for me, but if your baking sheet retains more heat, it might take a little longer—and then use the thinnest spatula you have to gently lift them off the baking sheet. Drape the soft mass over a narrow glass, and shape gently; the cups will be ready to fill in a few minutes.

Though they are best when fresh, the cups will retain both shape and flavor for a couple of hours.

PARMESAN CUPS WITH ORZO RISOTTO

MAKES 4 OR MORE APPETIZER SERVINGS   TIME: 30 MINUTES

A COUPLE OF years ago, on a trip to central Italy—where true Parmigiano-Reggiano is made—I learned yet another use for the world's most important cheese. A cook in a trattoria was taking handfuls of the grated stuff, sprinkling them in a skillet, and forming melted cheese pancakes. While they were still warm, he draped them over the back of a cup, to form crisp, edible, single-ingredient containers. He filled these with a mixture of zucchini, eggplant, and tomatoes and sent them out as a first course.

I found the idea intriguing, but not all that easy to duplicate at home, where my skillet seemed always too hot or too cool, the pancakes too thick or too thin. But when I took the task seriously and set about figuring out the most reliable way to produce these Parmigiano-Reggiano cups, it turned out to be fairly straightforward. Thanks to the miracle of the nonstick surface, just put four rounds of grated cheese on a baking sheet and, five minutes later, they're done.

VARIATIONS

- Cheese cups can be made with almost any hard cheese or a combination of cheeses. Manchego, pecorino, and other sheep's milk cheeses are especially good.

For fillings, try:
- Steamed and chopped spinach (other than a grating of pepper, no seasoning is necessary)
- Beef stew or other stewed meat
- Ratatouille or other stewed vegetables

2 cups good-quality chicken or other stock
1 cup orzo (rice-shaped pasta)
1 cup freshly grated Parmigiano-Reggiano cheese (about $1/4$ pound)

Salt and freshly ground black pepper
$1/2$ cup minced fresh parsley

1. Preheat the oven to 350°F.
2. Bring the stock to a boil in a 6- to 8-cup saucepan; stir in the orzo, cover, and turn the heat to medium-low. Set a timer for 15 minutes.
3. Use a $1/4$-cup measure to make 4 rounds of Parmigiano-Reggiano on a nonstick baking sheet. Smooth the rounds into thin pancakes, 5 or 6 inches across; the thickness need not be perfectly uniform. Put the baking sheet in the oven.
4. The Parmigiano-Reggiano rounds are done when the centers darken slightly and the edges begin to brown, 5 to 6 minutes. Remove the baking sheet from the oven and let it stand for about a minute, then carefully lift each of the rounds and drape it over the bottom of a narrow cup or glass to form a cup shape. Let dry for about 5 minutes.
5. The orzo is done when it is tender and all the liquid has been absorbed. Season it with pepper and very little salt, then stir in the parsley. Spoon a portion of orzo into each of the Parmigiano-Reggiano cups and serve.

RICE NOODLES WITH BASIL

MAKES 4 SERVINGS   TIME: 40 MINUTES

IN A STIR-FRY like this, you can get away with simply soaking rice noodles, but I believe boiling the noodles for 30 seconds or so after soaking improves them a bit. Try it and see. Substitute soy sauce for the nam pla if you like. Thai basil, which looks different from regular basil, can be found at many Asian markets; it's fabulously fragrant.

$3/4$ pound rice noodles ("rice stick")

2 tablespoons peanut or vegetable oil

1 tablespoon minced garlic

1 teaspoon minced fresh hot chiles or hot red pepper flakes, or to taste

1 teaspoon sugar

Salt and freshly ground black pepper

2 tablespoons nam pla (fish sauce) or soy sauce, or to taste

1 tablespoon fresh lime juice, or to taste

$1/2$ cup roughly chopped fresh Thai or other basil or mint

1. Soak the rice noodles in hot water to cover for 15 to 30 minutes, changing the water once or twice if possible to speed the softening. Meanwhile, bring a pot of water to a boil. When the noodles are soft, drain them, then immerse them in the boiling water for about 30 seconds. Drain and rinse in cold water.

2. Heat the oil in a deep skillet, preferably nonstick, over medium-high heat. Add the garlic and chiles and cook for about 30 seconds, stirring. Raise the heat to high, then add the noodles and sugar and toss to blend. Season with salt and pepper to taste.

3. When the noodles are hot, add the nam pla and lime juice. Taste and adjust the seasoning as necessary, then stir in the basil or mint and serve.

VARIATIONS

• Before adding the garlic, quickly stir-fry about 1 cup ground or chopped pork, beef, chicken, or turkey until the color is gone. Proceed as directed.

• Before adding the garlic, stir-fry 1 to 2 cups tender shredded vegetables, like leeks, cabbage, Chinese cabbage (like bok choy), celery, bean sprouts, sliced mushrooms, or a combination. Proceed as directed.

• Add about 1 tablespoon curry powder to the oil along with the garlic. Add more to taste if necessary. Proceed as directed.

STIR-FRIED COCONUT NOODLES

MAKES 4 SERVINGS   TIME: 45 MINUTES

YOU CAN SUBSTITUTE Italian linguine or spaghetti for the rice noodles in this dish. Although the texture will not be the same, the dish will still be good. Boil the noodles nearly to doneness in the normal fashion, then rinse before proceeding.

$3/4$ pound linguine-style rice noodles

3 tablespoons grapeseed, corn, or other neutral oil

1 pound minced or ground boneless pork or chicken

1 yellow or red bell pepper, minced

1 eggplant (about $1/2$ pound) cut into $1/2$-inch cubes

1 tablespoon minced garlic

One 12- to 14-ounce can coconut milk ($1^{1}/2$ to 2 cups)

Nam pla (fish sauce), soy sauce, or salt

Freshly ground black pepper

Minced fresh cilantro for garnish

1. Soak the noodles in very hot water to cover until you're ready to add them to the stir-fry. Meanwhile, put a tablespoon of the oil in a large skillet or wok and turn the heat to high. A minute later, add the meat and cook, stirring occasionally, until it browns and loses its raw look, about 5 minutes. Remove with a slotted spoon and set aside.

2. Add another tablespoon of the oil to the skillet, followed by the pepper and eggplant. Cook over medium-high heat, stirring occasionally, until the pepper and eggplant are browned and tender, about 10 minutes. Remove with a slotted spoon and combine with the meat.

3. Add the remaining tablespoon oil, followed immediately by the garlic and, about 30 seconds later, the coconut milk. Cook over medium-high heat, stirring and scraping with a wooden spoon, for about a minute. Add the drained noodles along with the meat and vegetables and cook until the noodles absorb most of the coconut milk, about 3 minutes.

4. Season with nam pla, soy sauce, or salt to taste, then add plenty of black pepper. Garnish with cilantro and serve.

ASIANS USE WHEAT and rice noodles with equal frequency—but not interchangeably. Rice noodles have no equivalent in European cooking. Made from rice powder, and almost always sold dried, they are nearly as convenient as fresh wheat noodles. Regardless of their name (rice stick, rice vermicelli, Oriental-style noodle, and so on), rice noodles are easily recognized by their grayish white, translucent appearance and by the fact that because of their somewhat irregular shapes they are never packed in as orderly a fashion as wheat noodles (they are quite long and are packaged folded up over themselves).

They're best when soaked for a few minutes in hot water, then boiled just until their raw flavor disappears. Finally, they're never really what you call al dente, but rather quite soft.

You might see fresh rice noodles from time to time, but for the most part they are sold dried, like most pasta, only in far fewer shapes, ranging from very thin to linguine-like to fettuccine-like; that's about it. The superthin ones (usually called "vermicelli") are best for soups. The two thicker varieties, usually called "rice sticks," are best for stir-fries.

PAD THAI

MAKES 4 SERVINGS   TIME: 30 MINUTES

HERE'S MY TAKE on Pad Thai. There are a lot of ingredients here, but most of them keep well in your pantry, and substituting is easy—you could use finely chopped cabbage in place of the bean sprouts or substitute soy or hoisin sauce for the nam pla.

6 dried black (shiitake) mushrooms or fresh shiitakes, trimmed of their stems and sliced

$3/4$ pound thin rice noodles ("vermicelli" or "rice stick")

2 tablespoons peanut, corn, grapeseed, or other neutral oil

1 tablespoon slivered or minced garlic

$3/4$ pound shrimp, peeled and, if you like, deveined, cut into bite-sized pieces

$1/2$ teaspoon chile paste or hot red pepper flakes, or to taste

2 eggs, lightly beaten

3 tablespoons nam pla (fish sauce),
   or more to taste

2 teaspoons sugar

Stock, water, or mushroom-soaking
   liquid as needed

Salt

1 cup bean sprouts (optional)

$^1/_2$ cup torn fresh basil leaves,
   preferably Thai basil (optional)

1. Put the dried mushrooms in a small bowl and cover them with boiling water. Put the noodles in a large bowl and cover them with hot water. When the mushrooms are soft, drain, reserving their soaking liquid; trim and slice them.

2. Put the oil in a large nonstick skillet over high heat. Add the garlic and stir; add the shrimp and cook, stirring occasionally, for about a minute. Stir in the mushrooms and chile paste.

3. Drain the noodles and add them to the skillet. Cook, stirring occasionally, for about a minute. Make a well in the center of the noodles and pour the eggs into this well. Scramble, gradually integrating the egg with the noodles; this will take less than a minute. Stir in the nam pla and sugar. If the noodles are clumpy, add about $^1/_2$ cup of liquid to allow them to separate and become saucy (use more liquid if necessary, but do not make the mixture soupy). Add salt to taste, then stir in the bean sprouts and basil if you like. Serve.

FRESH CHINESE NOODLES
WITH BROWN SAUCE

MAKES 4 SERVINGS   TIME: 20 MINUTES

YOU CAN FIND fresh Chinese-style (and Japanese-style) wheat noodles at most supermarkets these days. They're a great convenience food and, for some reason, seem to me more successful than prepackaged "fresh" Italian noodles. Here they're briefly cooked and then combined with a stir-fried mixture of pork, vegetables, and Chinese sauces; it's very much a Chinese restaurant dish.

Both ground bean sauce and hoisin sauce can be found at supermarkets (if you can't find ground bean sauce, just use a little more hoisin), but you can usually find a better selection (and higher-quality versions) at Chinese markets. Usually, the fewer ingredients they contain, the better they are.

VARIATIONS

• Toss the noodles with 1 cup bean sprouts or lightly stir-fried snow peas before dressing.

Fresh Chinese Noodles with Chicken, or Meatless Fresh Chinese Noodles
Substitute ground chicken or turkey for the pork; or eliminate the meat entirely, sautéing the scallion, ginger, and garlic in a couple tablespoons of peanut oil.

1/2 to 3/4 pound ground pork

1 cup minced scallion

1 tablespoon minced garlic

1 tablespoon minced peeled fresh
    ginger

1 cup chicken stock or water

2 tablespoons ground bean sauce

2 tablespoons hoisin sauce

1 tablespoon soy sauce

1 pound fresh egg or wheat noodles

1 tablespoon sesame oil

1. Bring a large pot of water to a boil. Meanwhile, put a large skillet over medium-high heat. Add the pork, crumbling it to bits as you add it and stirring to break up any clumps; add half the scallion, along with the garlic and ginger, and stir. Add the stock or water; stir in the bean, hoisin, and soy sauces and cook, stirring occasionally, until thick, about 5 minutes. Reduce the heat and keep warm.

2. Cook the noodles, stirring, until tender, 3 to 5 minutes. Drain and dress with the sauce. Garnish with the remaining scallion, drizzle the sesame oil over all, and serve.

SAUCES AND CONDIMENTS

FRESH SALSA

MAKES ABOUT 2 CUPS   TIME: 20 MINUTES

THIS RECIPE IS BASIC—make it a few times and you'll find ways to vary it to perfectly suit your tastes.

12 plum tomatoes	1 tablespoon chile powder, or to taste
1 large white onion, chopped	Salt
2 garlic cloves, minced	1 cup fresh cilantro leaves, chopped

1. Broil the tomatoes as close to the heat source as you can get them, until blistered and a little blackened, 5 to 10 minutes.
2. Put them in a blender, skins and all, with the onion, garlic, chile powder, and a big pinch of salt. Whir until chunky, then stir in the cilantro by hand. This is best used right away but will retain decent flavor, refrigerated, for a day or two.

PICO DE GALLO

MAKES 2 CUPS

TIME: AT LEAST 1 HOUR, LARGELY UNATTENDED

THIS IS WHAT most Americans are talking about when they say salsa. You can make it hot or not, as you like; it's a good use for less-than-perfect tomatoes and an excellent sauce–side dish accompaniment for anything grilled, particularly seafood.

4 medium tomatoes	Salt and freshly ground black pepper
1/2 cup chopped scallion	Minced fresh chiles or hot red
1 garlic clove, minced	pepper flakes (optional)
2 tablespoons fresh lime juice	1/2 cup chopped fresh cilantro

1. Core the tomatoes (cut a cone-shaped wedge out of the stem end) and chop them. Toss them with the scallion, garlic, lime juice, salt, pepper, and chiles if you like. Set aside until you're ready to eat, or for about an hour.

2. Toss in the cilantro and serve.

—————————

PAN-GRILLED TOMATO SALSA

MAKES 4 SERVINGS   TIME: 20 MINUTES

THIS RELISH IS good with a bit of minced jalapeño or habanero chile if you like hot food. If you have them on hand, don't hesitate to add up to a quarter cup of fresh herbs, like basil, oregano, or marjoram.

3 large, meaty tomatoes, cored and cut into thick slices

1/4 cup extra virgin olive oil

2 tablespoons sherry vinegar or balsamic vinegar

Salt and freshly ground black pepper

1. Heat a large skillet, preferably cast iron or nonstick, over medium-high heat for about 5 minutes. Add the tomatoes, raise the heat to high, and cook until lightly charred on one side, 3 to 5 minutes. Turn and cook the other side very lightly, about 1 minute. If necessary, work in batches to avoid crowding the tomatoes.

2. Combine the olive oil and vinegar in a large, shallow dish and, as the tomatoes are done, turn them in the mixture. Season and serve as a side dish or as a sauce for grilled or roasted fish or chicken. (This can be refrigerated for up to a day or two; bring to room temperature before serving.)

CHIPOTLE-PEACH SALSA

MAKES ABOUT 4 CUPS   TIME: 1 HOUR

"CHILES IN ADOBO" are chipotles (wood-smoked jalapeños) in tomato sauce, sold in cans. They're available at any market with a good selection of Mexican foods. If you can't find one, substitute hot chile powder or even cayenne. This is lovely with any grilled meat.

4 cups pitted peaches in $1/4$-inch dice

1 cup red bell pepper in $1/4$-inch dice

2 chiles in adobo, pureed

$1/4$ cup fresh lime juice

$1/2$ cup minced fresh cilantro

2 tablespoons sugar

Combine all the ingredients and let them marry for up to 1 hour before serving.

PARSLEY-VINEGAR SAUCE

MAKES ABOUT 1 CUP   TIME: 10 MINUTES

WHEN YOU GET past using parsley as a garnish and sprinkle a handful on top of a dish just before serving, you begin to appreciate the bright, clean flavor of this common herb. And when you realize that it remains in season far longer than basil, rosemary, or other popular herbs, you get a further sense of its value. You can also blend parsley with vinegar to make a sharp, spiky sauce that is an ideal accompaniment to the simplest grilled, broiled, or roasted meat—great on well-browned steaks, pork, or chicken, or on Salmon Burgers (page 107).

1 cup packed fresh parsley leaves (about 1 ounce)

1 tablespoon extra virgin olive oil

1 small garlic clove, peeled

Salt and freshly ground black pepper

$1/3$ cup rice vinegar, sherry vinegar, or other good-quality, fairly mild vinegar

• Add toasted walnuts or pine nuts, about 2 tablespoons, after the water. Pulse just until the nuts are chopped.
• Add the chopped white of a hard-cooked egg or two.
• Add grated Parmigiano-Reggiano or other hard cheese to taste, at least 2 tablespoons.
• Substitute a shallot for the garlic to weaken the sauce's bite.

1. Put the parsley in a food processor along with the oil, garlic, a pinch of salt, and $1/4$ teaspoon pepper. With the machine on, drizzle the vinegar through the feed tube until the parsley is pureed.

2. Add 1 tablespoon of water and pulse the machine on and off a couple of times; taste. The mixture should be sharp, but not overpoweringly so. If it seems too strong, add a little more water (the texture will be quite loose, something like thick orange juice). Taste and add more salt and pepper if necessary. Pass the sauce at the table, using a spoon to serve it.

MARJORAM "PESTO"

MAKES 4 SERVINGS   TIME: 30 MINUTES

MARJORAM IS RELATED to and resembles oregano, but its flavor is better. Oregano is a good but not perfect substitute. This sauce is excellent over simply cooked seafood.

2 cups fresh marjoram, leaves and small stems only

1 large or 2 small garlic cloves, peeled

2 teaspoons red wine vinegar

$1/3$ cup extra virgin olive oil

1 tablespoon capers, drained

2 anchovy fillets (optional)

Salt and freshly ground black pepper

1. Combine the marjoram and garlic in a blender or small food processor. Process until finely minced, scraping down the sides with a rubber spatula once or twice if necessary. Add the vinegar and most of the oil and process until smooth.

2. Add the capers and anchovies if you like and pulse the machine on and off a few times; you want to mince, not puree, the mixture, so don't overprocess.

3. Stir in the remaining oil, along with salt and pepper to taste. Serve at room temperature.

- Although many sources insist that flat-leaf parsley is better than the curly-leaf variety, blind tastings have not borne out that myth. What matters more is freshness—limp parsley has less flavor.
- The parsley's thick stems must be removed for preparations like these. Don't discard them: use them to bolster the flavor of chicken stock.
- Parsley may be sandy, so wash it well. In the quantity given below, it's worth using a salad spinner to dry it.

CREAMED PARSLEY SAUCE
MAKES 4 TO 6 SERVINGS   TIME: 10 MINUTES

PARSLEY IS THE most reliable and underrated herb in the western culinary world. Although we've come a long way from the days when its major role was as a decorative sprig on the side of a plate, we still don't use it in the kinds of quantities we could. Here it is cooked like a vegetable—like spinach, really—to create a delicious, fresh-tasting sauce that I frequently serve over pasta but that also makes an interesting foil for simply grilled or broiled chicken breasts.

2 tablespoons butter or extra virgin olive oil

1/4 cup minced shallot or onion

2 or 3 bunches (about 1 pound) parsley, stemmed

1 cup heavy cream or half-and-half

Salt and freshly ground black pepper

Freshly grated Parmigiano-Reggiano cheese (optional)

1. Put the butter or oil in a deep skillet and turn the heat to medium. When the butter melts or the oil is hot, add the shallot and cook, stirring occasionally, until softened, 3 to 5 minutes.

2. Add the parsley and cook, stirring, for about a minute. Add the cream and turn the heat to low. Season the parsley mixture with salt and pepper and serve at once, with the cheese if you like.

SUN-DRIED TOMATO SAUCE

MAKES ABOUT 4 SERVINGS

TIME: 2 HOURS, LARGELY UNATTENDED

YOU CAN BUY sun-dried tomatoes already reconstituted and soaked in olive oil, but they're expensive. It's certainly easy enough—and only slightly less convenient if you think ahead—to begin with dried tomatoes. They're almost as tough as shoe leather when you buy them but can easily be reconstituted: Soak them in hot water to cover until they're soft, about an hour. (You might change the water once it cools to hasten the softening.) Drain the tomatoes and marinate them in a good fruity olive oil to cover (a half cup or more) for at least an hour.

After that, making the tomato paste takes just a moment. Traditionally, the tomatoes are pounded, usually with garlic, in a mortar and pestle. I use a small food processor and like the resulting texture very much.

WHERE TO USE SUN-DRIED TOMATO SAUCE

Some of the many uses for this sauce:
• As a pasta sauce, but sparingly, and thinned with a little of the hot pasta-cooking water
• As a spread on bread or sandwiches
• As a dip for raw vegetables or crackers
• As a condiment for chicken or fish
• As a sauce for cooked bland vegetables, such as boiled potatoes

$1/2$ cup softened sun-dried tomatoes with their oil

1 small or $1/2$ large garlic clove, or to taste

Salt

4 fresh basil leaves, chopped (optional)

1 tablespoon fresh lemon juice (optional)

3 tablespoons pine nuts

Additional extra virgin olive oil if necessary

1. Put the tomatoes and a tablespoon or so of their oil in a small food processor along with the garlic and a good pinch of salt. Process until fairly smooth, stopping the machine and stirring down the mixture with a rubber spatula as necessary.

2. Add the basil and lemon juice if you like; pulse the machine a few times to blend. Remove the paste from the machine and stir in, by hand, the nuts and just enough additional oil to make the mixture silky rather than oily. Taste and adjust the seasoning. The sauce will keep, covered with a thin layer of oil and refrigerated in a tightly covered container, for at least a week. But its flavor is best when served immediately.

FIG RELISH

MAKES 4 SERVINGS TIME: 10 MINUTES

WHILE THE BEST way to eat figs is out of hand—few fruits are as delicious when ripe—there are rewarding ways to use them in recipes; this fig relish is one of them. It is especially brilliant on grilled swordfish or tuna (try it on Grilled Fish the Mediterranean Way, page 98), but nearly as good with grilled or broiled chicken (especially dark meat), pork, lamb, or beef. Note that all of these foods contain some fat; because the relish is so lean, combining it with nonfatty meats or fish—such as boneless chicken or flounder—produces a dish that seems to lack substance. Gently rinse and stem the figs; chop them into about $^1/_4$-inch pieces,

$^1/_2$ pound ripe fresh figs

1 tablespoon minced drained capers

Zest of 1 lemon, minced

Juice of 1 lemon

2 tablespoons olive oil

Salt and freshly ground black
    pepper

2 tablespoons chopped fresh
    parsley

2 tablespoons chopped fresh basil
    (optional)

being sure to catch all of their juices. Toss in a bowl with the capers, lemon zest and juice, olive oil, and salt and pepper to taste. Just before serving (you can wait up to 2 hours), add the herbs, then taste and adjust the seasonings.

• Add a tiny amount ($^1/_4$ teaspoon or so) of minced garlic. Alternatively, crush a garlic clove and let it sit in the mixture for a few minutes, then fish it out just before serving.
• Add 1 teaspoon or more minced shallot.
• Add a couple tablespoons chopped olives or anchovies.
• Substitute lime zest and juice or mild vinegar for the lemon.
• Change the herbs; 1 teaspoon minced fresh thyme or rosemary in place of the basil makes the relish considerably more pungent.

DRIED MUSHROOM PUREE

MAKES 4 SERVINGS   TIME: 20 MINUTES

IT ISN'T OFTEN that you can make a condiment with a single dried ingredient, but since dried mushrooms have become widely available, that occurrence has become more common. If you simmer dried mushrooms until tender, then toss them in a blender with their cooking liquid, you get a thick puree, potent and delicious, something you can use wherever you'd use salsa or even ketchup.

You can use any dried mushrooms for this condiment, from the extremely inexpensive shiitakes (also called "black mushrooms") sold at Asian markets to the prince of dried mushrooms, the porcini. Smoky porcini (usually imported from Chile or Poland) are really good here.

1 ounce dried porcini (about $^1/_2$ cup loosely packed)

Salt and freshly ground black pepper

1. Combine the mushrooms with $2^1/_2$ cups of water in a 4- or 6-cup saucepan and turn the heat to medium-high. Bring to a boil, then adjust the heat so the mixture simmers gently. Cook until the mushrooms are tender, about 15 minutes.
2. Remove the mushrooms with a slotted spoon and put in a blender. Strain the liquid through a paper towel put in a sieve or through a couple of layers of cheesecloth; there will be about 1 cup. Add most of the liquid to the mushrooms and puree, adding the remaining liquid if necessary to allow the machine to do its work.
3. Season to taste with salt and pepper and serve or cover and refrigerate for up to a couple of days.

VARIATIONS

While the basic sauce—mushroom, salt, pepper, and water—is surprisingly complex, you can give it additional depth by adding one—or all—of the following to the blender during step 2:
• A peeled shallot or small garlic clove
• 1 teaspoon or more fresh thyme leaves (or $^1/_2$ teaspoon dried)
• 1 tablespoon or more port, tomato paste, or soy sauce
In each case, be sure to taste the puree before you remove it from the blender; the mushroom flavor is so strong that it may take a relatively large quantity of a complementary ingredient to make an impression.

RED PEPPER PUREE

MAKES AT LEAST 4 SERVINGS   TIME: ABOUT 1 HOUR

ROASTED RED PEPPER puree is incredibly useful, easy to make, and delicious—you can eat it with a spoon. It contains two basic ingredients, red bell peppers and olive oil, and both are always readily available. And since making a batch is about as difficult as scrambling an egg, and the puree keeps fairly well, there's little reason not to have some on hand. If you are so inclined, you can flavor it with any number of herbs (thyme, basil, and parsley are fine) or spices, like cumin or chile powder (or minced chiles). I usually leave the sauce unadulterated.

Of course you can use bottled or canned preroasted peppers ("pimientos") here, though the results will not be as fresh tasting.

4 large red bell peppers (about 2 pounds)	Salt
	1/2 cup extra virgin olive oil

1. Preheat the oven to 500°F. Line a roasting pan with enough aluminum foil to fold over the top later. Put the bell peppers in the pan and the pan in the oven. Roast, turning the peppers about every 10 minutes, until they collapse, about 40 minutes.

2. Fold the foil over the peppers and allow them to cool. Working over a bowl, remove the core, skin, and seeds from each of the peppers, reserving some of the liquid.

3. Put the pepper pulp in a food processor with about 2 tablespoons of the reserved liquid. Add a large pinch of salt and turn on the machine; drizzle the oil in through the feed tube. Stop the machine, then taste and add more salt and/or olive oil if necessary. Store, well covered, in the refrigerator (for several days) or the freezer (up to a month).

VARIATIONS

- Add a couple tablespoons of puree to the cooking liquid of any simmering grain—rice, couscous, or quinoa, for example.
- Use in place of or with tomatoes in pasta sauce. For example, sauté several vegetables and bind them with the puree during the last minute of cooking.
- Fold into omelets or scrambled eggs, with or without cooked vegetables.
- Combine with chopped fresh basil, grated Parmigiano-Reggiano, and minced garlic for a pesto-like pasta sauce.
- Emulsify with fresh lemon juice, salt, and pepper to make a beautiful salad dressing.
- Spread on crostini or pizza before baking.
- Use as a finishing sauce for roasted eggplant, zucchini, or other vegetables.
- Serve as a condiment with grilled or roasted fish, meat, or chicken.
- Stir into soups or stews just before serving.
- Mash a couple tablespoons of puree, with a little olive oil, minced garlic, and cracked black pepper, into fresh, salty cheese—like feta or goat—to make a dip for bread or vegetables.

You can integrate almost
anything that appeals to
you into your vinaigrette.
Some quick ideas, many of
which may be combined:
• Any fresh or dried herb,
fresh by the teaspoon
or tablespoon, dried by
the pinch
• Minced fresh garlic and/or
peeled ginger to taste
• Soy sauce, Worcestershire
sauce, meat or vegetable
stock, or other liquid
seasonings, as much as
1 tablespoon
• Honey or other
sweeteners to taste
• Whole-grain or dry
mustard to taste
• Cayenne or hot red
pepper flakes, minced
fresh hot chiles, or grated
or prepared horseradish
to taste
• Freshly grated
Parmigiano-Reggiano or
other hard cheese, or
crumbled Roquefort or
other blue cheese, at least
1 tablespoon
• Capers or minced pickles,
preferably cornichons, at
least 1 tablespoon
• Sour cream, yogurt, or
pureed soft tofu, about
2 tablespoons
• Ground spices, such as
curry powder, five-spice
powder, or nutmeg, in very
small quantities

BASIC VINAIGRETTE

MAKES ABOUT $^2/_3$ CUP   TIME: 10 MINUTES

IT'S HARD TO IMAGINE five minutes in the kitchen better spent than those spent making vinaigrette, the closest thing to an all-purpose sauce.

The standard ratio for making vinaigrette is three parts oil to one part vinegar, but because the vinegars I use are mild and extra virgin olive oil is quite assertive, I usually wind up at about two parts oil to one part vinegar, or even a little stronger. Somewhere in that range you're going to find a home for your own taste; start by using a ratio of three to one and taste, adding more vinegar until you're happy. (You may even prefer more vinegar than olive oil; there's nothing wrong with that.)

Be sure to use good wine vinegar; balsamic and sherry vinegars, while delicious, are too dominant for some salads, fine for others. Lemon juice is a fine substitute, but because it is less acidic than most vinegars—3 or 4 percent compared to 6 or 7 percent—you will need more of it.

The ingredients may be combined with a spoon, a fork, a whisk, or a blender. Hand tools give you an unconvincing emulsion that must be used immediately. Blenders produce vinaigrettes that very much resemble thin mayonnaise in color and thickness—without using egg. They also dispose of the job of mincing the shallot; just peel, chop, and dump it into the container at the last minute (if you add it earlier, it will be pureed, depriving you of the pleasure of its distinctive crunch).

This is best made fresh but will keep, refrigerated, for a few days. Bring it back to room temperature and whisk briefly before using it.

$^1/_2$ cup extra virgin olive oil

3 tablespoons or more good-quality
   wine vinegar

Salt and freshly ground black
   pepper

1 heaping teaspoon Dijon mustard

1 large shallot (about 1 ounce),
   peeled and cut into chunks

1. Combine all ingredients except the shallot in a blender and turn the machine on; a creamy emulsion will form within 30 seconds. Taste and add more vinegar, a teaspoon or two at a time, until the balance tastes right to you.

2. Add the shallot and turn the machine on and off a few times until the shallot is minced within the dressing. Taste, adjust the seasoning, and serve.

MAYONNAISE

MAKES 1 CUP   TIME: 10 MINUTES

WHETHER YOU WORK by hand or with a blender or food processor, it takes just five minutes to make mayonnaise, and when you're done you have a flavorful, creamy dressing that is so far superior to the bottled stuff you may not recognize it as the same thing. Next to vinaigrette, it's the most useful of all dressings, and despite its luxurious nature it contains little saturated fat. If you're worried about the health aspects of using a raw egg, start with bottled mayonnaise and beat in a little oil and/or any of the suggested additions.

1 egg yolk

2 teaspoons Dijon mustard

Salt and freshly ground black
   pepper

1 cup olive or other oil

1 tablespoon fresh lemon juice or
   vinegar

1. To make the mayonnaise by hand: Combine the egg, mustard, and salt and pepper to taste in a medium bowl. Use a wire whisk to combine, then add the oil in a thin, steady stream, beating all the while. When the mixture becomes thick and creamy, you can add the oil a little faster. When it is all integrated, whisk in the lemon juice. Taste and adjust the seasoning.

   To make the mayonnaise in a blender or food processor: Combine

VARIATIONS

Like vinaigrette, the flavor of mayonnaise can be varied almost infinitely. Many of the suggested ingredients can be combined; use your judgment.

• Add a garlic clove at the beginning. Try adding 1/2 cup roasted red peppers (or canned pimiento) and a little cayenne at the same time.

• Vary the kind of acid you use: fresh lime or orange juice or any type of vinegar. If the acidity is too strong when you're done, beat in a little warm water.

• Add 2 or 3 anchovy fillets at the beginning.

• Add any fresh herbs you like. Start with a small amount and taste, adding more at the end if you wish. If you're using a machine, they will turn the mayonnaise green. If you're working by hand, you will have herb-flecked mayonnaise.

(continued)

(Variations, continued)

• Add horseradish, Worcestershire sauce, or spices or spice mixes to the finished mayonnaise, tasting as you go.

Tartar Sauce

Combine 1 cup mayonnaise with $1/4$ cup minced cornichons or other pickles, 2 tablespoons minced shallot, and horseradish to taste.

Aïoli

Combine 1 cup mayonnaise with 1 teaspoon finely minced garlic and a pinch of saffron. Let rest for an hour or so before using.

the egg, mustard, and salt and pepper in the machine's container and pulse on and off a few times. With the machine running, slowly add the oil through the top or feed tube. When the mixture becomes thick and creamy, you can add the oil a little faster. When it is all integrated, pulse in the lemon juice. Taste and adjust the seasoning.

2. If the mayonnaise is thicker than you like (a distinct possibility if you're using a machine), thin with warm water, sweet cream, or sour cream.

BETTER COCKTAIL SAUCE

MAKES ABOUT 1 CUP   TIME: 10 MINUTES

THIS IS A rich cocktail sauce, laced with butter but made spiky with vinegar and horseradish. Make it as hot as you like and serve it warm or cold. It is a natural partner for poached, grilled, or otherwise cooked shrimp.

1 cup ketchup

1 tablespoon vinegar

3 tablespoons butter

2 tablespoons prepared horseradish, or to taste

Combine the ketchup, vinegar, and butter in a small saucepan and cook over medium-low heat, stirring occasionally, until the butter melts. (At this point, you can keep the sauce warm for an hour—but make the heat as low as possible.) Add horseradish to taste.

SHALLOT-THYME BUTTER

MAKES 8 TABLESPOONS ($^1/_2$ CUP)   TIME: A COUPLE MINUTES

COMPOUND BUTTERS can be stored, well wrapped, in the freezer for two or three weeks.

8 tablespoons (1 stick) unsalted
   butter, softened slightly
$^1/_4$ teaspoon fresh thyme leaves
10 chives, minced

1 shallot, minced
Salt and freshly ground black
   pepper
$^1/_2$ teaspoon red wine vinegar

Cream the butter with a fork, integrating all the ingredients, using about $^1/_2$ teaspoon each of salt and pepper. Taste and add more of any ingredient you deem necessary.

HORSERADISH-GINGER BUTTER

MAKES 8 TABLESPOONS ($^1/_2$ CUP)   TIME: A COUPLE MINUTES

8 tablespoons (1 stick) unsalted
   butter, softened slightly
1 teaspoon prepared horseradish or
   wasabi

1 teaspoon finely minced peeled
   fresh ginger
1 teaspoon good-quality soy sauce
Freshly ground black pepper

Cream the butter with a fork, integrating all the ingredients. Taste and add more of any ingredient you deem necessary.

Compound butters can be made with any seasoning you like: mustard, garlic, ginger, chiles, vinegar, or citrus juice and zest, just to name a few. In good weather, you can easily experiment with adding the fresh herb of your choice—chervil is especially nice, as are dill and parsley.

GARLIC-OREGANO BUTTER

MAKES 8 TABLESPOONS (^{1}/$_2$ CUP)   TIME: A COUPLE MINUTES

8 tablespoons (1 stick) unsalted
    butter, softened slightly
1 teaspoon finely minced garlic or
    1 tablespoon roasted garlic
    puree

1 teaspoon finely minced fresh
    oregano or marjoram
Salt and freshly ground black
    pepper
1 teaspoon fresh lemon juice

Cream the butter with a fork, integrating all the ingredients, using about ^{1}/$_2$ teaspoon each of salt and pepper. Taste and add more of any ingredient you deem necessary.

CHILE-CILANTRO BUTTER

MAKES: 8 TABLESPOONS (^{1}/$_2$ CUP)   TIME: A COUPLE MINUTES

8 tablespoons (1 stick) unsalted
    butter, softened slightly
1 small fresh chile, seeded and
    finely minced

1 tablespoon minced fresh cilantro
Salt and freshly ground black
    pepper
1 teaspoon fresh lime juice

Cream the butter with a fork, integrating all the ingredients, using about ^{1}/$_2$ teaspoon each of salt and pepper. Taste and add more of any ingredient you deem necessary.

DESSERTS

SUGARED STRAWBERRIES

MAKES 4 SERVINGS   TIME: 20 MINUTES

THIS RECIPE AND the four that follow share one basic requirement: in-season, preferably locally grown strawberries. In the event that you can't find strawberries that match that description, substitute any other berries—blackberries, blueberries, raspberries—that are at their peak.

Look for strawberries that are dark red, inside and out. The sugar will juice up any strawberries and make them sweeter of course, but it cannot work miracles.

1 quart strawberries, rinsed, hulled, and sliced

1/4 cup sugar, or more to taste

Sweetened whipped cream or vanilla ice cream (optional)

Toss the strawberries with the sugar and let sit at room temperature for about 20 minutes, or until juicy. Serve, if you like, with whipped cream or ice cream.

STRAWBERRIES WITH BALSAMIC VINEGAR

MAKES 4 SERVINGS   TIME: 15 MINUTES

HERE'S A STRAWBERRY dessert that not only is delicious and intriguing but also can compete with plain fruit in lightness. Strawberries are sugared to juice them up a bit, then drizzled with balsamic vinegar and sprinkled with a pinch of black pepper. The result is so elegant that you'll find it in great restaurants from here to Emilia-Romagna, the home of balsamic vinegar. It's an ideal dessert after a heavy meal. Serve, if you like, with a few crisp cookies or a slice of pound, sponge, or angel food cake.

This will not hold for any length of time; you can sugar the berries an hour or two before you want to serve them, but no longer.

1 quart strawberries, rinsed, hulled, and sliced, or a mixture of several berries

1/4 cup sugar, or more to taste

1 teaspoon high-quality balsamic vinegar, or more to taste

About 1/8 teaspoon freshly ground black pepper

1/4 cup loosely packed fresh mint leaves, torn or coarsely chopped (optional)

1. Toss the berries with 1/4 cup sugar and let sit for 10 minutes or longer. Do not refrigerate.

2. Sprinkle with the vinegar; toss gently, then taste and add more sugar or vinegar if necessary. Sprinkle with the pepper and the mint if using, toss again, and serve.

STRAWBERRY FOOL

MAKES 4 SERVINGS   TIME: 20 MINUTES

A SIMPLE, TRADITIONAL, and super-rich dessert.

2 cups strawberries, picked over and trimmed of stems

1/2 cup superfine or confectioners' sugar, plus 1 1/2 teaspoons, plus more if needed

1 cup heavy cream, preferably not ultra-pasteurized

1. Slice about two-thirds of the berries and toss them with 1/4 cup sugar; set aside. Puree the remaining berries in a blender with 1/4 cup sugar. Force the puree through a sieve to remove the seeds. Taste; the puree should be quite sweet. If it is not, add a little more sugar.

2. Beat the cream with the remaining 1 1/2 teaspoons sugar, until it holds soft peaks. Beat in the puree, then fold in the sugared berries. Taste and add more sugar if necessary. Serve immediately or refrigerate for up to an hour.

STRAWBERRIES WITH SWEDISH CREAM

MAKES 4 SERVINGS   TIME: 15 MINUTES

THIS MIXTURE OF sour and whipped cream is akin to crème fraîche, but I find it more delicious. It's killer on strawberries.

1 cup heavy cream

1/2 cup sour cream

Sugar or honey to taste

1 quart strawberries, rinsed and hulled

1. Whip the sweet cream until it holds soft peaks, then fold it into the sour cream; add sweetener to taste.
2. Put the berries in 4 bowls or stemmed glasses and top with the cream.

COEURS À LA CRÈME WITH STRAWBERRIES

MAKES 4 SERVINGS   TIME: 24 HOURS, LARGELY UNATTENDED

"HEARTS OF CREAM," a lovely, classic dessert and one that takes very little attention or work.

1/2 pound cream cheese

1 cup whole-milk yogurt

1 teaspoon vanilla extract

3/4 cup sugar

1 quart strawberries, rinsed, hulled, and sliced

1. Use a fork or blender to cream together the cream cheese, yogurt, vanilla, and half the sugar. (If you use a blender and the mixture is too thick, add a little heavy cream or milk.) The mixture should be quite smooth. Put in a fine-mesh strainer lined with cheesecloth or a clean dishtowel and place over a bowl. Refrigerate until ready to serve.
2. About a half hour before serving, toss the strawberries with the remaining sugar and let sit at room temperature. Turn the cream

cheese mixture out onto a plate and divide into 4 portions or put some of the mixture in each of 4 bowls. Mix the berries, if you like, with a little more sugar.

3. Serve the coeurs à la crème topped with the berry mixture.

EASY SUMMER PUDDING

MAKES 4 SERVINGS

TIME: 20 MINUTES, PLUS OVERNIGHT RESTING

FROZEN POUND CAKE is fine for the summer pudding (homemade is better, of course, though not one in ten people will know the difference), but fresh berries are essential.

$1^1/_2$ pounds raspberries, fresh or frozen

$^1/_4$ cup sugar, or to taste

1 pound pound cake

Lightly sweetened whipped cream, sour cream, or crème fraîche

1. Rinse the berries, then combine in a saucepan with the sugar and 2 tablespoons of water. Cook gently, stirring occasionally, just until the berries soften and yield their liquid, 10 to 15 minutes. Cool.

2. Meanwhile, cut the pound cake into roughly $^1/_2$-inch-thick slices. Line a rounded bowl with just over half the slices of the pound cake to a depth of about 4 inches; pack the slices so they leave no (significant) gaps. When the berries are cool, strain them, reserving the liquid. Spoon the solids on top of the pound cake and drizzle with about half the liquid.

3. Cover with the remaining slices of pound cake, again packing them close together. Drizzle with all but a few tablespoons of the remaining liquid (refrigerate the rest).

4. Find a plate that will just fit in the bowl and press it down on top of the pudding. Weight it with a few cans (or whatever you can find that will do the trick) and refrigerate overnight.

5. To serve, run a knife around the edge of the pudding and invert onto a plate. Cut slices and serve with cream.

CITRUS WITH HONEY AND MINT

MAKES 4 SERVINGS

TIME: $1^1/_2$ HOURS, LARGELY UNATTENDED

THIS DESSERT—the kind of thing that Jell-O is supposed to imitate— is unusual these days, but it's easy and delicious, a nice use of fruit that's available year-round.

1 grapefruit

2 medium (or 1 large) navel oranges

2 tangerines

2 temple or other juice oranges

1 tablespoon honey, or to taste

1 tablespoon minced fresh mint, plus a few mint leaves for garnish

1 envelope unflavored gelatin

1. Over a bowl, cut the grapefruit in half and section as you would to serve it at the table, being sure to catch all the juice; you want small pieces with little or no membrane or pith. Peel the navel oranges and tangerines, then, over the same bowl, trim off most of the white pith that clings to their surface. Separate into sections and cut into small pieces if necessary, again being sure to catch all the juice. Strain the fruit. To the reserved juice, add the squeezed juice of the juice oranges.

2. Toss the fruits with the honey and mint and put them in 4 small bowls. Put the juice in a small saucepan and sprinkle the gelatin over the surface. Wait a couple of minutes, then warm the mixture over low heat, stirring to dissolve the gelatin. Cool slightly, then pour the juice mixture over the fruits in the bowls.

3. Refrigerate for about an hour, or until the liquid in the bowls gels. Serve, garnished with additional mint.

MACERATED FRUIT

MAKES AT LEAST 4 SERVINGS

TIME: 6 TO 48 HOURS, LARGELY UNATTENDED

THIS RECIPE, adapted from a classic by cookbook author Claudia Roden, is a longtime personal favorite. It becomes heavenly if you add a little rose and/or orange flower water.

1 pound assorted dried fruit:
    apricots, pears, peaches, prunes,
    raisins, etc.
$1^1/_2$ cup pine nuts or slivered
    blanched almonds
$1^1/_2$ teaspoons rose water
    (optional)

$1^1/_2$ teaspoons orange flower water
    (optional)
$^1/_4$ cup sugar, or to taste
Sour cream or crème fraîche

1. Combine everything but the sour cream in a bowl and add water to cover. Stir and let sit, at room temperature, for at least 6 hours. The fruit is ready when it is soft and the liquid is syrupy.
2. To serve, put some fruit in a bowl and garnish with sour cream.

POACHED CHERRIES

MAKES 4 SERVINGS   TIME: ABOUT 30 MINUTES

SOUR CHERRIES ARE too acidic to eat raw but are the best for cooking. This simple preparation amounts to cherry pie without the crust.

1 to 2 pounds cherries, preferably
    sour
$^1/_2$ cup sugar, or more to taste
$^1/_4$ teaspoon ground cinnamon
    (optional)

Fresh lemon juice, if using sweet
    cherries, or to taste

1. Pit the cherries and combine them with $^1/_2$ cup of water in a medium saucepan; turn the heat to medium-high and cook, stirring occasionally, until the cherries are very tender, about 20 minutes.

2. Stir in the sugar and the cinnamon if you are using it; taste and add more sugar or lemon juice if you like. Cool, then chill and serve the cherries cold, with their juice.

BUYING DRIED FRUIT

SINCE THE PREPARATION of this dish is absolutely foolproof, the challenge (and most of the fun) lies entirely in the shopping, especially since there is an incredible variety of dried fruits available, much of it of superhigh quality. In the course of fine-tuning this recipe, I tried not only the obvious prunes, figs, apricots, peaches, and pears, but also cherries, blueberries, strawberries, pineapple, and even banana. I tend toward the traditional but really enjoyed the tartness that dried pineapple added to the mixture and encourage you to experiment and find the mix of fruits that suits you best.

DRIED FRUIT POACHED IN PORT

MAKES 4 SERVINGS   TIME: 45 MINUTES

NOTHING CAN MATCH dried fruit for convenience and intensity of flavor. And when you poach an assortment with port and a few spices, the results belie the ease of preparation. This is not a summer dessert—no one would mistake this for fresh fruit—but it is delicious, low-fat, and a welcome change from heavy winter desserts. One tip: Use a port you'll enjoy drinking (or buy a half bottle), because you're going to use less than a third of a full-size bottle in this recipe.

12 prunes	3 pieces candied ginger
8 figs	1 clove
4 dried apricot or peach halves	5 allspice berries
4 dried pear halves	5 peppercorns

• Substitute almost any sweet or neutral liquid for the port: water, oloroso sherry, red wine (add a tablespoon of sugar), sweet white wine, orange juice, and so on.
• If you prefer less-than-sweet results, add a squeeze of fresh lemon juice at the end of cooking.
• Vary the spices. Try a tiny grating of nutmeg in place of the allspice, peppercorns, and star anise, for example. Some coriander seeds are also nice.

1 whole star anise

One 1-inch cinnamon stick

1 cup port, preferably ruby, late bottled vintage or vintage

1. Combine all the ingredients in a medium saucepan and bring to a boil. Turn the heat to very low and cover. Cook for about 30 minutes, at which point most of the port will have been absorbed.
2. If the fruit is tender, it's done. If not, add $1/2$ cup water, bring to a boil again, cover, and cook for another 15 minutes. Repeat once more if necessary.
3. Remove the fruit with a slotted spoon, then strain the liquid to remove the spices. Serve a portion of the fruit warm, cold, or at room temperature with a spoonful or two of its juice.

BAKED PEARS

MAKES 4 SERVINGS   TIME: 45 MINUTES

LOOK FOR LARGE PEARS, just about ripe; their "shoulders" should yield to gentle pressure, but they should not be mushy. Serve these, if you like, with a dollop of sweetened whipped cream, or ice cream, or sour cream.

2 large pears, peeled, halved, and cored

4 teaspoons unsalted butter

4 teaspoons brown sugar

1. Preheat the oven to 350°F. Put the pears, cavities up, in a baking pan filmed with a little water.
2. Fill the cavities with a dot each of butter and sugar. Cover the pan and bake until very soft, about 30 minutes; after about 15 minutes of cooking, brush the surface of the pears with the butter-sugar mixture, which will have softened. Serve warm or at room temperature.

SAUTÉED BANANAS

MAKES 4 SMALL SERVINGS   TIME: 15 MINUTES

THE IDEAL BANANAS for cooking are just ripe, yellow with barely any brown spots. Double this recipe if you want a more substantial dessert or serve with vanilla ice cream.

2 bananas, ripe but not too soft

$1^1/_2$ tablespoons unsalted butter

Flour for dredging

1 tablespoon sugar, plus more to
    pass at the table

Fresh lemon juice

1. Peel the bananas, cut them in half crosswise, then lengthwise, so that each banana has been made into 4 pieces. Put the butter in a large, deep skillet over medium-high heat.

2. Dredge the banana pieces lightly in the flour, shaking them to remove the excess. When the butter foam subsides, add the pieces to the skillet. Cook, turning frequently, until they are golden and beginning to brown, about 10 minutes. Sprinkle with the sugar and cook 1 minute more.

3. Serve, passing additional sugar and lemon juice at the table.

FIFTEEN-MINUTE FRUIT GRATIN

MAKES 4 SERVINGS   TIME: 15 MINUTES

IF YOU TAKE soft, ripe fruit, top it with a fancy sauce like crème Anglaise, and run the whole thing under the broiler, you have a four-star dessert. But if you top the fruit with something like sweetened heavy cream, whipped just enough so that it holds some body when broiled, or sweetened sour cream—which hardly needs to be whisked—you can produce a similarly glorious dessert in less than half the time.

Although this preparation is lightning-quick, it has to be constantly watched while cooking. Get the broiler hot, put the dish right under the heating element, and keep your eyes open. You want the topping to burn a little bit—it will smell like toasting marshmallows—but obviously not too much. When the topping is nearly uniformly brown, with a few black spots, it's done. The fruit will not have cooked at all.

1 to 1$^1/_2$ pounds perfectly ripe, soft fruit, such as peaches and/or berries	1 cup heavy cream
	3 tablespoons sugar
	1 teaspoon vanilla extract

1. Preheat the broiler; set the rack as close to the heat source as possible (even 2 inches is not too close).

2. Wash, pit, stem, and peel the fruit as necessary. Cut stone fruit in halves or slices as you prefer. Cut strawberries in thick slices; leave smaller berries whole. Put the fruit—there should be at least 2 cups—in a baking or gratin dish just large enough to hold it.

3. Whip the cream with 2 tablespoons of the sugar and the vanilla until it is thick and just barely holding soft peaks. Pour it over and around the fruit. Sprinkle with the remaining 1 tablespoon sugar.

4. Broil carefully, allowing the cream to brown all over and even burn in a couple of spots; rotate the baking dish during broiling if necessary. Remove and serve.

GRILLED FRUIT SKEWERS WITH GINGER SYRUP

MAKES 4 SERVINGS   TIME: 30 MINUTES

I MAKE THESE SKEWERS, the creation of my friend Johnny Earles, several times each summer. The bananas, especially, drive everyone wild.

¹/₂ cup sugar

¹/₄ cup thinly sliced fresh ginger
    (don't bother to peel it)

2 large or 3 medium bananas, not
    overly ripe

¹/₂ pineapple

2 large peaches

1. Start a grill; the fire should be quite hot and the rack positioned 4 to 6 inches from the heat source. Combine the sugar, ginger, and ¹/₂ cup of water in a saucepan over medium heat. Bring to a boil and simmer for 3 minutes. Remove from the heat and let sit while you prepare the fruit.

2. Do not peel the bananas; cut them into 2-inch-long chunks and make a shallow vertical slit in the skin to facilitate peeling at the table. Peel and core the pineapple, then cut it into 2-inch chunks. Pit the peaches and cut them into large chunks.

3. Skewer the fruit. Strain the syrup and brush the fruit lightly with it. Grill the fruit until the pineapple is nicely browned, 2 to 4 minutes per side. As it is grilling, brush occasionally with the syrup.

4. When the fruit is done, brush once more with syrup; serve hot or warm.

LIME GRANITA

MAKES 4 SERVINGS

TIME: AT LEAST 2 HOURS, LARGELY UNATTENDED

UNLIKE ALMOST EVERY other frozen dessert, granitas take no special equipment. They do take some time, however, and do not keep well, so timing is important. Figure two to three hours for this, start to finish.

²/₃ cup sugar, or to taste

1 cup fresh lemon or lime juice

1 tablespoon minced or grated
    lemon or lime zest

1. Mix the sugar with $^2/_3$ cup of boiling water and stir to dissolve. Add another cup of water and combine with the citrus juice and zest. Taste and add more sugar if necessary.

2. Pour the prepared mixture into a shallow metal or glass pan or bowl. Freeze for about 30 minutes, or until ice crystals begin to form at the edges. Gently stir the crystals back into the liquid, not breaking them up entirely; a large fork is a good tool for this task.

3. Continue to stir and break up clumps of crystals every half hour or so. When the entire mixture has the texture of soft crushed ice, it's ready to serve. Serve immediately or continue to stir every half hour or so until ready to serve.

===========

PINEAPPLE-GINGER SORBET

MAKES 4 SERVINGS   TIME: 10 MINUTES, PLUS TIME TO FREEZE

A SPECIAL COMBINATION, decidedly Asian. Use fresh ginger if at all possible.

$^1/_2$ cup sugar

$1^1/_2$ teaspoons very finely minced peeled fresh or candied ginger or $^1/_2$ teaspoon dried ginger, or to taste

1 medium pineapple, peeled, cored, and pureed in a food processor (about 2 cups)

Whisk the sugar and ginger into the puree and freeze in an ice cream machine, according to the manufacturer's directions. This is best served straight from the machine or after no more than an hour or two in the freezer.

COCONUT SORBET

MAKES 1 QUART   TIME: 5 MINUTES, PLUS TIME TO FREEZE

IF YOU HAVE an ice cream machine, this is one of the fastest, easiest, most satisfying desserts you can make.

3 cans coconut milk (about 1 quart)   2 teaspoons vanilla extract
1 cup sugar, or to taste

1. Combine the coconut milk with the sugar and taste; add more sugar if you like. Add the vanilla and stir.
2. Freeze in an ice cream machine according to the manufacturer's instructions. Serve as soon as possible after making or freeze and let "warm" in the refrigerator for 30 minutes before serving. Best the day it is made.

COOKIE DOUGH

MAKES ABOUT 4 DOZEN   TIME: 30 MINUTES

COOKIES ARE ALWAYS easy to make, but even they can use streamlining. One solution is to whip up a single dough in a food processor and finish it in different ways. This basic dough is great plain (with white sugar or brown or even molasses), but it can be varied with ginger or a mix of spices, chocolate chips, or orange. Or with one batch of dough you can make four different types of cookies—add lemon juice and zest to one-fourth of it, for example, chopped walnuts to the second, raisins to the third, and coconut to the fourth. Finally, it can produce rolled-out, cut, and decorated cookies; just chill it first to make it easier to handle. You might call this "the mother of all butter cookies."

Make these with more flour and they're cakey; use more butter and they're delicate, with better flavor; here, I go for the second option.

Bake at 350°F for a minute or two longer. The cookies won't brown on the edges as they will at 375°F, but they will be crisp. Or bake for an extra minute or two at 375°F for browned *and* crisp cookies.

Eight Cookies Using Butter Cookie Dough

Butterscotch Cookies

Substitute half or more brown sugar for the white sugar or simply add 1 tablespoon molasses along with the egg.

Citrus Cookies

Do not use the vanilla; add 1 tablespoon fresh lemon juice and 2 teaspoons grated lemon zest along with the egg. The same can be done with orange juice and zest. A couple tablespoons of poppy seeds go well here also.

Chocolate Chip Cookies

Stir about 1 cup chocolate chips into the finished batter. (The butterscotch batter variation is good here.)

Spice Cookies

Add 1 teaspoon ground cinnamon, $1/4$ teaspoon each ground allspice and ground ginger, and 1 pinch ground cloves and mace or nutmeg to the dry ingredients.

(continued)

$1^1/2$ cups all-purpose flour
$1/2$ cup cornstarch
$3/4$ cup sugar
Pinch of salt
1 cup (2 sticks) chilled unsalted butter, cut into bits

1 teaspoon vanilla extract
1 egg
$1/2$ cup milk, more or less

1. Preheat the oven to 375°F.

2. Combine the flour, cornstarch, sugar, and salt in a food processor and pulse once or twice. (It's important to process the ingredients gently, letting the machine run no longer than necessary at each stage so as not to toughen the batter.) Add the butter and pulse 10 or 20 times, until the butter and flour are well combined. Add the vanilla and the egg and pulse 3 or 4 times. Add about half the milk and pulse 2 or 3 times. Add the remaining milk a little at a time, pulsing once or twice after each addition, until the dough holds together in a sticky mass. (You can, of course, also make this batter in a standing mixer or by hand. In either case, cream together the butter and sugar first, then add the mixed dry ingredients.)

3. Drop rounded teaspoons of dough (you can make the cookies larger or smaller if you like) onto a nonstick baking sheet, a sheet lined with parchment paper, or a lightly buttered baking sheet. If you want flat cookies, press the balls down a bit with your fingers or the back of a spatula or wooden spoon. Bake for 10 to 12 minutes, checking every minute or so after 8 minutes since most oven temperatures are slightly inaccurate, or until the cookies are done as you like them. Cool on a rack, then serve or store in a covered container for up to 3 days.

OLIVE OIL COOKIES
WITH RED WINE AND ROSEMARY

MAKES ABOUT 4 DOZEN   TIME: 30 MINUTES

YOU NEED NOT use your best olive oil for these cookies, but extra virgin olive oil will make them more interesting than "pure" or "light" olive oil.

2¹/2 cups flour	3/4 cup sugar

2^1/2 cups flour ^{3}/4 cup sugar
^{1}/2 teaspoon baking powder   2 eggs
Pinch of salt ^{1}/2 cup olive oil
^{1}/8 teaspoon freshly ground black ^{3}/4 cup dry red wine, or a little
   pepper   more
1 teaspoon minced fresh rosemary
   or ^{1}/2 teaspoon dried

1. Preheat the oven to 375°F. Combine the dry ingredients. Beat the eggs with the olive oil and wine. Use a rubber spatula to stir the liquid mix into the dry one, just until well combined; if the mixture is stiff, add a little more wine.

2. Drop by rounded teaspoons onto a lightly oiled cookie sheet and bake for 12 to 15 minutes, or until lightly browned. Cool for a couple of minutes, then transfer the cookies to a rack to cool further. Store in a covered tin for up to 3 days.

APPLE CRISP

MAKES 4 SERVINGS   TIME: ABOUT 1 HOUR

IN PLACE OF APPLES, you can use pears here or a mixture. In fact, this is a universal crisp recipe and will work with just about any fruit. Almost needless to say, it's great with vanilla ice cream.

(Variations, continued)

Ginger Cookies
Add 1 tablespoon ground ginger to the dry ingredients. For even better flavor, add ^{1}/4 cup minced crystallized ginger to the batter by hand (this works well in addition to or in place of the ground ginger).

Chunky Cookies
To the finished batter, add about 1 cup M&Ms (or other similar candy) or roughly chopped walnuts, pecans, or cashews; slivered almonds; raisins; coconut; dried cherries; and so on. Or combine any chunky ingredients you like.

Rolled Cookies
Freeze the dough for 15 minutes or refrigerate it for about 1 hour (or longer). Work half the batter at a time and roll it on a lightly floured surface; it will absorb some flour at first but will soon become less sticky. Do not add more flour than necessary. Roll about ^{1}/4 inch thick and cut with any cookie cutter; decorate as you like. Bake as directed, reducing the cooking time to 8 to 10 minutes.

Puffy Cookies
The basic cookies are flat. For airier cookies, add ^{1}/2 teaspoon baking powder to the dry ingredients.

3 cups peeled, cored, and sliced
   apples or other fruit
$1/2$ teaspoon ground cinnamon
Juice of $1/2$ lemon
$1/3$ cup brown sugar, or to taste
$2^1/2$ tablespoons cold unsalted
   butter, cut into bits, plus butter
   for greasing the pan

$1/4$ cup rolled oats
$1/4$ cup all-purpose flour
2 tablespoons shredded
   unsweetened coconut (optional)
2 tablespoons chopped nuts
   (optional)
Dash of salt

1. Preheat the oven to 400°F. Toss the fruit with half the cinnamon, the lemon juice, and 1 tablespoon of the sugar and spread it in a lightly buttered 8-inch square or 9-inch round baking pan.

2. Combine all the other ingredients, including the remaining cinnamon and sugar, in a food processor and pulse a few times, then process for a few seconds more, until everything is well incorporated but not uniform. (To mix the ingredients by hand, soften the butter slightly, toss together the dry ingredients, and then work in the butter with your fingertips, a pastry blender, or a fork.)

3. Spread the topping over the apples and bake for 30 to 40 minutes, until the topping is browned and the apples are tender. Serve hot, warm, or at room temperature.

CHOCOLATE MOUSSE
MAKES 4 TO 6 SERVINGS
TIME: 20 TO 30 MINUTES, PLUS TIME TO CHILL

THE RICHEST, most elegant dessert you can make with so little work.

2 tablespoons unsalted butter
4 ounces bittersweet or semisweet
   chocolate, chopped
3 eggs, separated

$1/4$ cup sugar
$1/2$ cup heavy cream
$1/2$ teaspoon vanilla extract

1. In a double boiler, a small saucepan over low heat, or the microwave, melt the butter and chocolate together. Just before the chocolate finishes melting, remove it from the heat and beat with a wooden spoon until smooth.

2. Transfer the chocolate mixture to a bowl and beat in the egg yolks with a whisk. Put the bowl in the refrigerator.

3. Beat the egg whites with half the sugar until they hold stiff peaks but are not dry. Set aside. Beat the cream with the remaining sugar and vanilla until it holds soft peaks.

4. Stir a couple of spoonfuls of the whites into the chocolate mixture to lighten it a bit, then fold in the remaining whites thoroughly but gently. Fold in the cream and refrigerate until chilled. If you are in a hurry, divide the mousse among 4 to 6 serving cups; it will chill much faster. Serve within a day of making.

FLAN

MAKES 4 SERVINGS   TIME: ABOUT 45 MINUTES

IF YOU USE vanilla in place of the cinnamon and omit the caramel (step 2), you can call these *pots de crème*. No matter how you make them, though, be careful not to overcook, or the eggs will curdle instead of becoming silky and creamy.

2 cups milk, cream, or a mixture

1 cinnamon stick or $1/2$ teaspoon ground cinnamon

1 cup sugar

2 eggs plus 2 yolks

Pinch of salt

1. Preheat the oven to 300°F and put a kettle of water on to boil. Put the milk in a small saucepan with the cinnamon; turn the heat to medium. Cook just until it begins to steam, then cool a bit.

2. Meanwhile, combine $1/2$ cup of the sugar with $1/4$ cup of water in a small, heavy saucepan. Turn the heat to low and cook, shaking the

pan occasionally (it's best not to stir), until the sugar liquefies, turns clear, then golden brown, about 15 minutes. Remove from the heat and immediately pour the caramel into the bottom of a large heat-proof bowl or 4 ramekins.

3. Beat the eggs and yolks with the salt and remaining $1/2$ cup sugar until pale yellow and fairly thick. Remove the cinnamon stick (if you used it) from the milk and add the milk gradually to the egg mixture, stirring constantly. Pour the mixture into the prepared bowl or ramekins and put it/them in a baking pan, adding hot water to within about 1 inch of the top.

4. Bake for about 30 (for the ramekins) to 40 (for the bowl) minutes, or until the center is barely set. (Start checking after 20 minutes or so and remember that cream will set faster than milk.) Serve warm or at room temperature or cover and refrigerate for a day or so.

═══════════════

GINGER POTS DE CRÈME

MAKES 4 SERVINGS   TIME: ABOUT 1 HOUR

POTS DE CRÈME are always great, but flavored with ginger they become exotic—yet there's nothing to it.

2 cups heavy cream, light cream, or half-and-half

10 slices fresh ginger (don't bother to peel it)

5 egg yolks

$1/2$ cup sugar

1 tablespoon minced candied ginger (optional)

1. Preheat the oven to 300°F. Combine the cream and fresh ginger in a small saucepan and heat over medium-low heat until steam rises. Cover the pan, turn off the heat, and steep for 10 to 15 minutes.

2. Beat the yolks and sugar together until light. Remove the ginger slices from the cream and pour about a quarter of the cream into the egg mixture, then pour the sugar-egg mixture into the cream and stir.

If you're using the candied ginger, add it now. Pour into four 6-ounce ramekins and put the ramekins in a baking dish; pour water into the dish to come halfway up the side of the ramekins and cover with foil.

3. Bake for 30 to 45 minutes, or until the center is barely set. (Heavy cream sets fastest, half-and-half more slowly.) Cool or chill, then serve.

CRANBERRY CLAFOUTI

MAKES 4 SERVINGS   TIME: 1 HOUR

THE CLAFOUTI IS essentially a fruit-laden baked pancake. I love this Americanized version, which is crunchy and sweet.

Butter for the dish

$1/2$ cup sugar

1 egg

$1/2$ cup all-purpose flour

$1/2$ cup half-and-half or whole milk

Pinch of salt

1 cup cranberries

$1/2$ cup walnuts

Confectioners' sugar

1. Preheat the oven to 425°F. Butter a deep 9- or 10-inch pie plate, round porcelain dish, or gratin dish of similar size. Sprinkle it with a tablespoon or so of the sugar, then swirl the dish to coat evenly with sugar; invert to remove the excess.

2. Beat the egg well, then add the remaining sugar; beat until smooth. Add the flour and beat again until smooth. Add the half-and-half and salt and whisk once more until smooth.

3. Coarsely chop the cranberries and walnuts; you can do this in a food processor if you like (it's very fast), but be careful not to overprocess—you want to break up the cranberries, not mince them. Put the cranberry mixture in the bottom of the dish and pour the batter over it.

4. Bake for 20 to 30 minutes, or until the clafouti is nicely browned on top and a knife inserted into it comes out clean. Sift some confectioners' sugar over it and serve warm or at room temperature.

MAPLE BREAD PUDDING

MAKES 4 SERVINGS

TIME: ABOUT 1 HOUR, LARGELY UNATTENDED

USE GOOD WHITE BREAD for this, and don't bother to remove the crusts; the different textures make it more interesting.

4 tablespoons ($^1/_2$ stick) unsalted butter

$^1/_2$ pound white bread, cut or torn into chunks no smaller than 1 inch in diameter

1 cup milk plus 1 cup cream or a total of 2 cups half-and-half

4 eggs

$^3/_4$ cup maple syrup or sugar

$^1/_2$ teaspoon ground cinnamon

Small grating of nutmeg

Pinch of salt

Whipped cream for serving (optional)

1. Butter a 10- or 12-inch soufflé or baking dish and put the bread in it. Cut the remaining butter into bits and combine it with all the other ingredients; pour over the bread. Submerge the bread with a weighted plate and turn the oven to 350°F.

2. When the oven is hot, remove the plate (scrape any butter back onto the bread) and bake until the pudding is just set but not dry, 45 to 60 minutes. The top will be crusty and brown. Serve hot, warm, or at room temperature, with or without whipped cream.

INDEX

Aïoli, 306
Anchovy(ies), 224
  canapés with piquillo peppers and,
    230
  cauliflower with garlic and, 223–24
  dipping sauce, grilled chicken wings
    with, 135
  green sauce, grilled swordfish
    "sandwich" with, 115–16
  pasta with arugula and, 263
  –red wine sauce, rib-eye steak with,
    166
  tomato-anchovy sauce, linguine with,
    271–72
Anise-flavored lamb shanks, 188
Apples
  apple crisp, 325–26
  braised goose with, 152–53
  cabbage soup with, 27
  pumpkin and apple soup, 31
Applesauce, roast pork with, 210–11

Apricots
  chicken with, 145–46
  curried sweet potato soup with, 35
Artichoke soup, creamy, 20
Arugula
  pasta with anchovies and, 263
  pasta with Gorgonzola and, 262
  pizza with corn, bacon, and, 259
Asian-style dishes. *See also* Noodles;
    specific countries
  Asian meat sauce, roast monkfish
    with, 105
  chicken salad with greens, 50–51
  cucumber soup, 10
  one-pot pasta and greens, 261
  pot roast with turnips, 171–72
  shrimp with Asian flavors, 69
  steamed mussels, 64–65
Asparagus
  grilled, with lemon dressing,
    218–19

  pan-roasted asparagus soup with
    tarragon, 26
  pasta, risotto style, 283–84
  roasted, with Parmesan, 217–8
Avgolemono, 15

Bacon, 282
  chestnut soup with, 34
  and cream, corn chowder with,
    20
  pasta alla gricia, 281–82
  pizza with arugula, corn, and,
    259
  shad roe with, 117
  spaghetti carbonara, 281
  veal brisket with onion and, 180–81
Balsamic vinegar
  broiled Cornish hens with lemon and,
    137–38
  strawberries with, 311–12

Bananas
grilled fruit skewers with ginger
syrup, 320–21
sautéed, 319
Bangers and mash, Italian style, 205
Barbecue sauce, grilled lamb ribs with,
197
"Barbecue" sauce, shrimp with, 72–73
Barley-mushroom soup, 40
Basil. *See also* Pesto
rice noodles with, 287
tomato salad with, 49
Bay leaves, roast monkfish with crisp
potatoes, olives, and, 103–4
Bay scallops. *See also* Scallop(s)
roasted, with brown butter and
shallots, 84–85
Beans, 32. *See also* Black-eyed peas;
Chickpea(s); Green beans
forty-minute cassoulet, 206–7
rosemary-lemon white bean dip,
219–20
Beef, 159–77
braises, about, 173
with caramelized sugar, 174–75
negima (Japanese beef-scallion
rolls), 168–69
poached tenderloin with garnishes,
170–71
pot roast, 173; Asian, with turnips,
171–72; with cranberries, 172–74;
European, with carrots, 171
sautéed chickpeas with meat, 177
sirloin, roast, 169–70
steak: with butter and ginger sauce,
162; grilled, with Roquefort sauce,
164–65; grilled flank steak with
Provençal spices, 163; marinated,
the Minimalist's, 159–60; oven-
"grilled," 160; rib-eye, with
anchovy–red wine sauce, 166;
sirloin, with chimichurri sauce,
165–66; skirt steak with compound
butter, 161
stew, Japanese-style, with winter
squash, 175–76
wrapped in lettuce leaves, Korean
style, 167–68
Beet(s)
beet roesti with rosemary, 221
salad, raw, 46–47
soup, creamy, 28
Bell peppers. See Pepper(s)

Berries. *See also* Raspberries;
Strawberry(ies)
fifteen-minute fruit gratin, 319–20
Beurre noisette, steamed broccoli with,
222
Black beans, salmon with soy and, 110
Black-eyed pea soup with ham and
greens, 32
Black mushrooms, 25
Black skillet mussels, clams, or oysters,
65–66
Blue cheese. *See also* Gorgonzola;
Roquefort
fennel gratin with, 228
Bocuse, Paul, 144
Bouillabaisse, 90–91
Bread(s)
bread stuffing, fastest, 125
corn bread, 250
fastest French bread, 249
grilled bread salad, 59–60
olive oil croutons, 251
Bread pudding
maple, 330
with shiitake mushrooms, 252
Broccoli
soup, creamy, 29
steamed, with beurre noisette, 222
Brown butter and shallots, roasted bay
scallops with, 84–85
Brown sauce, fresh Chinese noodles
with, 291
Burgers, salmon, 107–8
Butter
beurre noisette, steamed broccoli
with, 222
compound: chile-cilantro, 308;
garlic-oregano, 308; horseradish-
ginger, 307; shallot-thyme, 307;
skirt steak with, 161
and ginger sauce, steak with, 162
new potatoes with mint and, 237–38
salmon roasted in, 111–12
sauce, grilled or broiled fish on
fennel or dill with, 98
ziti with sage, Parmigiano-Reggiano,
and, 278–79
Butter cookies with variations,
323–25
Butternut squash. *See also* Winter
squash
penne with, 265
Butterscotch cookies, 324

Cabbage
salad, Vietnamese-style pork chops
with, 202
soup, with apples, 27
Canapés with piquillo peppers and
anchovies, 236
Capers, shad roe with vinegar and, 117
Caramelized sugar, beef with, 174–75
Carrot(s)
carrot, spinach, and rice stew, 33
European pot roast with, 171
glazed, 223
soup, creamy, 28
Cassoulet, forty-minute, 206–7
Cauliflower
with garlic and anchovy, 223–24
pasta with, 266
Celery soup, creamy, 28
Cheese. *See also specific types*
cheese cups, 286
coeurs à la crème with strawberries,
313–14
Cherries, poached, 316–17
Chestnuts, 276
roasted chestnut soup, 33–34
ziti with mushrooms and, 275–76
Chicken
with apricots, 145–46
bread salad with, 59
breasts: grilled, with eggplant,
shallots, and ginger sauce, 130–31;
seared and steamed, 153–54
chicken curry in a hurry, 147–48
with coconut and lime, 148–49
coq au vin with prunes, 146–47
cucumber salad with, 54
cutlets meunière, 141–42
grilled chicken, sausage, and
vegetable skewers, 132–33
with onion confit, 113
with Riesling, 143
roast, fastest, 121
salad: Asian, with greens, 50–51;
spicy, 53
sautéed, simplest, with garlic, 140
soy-poached, 154–55
spicy, with lemongrass and lime,
149–50
stir-fried coconut noodles, 288
with sweet-and-sour sherry sauce,
128–29
ten-minute stir-fried chicken with
nuts, 138–39

thighs: deviled, 126–27; grilled, with sauce au chien, 129–30; with Mexican flavors, 131–32
under a brick, 133–34
with vinegar, 144–45
wings, grilled, with anchovy dipping sauce, 135
Chicken noodle soup
rich, with ginger, 39
whole-meal, Chinese style, 37–38
Chickpea(s), 32, 36
cod with sherry and, 101–2
sautéed, with meat, 177
soup, with sausage, 36–37
Chile-cilantro butter, 308
Chimichurri sauce, sirloin steak with, 165–66
Chinese-style dishes
fresh Chinese noodles with brown sauce, 291
slow-cooked ribs, 214
soy-poached chicken, 154–55
whole-meal chicken noodle soup, 37–38
Chipotle-peach salsa, 297
Chocolate chip cookies, 324
Chocolate mousse, 326–27
Chopped salad with vinaigrette, 45–46
Choucroute, the Minimalist's, 212–13
Chowder
clam, 21–22
corn, the Minimalist's, 20–21
Chutney, mint, broiled lamb chops with, 196
Cider-poached fish, 97
Cilantro-chile butter, 308
Citrus fruit. See also specific types
citrus cookies, 324
citrus gravlax, 106
citrus with honey and mint, 315
Clafouti, cranberry, 329
Clam(s), 21
black skillet clams, 66
bouillabaisse, 90–91
chowder, 22–23
clambake in a pot, 89–90
pasta with tomatoes and, 272–73
steamed, with soy, 65
stew, with potatoes and parsley puree, 22–23
white pasta with, 272
Cocktail sauce, better, 306

Coconut, coconut milk, 75
chicken with lime and, 148–49
coconut sorbet, 323
cucumber-coconut soup, 10
lemongrass-coconut sauce, steamed shrimp with, 74–75
stir-fried coconut noodles, 288
Cod
cakes, with ginger and scallions, 100–101
with chickpeas and sherry, 101–2
Emma's cod and potatoes, 102–3
Coeurs à la crème with strawberries, 313–14
Collards. See Greens
Compote, fennel-orange, roast pork chops with, 203–4
Compound butter(s), 307–8
skirt steak with, 161
Condiments. See also Butter; Relish; Salsa; Sauce(s)
dried mushroom puree, 302
gremolata, 179
mint chutney, broiled lamb chops with, 196
red pepper puree, 303
Confit, onion, with tuna, swordfish, or chicken, 113–14
Cookies
butter, with variations, 323–25
olive oil, with red wine and rosemary, 325
Coq au vin with prunes, 146–47
Coriander, grilled boneless leg of lamb with ginger and, 193
Corn
chowder, the Minimalist's, 20–21
grilled, 225
pizza with arugula, bacon, and, 259
Corn bread, 250
Cornish hens, broiled
with lemon and balsamic vinegar, 137–38
with spicy salt, 136
Crab(s)
crabby crab cakes, 66–67
softshell, broiled or grilled, 86–87
Cranberries
cranberry clafouti, 329
pot roast with, 172–74
Cream, Swedish, strawberries with, 313
Crisp, apple, 325–26
Croutons, olive oil, 251

Cucumber(s)
big chopped salad with vinaigrette, 45–46
salad: cumin-rubbed lamb chops with, 195–96; with scallops, chicken, or shrimp, 54–55; simple, 47–48
salsa, grilled lamb ribs with, 198
seaweed salad with, 48–49
soup: Asian-style, 10; cucumber-coconut, 10; European-style, 11
Cumin-rubbed lamb chops with cucumber salad, 195–96
Curry, curried dishes
chicken curry in a hurry, 147–48
curried boneless leg of lamb, 193
curried corn chowder, 20
curried scallops with tomatoes, 82–83
curried steamed mussels, 64
curried sweet potato soup with apricot, 35
curried tofu with soy sauce, 243
shrimp in yellow curry, 73–74

Dashi, 7, 176
Desserts, 311–30
apple crisp, 325–26
baked pears, 318
butter cookie dough, 323–24
chocolate mousse, 326–27
citrus with honey and mint, 315
coconut sorbet, 323
cranberry clafouti, 329
dried fruit poached in port, 317–18
easy summer pudding, 314–15
fifteen-minute fruit gratin, 319–20
flan, 327–28
ginger pots de crème, 328–29
grilled fruit skewers with ginger syrup, 320–21
lime or lemon granita, 321–22
macerated fruit, 316
maple bread pudding, 330
olive oil cookies with red wine and rosemary, 325
pineapple-ginger sorbet, 322
poached cherries, 316–17
sautéed bananas, 319
strawberries: with balsamic vinegar, 311–12; coeurs à la crème with, 313–14; fool, 312; sugared, 311; with Swedish cream, 313–14

Deviled chicken thighs, 126–27
Dill
　grilled or broiled fish on, 98
　veal stew with, 183
Dip
　grilled eggplant, 225–26
　rosemary-lemon white bean, 219–20
Dipping sauce
　anchovy, grilled chicken wings with, 135
　olive oil, fennel with, 227
　soy-dipped shrimp, 78–79
Dough
　butter cookies, 323–24
　pizza, 253–54
Dressing. See also Vinaigrette
　lemon, grilled asparagus with, 218–19
　soy-ginger, grilled asparagus with, 218
Dried fruit, 317. See also specific types
　macerated fruit, 316
　poached in port, 317–18
Dried mushroom(s), 25, 232. See also
　Mushroom(s); Porcini
Duck
　forty-minute cassoulet, 206–7
　legs, slow-cooked, with olives, 151
　panfried, 142
　roast duck in one hour, 122
　roasted and braised, with sauerkraut, 156

Earles, Johnny, 320
Eggplant
　grilled chicken, sausage, and vegetable skewers, 132–33
　grilled chicken breasts with shallots, ginger sauce, and, 130–31
　grilled eggplant dip, 225–26
　stir-fried coconut noodles, 288
Eggs
　in soups, 13; avgolemono, 15; egg drop soup, 13–14; stracciatella, 14–15
　spaghetti carbonara, 281
　Spanish tortilla, 245–46
Emma's cod and potatoes, 102–3
Endives braised in broth with Parmesan, 226–27

Fennel
　fennel-steamed mussels, Provence style, 63

gratin, 228
grilled or broiled fish on, 98
with olive oil dipping sauce, 227
-orange compote, roast pork chops with, 203–4
soup, creamy, 28
Fettuccine Alfredo, 264
Figs
　fig relish, 301
　stuffed with goat cheese, 229
Fish, 95–118. See also Cod; Monkfish; Salmon; Swordfish; Tuna
　baked with leeks, 99–100
　bouillabaisse, 90–91
　cakes, panfried, 100
　with fennel-orange compote, 203
　flounder poached in broth, 96
　grilled, the Mediterranean way, 98–99
　shad roe with mustard, 116–17
　simplest steamed fish, 95
　sparkling cider-poached, 97
　tacos, with fresh salsa, 117–18
Flan, 327–28
　garlic-mushroom, 233
Flounder poached in broth, 96
Fool, strawberry, 312
Franey, Pierre, 124, 240
French bread, fastest, 249
Fruit. See also Dried fruit; specific fruits
　gratin, fifteen-minute, 319–20
　skewers, grilled, with ginger syrup, 320–21

Garlic
　aïoli, 306
　cauliflower with anchovy and, 223–24
　garlic-mushroom flan, 233
　garlic-oregano butter, 308
　gremolata, 179
　and oil, linguine with, 260
　simplest sautéed chicken with, 140
　soup: with shrimp, 16–17; Thai, 16
　vichyssoise with, 19
Gazpacho, tomato-melon, 9
Ginger
　and butter sauce, steak with, 162
　cod cakes with scallions and, 100–101
　cookies, 325
　grilled boneless leg of lamb with coriander and, 193
　grilled soy-and-ginger boneless lamb leg, 193

horseradish-ginger butter, 307
lemongrass-ginger soup with mushrooms, 23–24
pea and ginger soup, 12–13
pineapple-ginger sorbet, 322
pots de crème, 328–29
rich chicken noodle soup with, 39
sauce, grilled chicken breasts with eggplant, shallots, and, 130–31
soy-ginger dressing, grilled asparagus with, 218
stir-fried leeks with, 230–31; with shrimp, 77–78
syrup, grilled fruit skewers with, 320–21
Goat cheese, figs stuffed with, 229
Goose, braised, with pears or apples, 152–53
Gorgonzola. See also Blue cheese
　pasta with arugula and, 262
　and pear green salad, with walnuts, 44–45
Granita, lime or lemon, 321–22
Grapefruit. See also Citrus fruit
　and shrimp salad, Southeast Asian, 51–52
Grapes, sausage with, 204–5
Gratin
　fennel, 228
　fruit, fifteen-minute, 319–20
　potato, fast, 238–39
Gravlax, 106
Gravy
　pan gravy, roast sirloin with, 170
　sherry reduction, 126
Green beans
　pasta with potatoes, pesto, and, 268–69
　and tomatoes, 220
Greens. See also Salad(s); specific types
　Asian chicken salad with, 50–51
　black-eyed pea soup with ham and, 32
　cool cooked greens with lemon, 229–30
　one-pot pasta and greens, Asian style, 261
　prosciutto soup with, 17–18
　Spanish tortilla with, 245
　stuffed scallops with, 79
Green salad. See also Salad(s)
　herbed, two ways, 43–44

pear and Gorgonzola, with walnuts, 44–45

simple, 43

Green sauce, grilled swordfish "sandwich" with, 115–16

Green tomatoes

creamy green tomato soup, 28

pizza with, 257

Gremolata, 179

Ham. *See also* Prosciutto

black-eyed pea soup with greens and, 32

Herbs. *See also* Pesto; *specific herbs*

herbed green salad, two ways, 43–44

herb paste, sautéed scallops with, 79

herb-roasted turkey breast, 123

herb-rubbed salmon, 108

linguine with fresh herbs, 267

Honey, citrus with mint and, 315

Horseradish-ginger butter, 307

Italian-style bangers and mash, 205

Japanese-style dishes

beef-scallion rolls (negima), 168–69

beef stew with winter squash, 175–76

Jerk seasonings, crispy pork bits with, 211–12

Kale. *See also* Greens

kale, sausage, and mushroom stew, 205–6

Korean-style dishes

beef wrapped in lettuce leaves, 167–68

spareribs, 208

Lamb, 187–98

boneless leg of, grilled, 193–94

boneless shoulder roast, 192

braised and browned, with peaches, 189–90

chops: broiled, with mint chutney, 196; cumin-rubbed, with cucumber salad, 195–96

cutlets, breaded, 194–95

with peppers and yogurt sauce, 191

rack of, crisp roasted, 187–88

ribs, grilled, 197–98

shanks, braised and grilled, 188–89

Leeks

fish baked with, 99–100

stir-fried: with ginger, 230–31; with ginger and shrimp, 77–78

vichyssoise with garlic, 19

Lemon(s). *See also* Citrus fruit

avgolemono, 15

broiled Cornish hens with balsamic vinegar and, 137–38

chicken cutlets meunière, 141–42

cool cooked greens with, 229–30

dressing, grilled asparagus with, 218–19

granita, 321–22

gremolata, 179

rosemary-lemon white bean dip, 219–20

Lemongrass, 202

-coconut sauce, steamed shrimp with, 74–75

-ginger soup with mushrooms, 23–24

spicy chicken with lime and, 149–50

Lettuce leaves, beef wrapped in, Korean style, 167–68

Lime. *See also* Citrus fruit

chicken with coconut and, 148–49

granita, 321–22

juice, shrimp cooked in, 76–77

sauce au chien, grilled chicken thighs with, 129–30

spicy chicken with lemongrass and, 149–50

Linguine. *See* Pasta

Lobster, grilled or broiled, 87–88

Mango relish, grilled lamb ribs with, 198

Maple bread pudding, 330

Ma-po tofu, 244

Marjoram "pesto," 298

Mayonnaise, 305–6

Meat. *See also* Beef; Lamb; Pork; Sausage; Veal

sautéed chickpeas with, 177

Meat sauce, roast monkfish with, 104–5

Meaty bones, pasta with, 277–78

Mediterranean grilled fish, 98–99

Melon

tomato-melon gazpacho, 9

watermelon, Thai style, 50

Mexican flavors, chicken thighs with, 131–32

Mint

chutney, broiled lamb chops with, 196

citrus with honey and, 315

minty broiled shrimp salad, 52–53

new potatoes with butter and, 237–38

Miso, 7

miso-broiled scallops, 80

-red wine sauce, pork chops with, 201

soup, nearly instant, with tofu, 7

Monkfish, roast

with crisp potatoes, olives, and bay leaves, 103–4

with meat sauce, 104–5

Moroccan-style tomato sauce, shrimp in, 69–70

Mousse, chocolate, 326–27

Mozzarella, pizza with, 259

Mushroom(s), 24–25, 232

braised veal breast with, 179–81

dried mushroom puree, 302

garlic-mushroom flan, 233

kale, sausage, and mushroom stew, 205–6

lemongrass-ginger soup with, 23–24

mushroom-barley soup, 40

porcini-scented "wild" mushroom sauté, 231

pumpkin and mushroom soup, 31

and shallots, with sweet-and-sour sherry sauce, 128–29

shiitake: bread pudding with, 252; chestnut soup with, 34; sautéed, 232

soup, creamy, 24–25

ziti with chestnuts and, 275–76

Mussel(s), 64

black skillet mussels, 65–66

bouillabaisse, 90–91

clambake in a pot, 89–90

and potato salad, 56–57

steamed: Asian style, 64–65; curried, 64; with fennel, Provence style, 63

Mustard

deviled chicken thighs, 126–27

pork and turnips with, 209–10

shad roe with, 116–17

Negima (Japanese beef-scallion rolls), 168–69

Noodles, 287–91. *See also* Pasta
　chicken noodle soup: rich, with
　　ginger, 39; whole-meal, Chinese
　　style, 37–38
　Chinese, fresh, with brown sauce, 291
　one-pot pasta and greens, Asian
　　style, 261
　pad Thai, 289–90
　rice noodles, 289; with basil, 287
　stir-fried coconut noodles, 288
Nuts. *See also* Walnuts
　curried tofu with soy sauce, 243
　nut vinaigrette, 44
　sea scallops with, 83–84
　ten-minute stir-fried chicken with,
　　138–39

Olive oil
　cookies, with red wine and rosemary,
　　325
　dipping sauce, fennel with, 227
　linguine with garlic and, 260
　olive oil croutons, 251
Olives
　marinated, 234
　pizza with tomatoes, onions, and, 255
　roast monkfish with crisp potatoes,
　　bay leaves, and, 103–4
　slow-cooked duck legs with, 151
Onion(s). *See also* Scallions
　confit, tuna, swordfish, or chicken
　　with, 113–14
　pizza with tomatoes, olives, and, 255
　potato and onion soup, 30
　Spanish tortilla with, 245
　veal brisket with bacon and, 180–81
Orange(s). *See also* Citrus fruit
　fennel-orange compote, roast pork
　　chops with, 203–4
Oregano-garlic butter, 308
Orzo risotto, Parmesan cups with,
　285–86
Osso buco, 178–79
Oysters, black skillet, 66

Pad Thai, 289–90
Paella, fast and easy, 88–89
Pancakes, scallion, quick, 240–41
Paprika, veal stew with, 182
Parmesan (Parmigiano-Reggiano)
　cups, with orzo risotto, 285–86

endives braised in broth with,
　226–27
pizza with sage and, 258
roasted asparagus with, 217–18
ziti with butter, sage, and, 278–79
Parsley, 299
　chimichurri sauce, sirloin steak with,
　　165–66
　creamed parsley sauce, 299
　green sauce, grilled swordfish
　　"sandwich" with, 115–16
　gremolata, 179
　parsley-vinegar sauce, 297–98
　puree, clam stew with potatoes and,
　　22–23
　rack of lamb persillade, 187
Parsnip and turnip soup, creamy, 28
Pasta, 260–86. *See also* Noodles
　all'amatriciana, 282
　with anchovies and arugula, 263
　with cauliflower, 266
　with clams and tomatoes, 272–73
　with fast sausage ragu, 274–75
　fettuccine Alfredo, 264
　with Gorgonzola and arugula, 262
　with green beans, potatoes, and
　　pesto, 268–69
　alla gricia, 281–82
　linguine: with fresh herbs, 267; with
　　garlic and oil, 260; with spinach,
　　261; with tomato-anchovy sauce,
　　271–72
　with meaty bones, 277–78
　Parmesan cups with orzo risotto,
　　285–86
　penne with butternut squash, 265
　with potatoes, 279–81
　risotto style, 283–84
　with sausage, 273–74
　shrimp, Roman style with, 71
　spaghetti: carbonara, 281; with fresh
　　tomato sauce, 270; with red wine
　　sauce, 282–83; with zucchini, 264
　with walnuts, 269
　ziti: with butter, sage, and
　　Parmigiano-Reggiano, 278–79; with
　　chestnuts and mushrooms,
　　275–76
Peach(es)
　braised and browned lamb with,
　　189–90
　chipotle-peach salsa, 297
　fifteen-minute fruit gratin, 319–20

grilled fruit skewers with ginger
　syrup, 320–21
relish, grilled lamb ribs with, 198
Peanut sauce, sautéed scallops stuffed
　with, 80
Pear(s)
　baked, 318
　braised goose with, 152–53
　and Gorgonzola green salad, with
　　walnuts, 44–45
Peas. *See also* Black-eyed peas
　rice salad with soy and, 58
　soup: cold, 12; creamy, 28; pea and
　　ginger, 12–13
　veal stew of spring, 181–82
Penne. *See* Pasta
Peppers
　big chopped salad with vinaigrette,
　　45–46
　grilled chicken, sausage, and
　　vegetable skewers, 132–33
　lamb with yogurt sauce and, 191
　piquillo, canapés with anchovies and,
　　236
　red, grilled, with olive oil and sherry
　　vinegar, 235–36
　red pepper and tomato soup,
　　creamy, 28
　red pepper puree, 303
　roasted, 234–35
Pesto
　grilled lamb ribs with, 197
　marjoram, 298
　pasta with green beans, potatoes,
　　and, 268–69
　pesto pizza, 259
Pico de gallo, 295–96
Pineapple
　grilled fruit skewers with ginger
　　syrup, 320–21
　pineapple-ginger sorbet, 322
Pinot Noir syrup, roast salmon steaks
　with, 109–10
Piquillo peppers, canapés with
　anchovies and, 236
Pizza, 253–59
　with arugula, corn, and bacon, 259
　dough, 253–54
　with four cheeses and basil, 258
　with green tomatoes, 257
　with tomatoes, onions, and olives,
　　255
　with zucchini and sausage, 256

Porcini, 25. *See also* Mushroom(s)
    porcini-scented "wild" mushroom
        sauté, 231
    seed-rubbed salmon, 108
Pork, 201–14. *See also* Bacon; Ham;
    Prosciutto; Sausage
    braised, with turnips, 209–10
    chops: with miso–red wine sauce, 201;
        roast, with fennel-orange compote,
        203–4; Vietnamese-style, 202
    crispy pork bits with jerk seasonings,
        211–12
    forty-minute cassoulet, 206–7
    fresh Chinese noodles with brown
        sauce, 291
    ground, simmered tofu with (ma-po
        tofu), 244
    Minimalist's choucroute, 212–13
    ribs: pasta with, 277; slow-cooked,
        Chinese-style, 214; slow-grilled,
        213–14; spareribs, Korean style,
        208
    roast, with applesauce, 210–11
    stir-fried coconut noodles, 288
Port, dried fruit poached in, 317–18
Potato(es)
    clam stew with parsley puree and,
        22–23
    crisp, roast monkfish with olives, bay
        leaves, and, 103–4
    Emma's cod and potatoes, 102–3
    gratin, fast, 238–39
    mashed, 239; bangers and mash,
        Italian style, 205
    and mussel salad, 56–57
    new: with butter and mint, 237–30;
        roast, with rosemary, 237
    and onion soup, 30
    pan-crisped, 240
    pasta with, 279–81
    pasta with green beans, pesto, and,
        268–69
    Spanish tortilla, 245–46
    squid in red wine sauce with, 85
    vichyssoise with garlic, 19
Pot roast. *See* Beef
Pots de crème, ginger, 328–29
Poultry. *See* Chicken; Cornish hens;
    Duck; Goose; Turkey
Prosciutto soup, 17–18
Provençal spices, grilled flank steak
    with, 163
Provençal-style veal stew, 182

Provence-style fennel-steamed
    mussels, 63
Prunes, coq au vin with, 146–47
Pudding. *See also* Bread pudding
    easy summer pudding, 314–15
Pumpkin
    Japanese-style beef stew with, 175–76
    soup, 30–31
Puree
    dried mushroom, 302
    red pepper, 303

Ragu, fast sausage, pasta with,
    274–75
Raspberries
    easy summer pudding, 314–15
Red peppers. *See* Peppers
Red wine, olive oil cookies with
    rosemary and, 325
Red wine sauce
    anchovy–red wine, rib-eye steak
        with, 166
    miso–red wine, pork chops with, 201
    roast sirloin with, 170
    spaghetti with, 282–83
    squid in, 85–86
Relish
    fig, 301
    mango or peach, grilled lamb ribs
        with, 198
Ribs. *See also* Pork: ribs
    lamb, grilled, 197–98
Rice
    avgolemono, 15
    carrot, spinach, and rice stew, 33
    fast and easy paella, 88–89
    salad, with peas and soy, 58
Rice noodles, 289. *See also* Noodles
    with basil, 287
Riesling, chicken with, 143
Risotto, orzo, Parmesan cups with,
    285–86
Risotto-style pasta, 283–84
Roden, Claudia, 316
Roesti, beet, with rosemary, 221
Roman-style shrimp, squid, or scallops,
    71–72
Roquefort. *See also* Blue cheese
    sauce, grilled steak with, 164–65
Rosemary
    beet roesti with, 221
    cold tomato soup with, 8

grilled chicken, sausage, and
    vegetable skewers, 132–33
olive oil cookies with red wine and,
    325
roast new potatoes with, 237
rosemary-lemon white bean dip,
    219–20

Sage
    pizza with Parmigiano-Reggiano
        and, 258
    ziti with butter, Parmigiano-
        Reggiano and, 278–79
Salad(s), 43–60
    beet, raw, 46–47
    big chopped salad with vinaigrette,
        45–46
    chicken: Asian, with greens, 50–51;
        spicy, 53
    cucumber: cumin-rubbed lamb
        chops with, 195–96; with scallops,
        chicken, or shrimp, 54–55; simple,
        47–48
    grilled bread salad, 59–60
    herbed green, two ways, 43–44
    mussel and potato, 56–57
    pear and Gorgonzola green salad
        with walnuts, 44–45
    rice, with peas and soy, 58
    seaweed, with cucumber, 48–49
    shrimp: minty broiled shrimp, 52–53;
        Southeast Asian shrimp and
        grapefruit, 51–52
    simple green, 43
    tomato, with basil, 49
    triple sesame salad with scallops,
        55–56
    watermelon, Thai style, 50
Salad dressings. *See* Vinaigrette
Salmon
    burgers, 107
    gravlax, 106
    herb-rubbed, 108
    roast, with spicy soy oil, 110–11
    roasted in butter or olive oil, 111–12
    steaks, roast, with Pinot Noir syrup,
        109–10
    and tomatoes, cooked in foil, 112
Salsa
    chipotle-peach, 297
    fresh, 295; fish tacos with, 117–18
    grilled lamb ribs with, 198

pan-grilled tomato, 296
pico de gallo, 295–96
Sauce(s). *See also* Condiments;
     Dipping sauce; Dressing; Gravy;
     Pasta; Vinaigrette; *specific types of
     meat, poultry, and seafood*
     better cocktail sauce, 306
     brown, fresh Chinese noodles with,
       291
     creamed parsley sauce, 299
     dried mushroom puree, 302
     marjoram "pesto," 298
     mayonnaise, 305–6
     parsley-vinegar, 297–98
     sun-dried tomato, 300
     tartar sauce, 306
Sauerkraut, 156
     Minimalist's choucroute, 212–13
     roasted and braised duck with, 156
Sausage
     bangers and mash, Italian style, 205
     chickpea soup with, 36–37
     clambake in a pot, 89–90
     fast sausage ragu, pasta with,
       274–75
     forty-minute cassoulet, 206–7
     with grapes, 204–5
     grilled chicken, sausage, and
       vegetable skewers, 132–33
     kale, sausage, and mushroom stew,
       205–6
     Minimalist's choucroute, 212–13
     pasta with, 273–74
     pizza with zucchini and, 256
Scallions
     cod cakes with ginger and, 100–101
     Japanese beef-scallion rolls, 168–69
     quick scallion pancakes, 240–41
     Spanish tortilla with, 245
Scallop(s), 81
     cucumber salad with, 54–55
     curried, with tomatoes, 82–83
     miso-broiled, 80
     a la plancha, 81–82
     roasted bay scallops with brown
       butter and shallots, 84–85
     Roman style, 71–72
     sautéed, with herb paste, 79
     sea scallops with nuts, 83–84
     seviche, 76
     stuffed, 79–80
     triple sesame salad with, 55–56
Sea scallops. *See* Scallop(s)

Seaweed
     dashi, 7, 176
     salad, with cucumber, 48–49
Seed-rubbed salmon, 108
Sesame
     roast asparagus with soy and, 217
     triple sesame salad with scallops,
       55–56
Seviche, shrimp or scallop, 76
Shad roe with mustard, 116–17
Shallots
     crisp, tender spinach and, 241–42
     grilled chicken breasts with
       eggplant, ginger sauce, and, 130–31
     and mushrooms, with sweet-and-
       sour sherry sauce, 128–29
     roasted bay scallops with brown
       butter and, 84–85
     shallot-thyme butter, 307
     and thyme, pizza with, 258
Shellfish, 61–91. *See also specific types*
Sherry
     cod with chickpeas and, 101–2
     sauce, sweet-and-sour, chicken with,
       128–29
     sherry reduction gravy, 126
Sherry vinegar
     grilled red peppers with olive oil
       and, 235–36
     spicy sherry vinegar oil, salmon with,
       110
Shiitake mushrooms, 25. *See also*
     Mushroom(s)
Shrimp, 68
     with Asian flavors, 69
     with "barbecue" sauce, 72–73
     bouillabaisse, 90–91
     bread salad with, 59
     cooked in lime juice, 76–77
     cucumber salad with, 55
     fast and easy paella, 88–89
     garlic soup with, 16–17
     and grapefruit salad, Southeast
       Asian, 51–52
     minty broiled shrimp salad, 52–53
     in Moroccan-style tomato sauce,
       69–70
     pad Thai, 289–90
     a la plancha, 81
     poached, cold, 67
     Roman style, 71–72
     scampi style, 69
     seviche, 76

soy-dipped, 78–79
     Spanish-style, 68–69
     spicy, 70–71
     steamed, with lemongrass-coconut
       sauce, 74–75
     stir-fried leeks with ginger and, 77–78
     stock, 16
     in yellow curry, 73–74
Softshell crabs, broiled or grilled,
     86–87
Sorbet
     coconut, 323
     pineapple-ginger, 322
Soup(s), 7–40. *See also* Chowder;
     Stew(s)
     avgolemono, 15
     black-eyed pea, with ham and
       greens, 32
     broccoli, creamy, 29
     cabbage, with apples, 27
     chicken noodle: rich, with ginger, 39;
       whole-meal, Chinese style, 37–38
     chickpea, with sausage, 36–37
     creamy vegetable soups, 28
     cucumber: Asian-style, 10; cucumber-
       coconut, 10; European-style, 11
     curried sweet potato, with apricot, 35
     egg drop, 13–14
     garlic: with shrimp, 16–17; Thai, 16
     lemongrass-ginger, with mushrooms,
       23–24
     miso, nearly instant, with tofu, 7
     mushroom, creamy, 24–25
     mushroom-barley, 40
     pan-roasted asparagus, with
       tarragon, 26
     pea: cold, 12; pea and ginger, 12–13
     potato and onion, 30
     prosciutto soup, 17–18
     pumpkin or winter squash, 30–31
     roasted chestnut, 33–34
     stracciatella, 14–15
     tomato: cold, with rosemary, 8;
       tomato-melon gazpacho, 9
     vichyssoise with garlic, 19
Southeast Asian–style broiled shrimp
     salad, 53
Soy
     and black beans, salmon with, 110
     curried tofu with soy sauce, 243
     grilled soy-and-ginger boneless lamb
       leg, 193
     rice salad with peas and, 58

roast asparagus with sesame and, 217
roast salmon with spicy soy oil, 110–11
simplest steamed fish with, 95
soy-dipped shrimp, 78–79
soy duck, 142
soy-ginger dressing, grilled asparagus with, 218
soy-poached chicken, 154–55
soy vinaigrette, 44
steamed clams with, 65
Spaghetti. See Pasta
Spanish-style broiled shrimp salad, 53
Spanish-style shrimp, 68–69
Spanish tortilla, 245–46
Spareribs. See Pork: ribs
Spice cookies, 324
Spice-rubbed salmon, 108
Spicy salt, broiled Cornish hens with, 136
Spinach. See also Greens
carrot, spinach, and rice stew, 33
linguine with, 261
soup, creamy, 28
tender spinach and crisp shallots, 241–42
Squash. See Summer squash; Winter squash; Zucchini
Squid, 86
a la plancha, 81
in red wine sauce, 85–86
Roman style, 71–72
Steak. See Beef
Stew(s)
beef, 173; Japanese-style, with winter squash, 175–76
bouillabaisse, 90–91
carrot, spinach, and rice, 33
clam, with potatoes and parsley puree, 22–23
kale, sausage, and mushroom, 205–6
veal: with dill, 183; veal stew of spring, 181–82
Stir-fries, 139
chicken with nuts, ten-minute, 138–39
leeks: with ginger, 230–31; with ginger and shrimp, 77–78
rice noodles with basil, 287
stir-fried coconut noodles, 288
Stock(s)
dashi, 7, 176
shrimp, 16
Stracciatella, 14–15

Strawberry(ies)
with balsamic vinegar, 311–12
coeurs à la crème with, 313–14
fool, 312
sugared, 311
with Swedish cream, 313
Stuffing, bread, fastest, 125
Sugared strawberries, 311
Summer pudding, easy, 314–15
Summer squash. See also Zucchini
grilled chicken, sausage, and vegetable skewers, 132–33
Sun-dried tomato sauce, 300
Swedish cream, strawberries with, 313
Sweet-and-sour sherry sauce, chicken with, 128–29
Sweet potato(es)
Japanese-style beef stew with, 175–76
soup, curried, with apricot, 35
Swordfish
grilled "sandwich" with green sauce, 115–16
with onion confit, 113–14
Syrup
ginger, grilled fruit skewers with, 320–21
Pinot Noir, roast salmon steaks with, 109–10

Tacos, fish, with fresh salsa, 117–18
Tarragon, pan-roasted asparagus soup with, 26
Tartar sauce, 306
Thai-style dishes
lemongrass-ginger soup with mushrooms, 23–24
pad Thai, 289–90
spicy chicken with lemongrass and lime, 149–50
Thai garlic soup, 16
Thai steamed mussels, 64
Thai-style watermelon, 50
Thanksgiving turkey, the Minimalist's, 124–26
Thyme
and shallots, pizza with, 258
shallot-thyme butter, 307
Tofu
curried, with soy sauce, 243
nearly instant miso soup with, 7
simmered, with ground pork (ma-po tofu), 244

Tomatillo soup, creamy, 28
Tomato(es), 271
curried scallops with, 82–83
green: creamy green tomato soup, 28; pizza with, 257
green beans and tomatoes, 220
grilled bread salad with, 59–60
pastas: linguine with tomato-anchovy sauce, 271–72; pasta all'amatriciana, 282; pasta with clams and tomatoes, 272–73; pasta with fast sausage ragu, 274–75; pasta with meaty bones, 277–78; pasta with potatoes, 279–81; spaghetti with fresh tomato sauce, 270
pizza with onions, olives, and, 255
salad, with basil, 49
salmon and, cooked in foil, 112–13
salsas: fresh salsa, 295; pan-grilled tomato salsa, 296; pico de gallo, 295–96
sauce, Moroccan-style, shrimp in, 69
soups: cold, with rosemary, 8; creamy red pepper and tomato, 28; tomato-melon gazpacho, 9
squid in red wine sauce with, 85
sun-dried tomato sauce, 300
Tortilla, Spanish, 245–46
Triple sesame salad with scallops, 55–56
Tuna
bread salad with, 59
with onion confit, 113–14
au poivre, 114–15
Turkey, 124
Minimalist's Thanksgiving turkey, 124–26
roast turkey breast, 123
Turnip(s)
Asian pot roast with, 171–72
braised pork with, 209–10
and parsnip or potato soup, creamy, 28

Veal, 178–83
breast, braised, with mushrooms, 179–81
brisket, with bacon and onion, 180–81
osso buco, 178–79
pasta with meaty bones, 277–78
stew, with dill, 183
veal stew of spring, 181–82

Vegetables, 217–46. *See also specific vegetables*
    creamy vegetable soups, 28
Vichyssoise with garlic, 19
Vietnamese-style pork chops, 202
Vinaigrette. *See also* Dressing
    basic, 304–5
    nut, 44
    soy, 44
Vinegar, 297–98. *See also* Balsamic vinegar; Sherry vinegar
    chicken with, 144–45
    shad roe with capers and, 117
Vongerichten, Jean-Georges, 9

Walnuts
    pasta with, 269
    pear and Gorgonzola green salad with, 44–45
    sea scallops with nuts, 83–84
    ten-minute stir-fried chicken with nuts, 138–39
Watermelon, Thai style, 50
White pizza, 258
Winter squash
    Japanese-style beef stew with, 176
    penne with butternut squash, 265
    soup, 30–31

Yellow curry, shrimp in, 73–74
Yogurt
    chicken curry with, 147
    European-style cucumber soup, 11
    sauce, lamb with peppers and, 191

Ziti. *See* Pasta
Zucchini
    grilled chicken, sausage, and vegetable skewers, 132–33
    pizza with sausage and, 256
    spaghetti with, 264

MARK BITTMAN is the author of the blockbuster *Best Recipes in the World* (Broadway, 2005) and the classic bestseller *How to Cook Everything,* which has sold more than one million copies. He is also the coauthor, with Jean-Georges Vongerichten, of *Simple to Spectacular* and *Jean-Georges: Cooking at Home with a Four-Star Chef.* Mr. Bittman is a prolific writer, makes frequent appearances on radio and television, and is the host of *The Best Recipes in the World,* a thirteen-part series on public television. He lives in New York and Connecticut.

Also by Mark Bittman

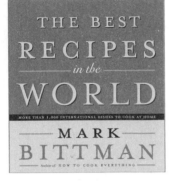

Shop locally, cook globally. Mark Bittman gathers the best recipes that people from dozens of countries around the world cook every day. And when he brings his distinctive no-frills approach to dishes that were once considered esoteric, America's home cooks will eagerly follow where they once feared to tread.

The cooking of Jean-Georges Vongerichten has earned endless raves and accolades from every quarter. Now, Jean-Georges and Mark Bittman help home cooks turn their kitchens into four-star restaurants, with uncomplicated recipes that use readily available ingredients, many of which can be prepared in thirty minutes or less.

A four-star chef and a bestselling cookbook author come together to create a delicious style of cooking that adapts to every occasion.